PROVERBS AND ECCLESIASTES

BELIEF

A Theological Commentary on the Bible

GENERAL EDITORS

Amy Plantinga Pauw
William C. Placher†

PROVERBS AND ECCLESIASTES

AMY PLANTINGA PAUW

First edition
Published by Westminster John Knox Press
Louisville, Kentucky

15 16 17 18 19 20 21 22 23 24—10 9 8 7 6 5 4 3 2 1

Book design by Drew Stevens
Cover design by Lisa Buckley
Cover illustration: © David Chapman/Design Pics/Corbis

Library of Congress Cataloging-in-Publication Data

Pauw, Amy Plantinga.
Proverbs and Ecclesiastes : a theological commentary on the Bible / Amy Plantinga Pauw.
-- First edition.
pages cm. -- (Belief: a theological commentary on the Bible)
Includes bibliographical references and index.
ISBN 978-0-664-23210-8 (alk. paper)
1. Bible. Proverbs--Commentaries. 2. Bible. Ecclesiastes--Commentaries. I. Title.
BS1465.53.P38 2015
223'.707--dc23

2014029873

♾ The paper used in this publication meets the minimum requirements of the American National Standard for Information Sciences—Permanence of Paper for Printed Library Materials, ANSI Z39.48-1992.

In loving memory of Jan Winsemius Pauw,
Lettie Plantinga, and Connie Ottenhoff,
wise women, all of them

Contents

ECCLESIASTES

Publisher's Note

William C. Placher worked with Amy Plantinga Pauw as a general editor for this series until his untimely death in November 2008. Bill brought great energy and vision to the series, and was instrumental in defining and articulating its distinctive approach and in securing theologians to write for it. Bill's own commentary for the series was the last thing he wrote, and Westminster John Knox Press dedicates the entire series to his memory with affection and gratitude.

William C. Placher, LaFollette Distinguished Professor in Humanities at Wabash College, spent thirty-four years as one of Wabash College's most popular teachers. A summa cum laude graduate of Wabash in 1970, he earned his master's degree in philosophy in 1974 and his PhD in 1975, both from Yale University. In 2002 the American Academy of Religion honored him with the Excellence in Teaching Award. Placher was also the author of thirteen books, including *A History of Christian Theology, The Triune God, The Domestication of Transcendence, Jesus the Savior, Narratives of a Vulnerable God,* and *Unapologetic Theology.* He also edited the volume *Essentials of Christian Theology,* which was named as one of 2004's most outstanding books by both *The Christian Century* and *Christianity Today* magazines.

Series Introduction

Belief: A Theological Commentary on the Bible is a series from Westminster John Knox Press featuring biblical commentaries written by theologians. The writers of this series share Karl Barth's concern that, insofar as their usefulness to pastors goes, most modern commentaries are "no commentary at all, but merely the first step toward a commentary." Historical-critical approaches to Scripture rule out some readings and commend others, but such methods only begin to help theological reflection and the preaching of the Word. By themselves, they do not convey the powerful sense of God's merciful presence that calls Christians to repentance and praise; they do not bring the church fully forward in the life of discipleship. It is to such tasks that theologians are called.

For several generations, however, professional theologians in North America and Europe have not been writing commentaries on the Christian Scriptures. The specialization of professional disciplines and the expectations of theological academies about the kind of writing that theologians should do, as well as many of the directions in which contemporary theology itself has gone, have contributed to this dearth of theological commentaries. This is a relatively new phenomenon; until the last century or two, the church's great theologians also routinely saw themselves as biblical interpreters. The gap between the fields is a loss for both the church and the discipline of theology itself. By inviting forty contemporary theologians to wrestle deeply with particular texts of Scripture, the editors of this series hope not only to provide new theological resources for the church but also to encourage all theologians to pay more attention to Scripture and the life of the church in their writings.

We are grateful to the Louisville Institute, which provided funding for a consultation in June 2007. We invited theologians, pastors, and biblical scholars to join us in a conversation about what this series could contribute to the life of the church. The time was provocative and the results were rich. Much of the series' shape owes to the insights of these skilled and faithful interpreters, who sought to describe a way to write a commentary that served the theological needs of the church and its pastors with relevance, historical accuracy, and theological depth. The passion of these participants guided us in creating this series and lives on in the volumes.

As theologians, the authors will be interested much less in the matters of form, authorship, historical setting, social context, and philology—the very issues that are often of primary concern to critical biblical scholars. Instead, this series' authors will seek to explain the theological importance of the texts for the church today, using biblical scholarship as needed for such explication but without any attempt to cover all of the topics of the usual modern biblical commentary. This thirty-six-volume series will provide passage-by-passage commentary on all the books of the Protestant biblical canon, with more extensive attention given to passages of particular theological significance.

The authors' chief dialogue will be with the church's creeds, practices, and hymns; with the history of faithful interpretation and use of the Scriptures; with the categories and concepts of theology; and with contemporary culture in both "high" and popular forms. Each volume will begin with a discussion of *why* the church needs this book and why we need it *now*, in order to ground all of the commentary in contemporary relevance. Throughout each volume, text boxes will highlight the voices of ancient and modern interpreters from the global communities of faith, and occasional essays will allow deeper reflection on the key theological concepts of these biblical books.

The authors of this commentary series are theologians of the church who embrace a variety of confessional and theological perspectives. The group of authors assembled for this series represents more diversity of race, ethnicity, and gender than any other commentary series. They approach the larger Christian tradition with a critical respect, seeking to reclaim its riches and at the same time to acknowledge its shortcomings. The authors also aim to make available to readers a wide range of contemporary theological voices from many parts of the world. While it does recover an older genre of writing, this series is not an attempt to retrieve some idealized past. These commentaries have learned from tradition, but they are most importantly commentaries for today. The authors share the conviction that their work will be more contemporary, more faithful, and more radical, to the extent that it is more biblical, honestly wrestling with the texts of the Scriptures.

William C. Placher
Amy Plantinga Pauw

Acknowledgments

I have been the sole general editor of the Belief series since Bill Placher's unexpected death in 2008. The two of us had agreed at the outset that we would each write a commentary for the series. Bill's powerful commentary on Mark was the first volume to be published. Mine has taken considerably longer to appear, in part because of my editorial responsibilities. I hope that the process of writing my own commentary for the series has made me a wiser and more compassionate editor.

Writing a biblical commentary has given me fresh appreciation for biblical scholars, and my debts to them feel very direct. My first Hebrew teacher was Raymond Van Leeuwen, and his discerning work on biblical wisdom literature has given me the welcome opportunity to become his student once again. My Bible colleague at Louisville Seminary, Johanna van Wijk-Bos, graciously agreed to teach a course on the wisdom literature with me and taught me a great deal in the process. Three scholars from the Atlanta area—Bill Brown, Carol Newsom, and Christine Roy Yoder—provided not only exemplary scholarship but also personal encouragement along the way. Pat Miller has been a friend and a source of support and guidance throughout this project. Melisa Scarlott helped prepare the manuscript. Fellow theologians David Kelsey and Daniel Treier generously shared with me their own theological work on Proverbs and Ecclesiastes. I am indebted to many others who are not named here.

Worship and Christian education have been important contexts for me as I lived with these texts. To my surprise, I found Proverbs and Ecclesiastes to be eminently "preachable" on occasions as varied as a meeting of the Association of Theological Librarians and World AIDS day services. My immediate family cheered me on by designating Monday as "Proverbs night" for our dinnertime devotions. My home congregation, Crescent Hill Presbyterian in Louisville; the community at Louisville Seminary; as well as congregations in Birmingham and Mobile, Alabama; Knoxville, Tennessee; and Washington, D.C., have all been valued fellow travelers in this journey.

In one of his charming theological speculations, Augustine suggests that God could have taught all persons individually and immediately by means of angels. Had God so chosen, all the wisdom every human being needed could have been obtained in this direct and effortless way. Instead, according to Augustine, God's good plan was for us humans to learn wisdom from one another, because, he says, it makes a "way for love, which ties people together in the bonds of unity, [and] make[s] souls overflow and as it were intermingle with each other." God has bound us together in the laborious and precarious enterprise of seeking wisdom so that we will learn at the same time to love one another. I offer this commentary in grateful testimony to this hope.

Abbreviations

DBW	*Dietrich Bonhoeffer Works*
KJV	King James Version
KW	*Kierkegaard's Writings*
LCC	Library of Christian Classics
LW	*Luther's Works*
NIB	New Interpreter's Bible
NIV	New International Version
NRSV	New Revised Standard Version
WBC	Westminster Bible Companion

Introduction: Why Proverbs and Ecclesiastes? Why Now?

Proverbs and Ecclesiastes may seem to be among the least promising biblical books for contemporary theological reflection. Until rather recently, Proverbs and Ecclesiastes were viewed by many modern Christian biblical scholars as stepchildren of the canon, awkward presences whose concerns were largely alien to the center of Israel's faith. As John Bright put it, "Some parts of the Old Testament are far less clearly expressive of Israel's distinctive understanding of reality than others; some parts (and one thinks of such a book as Proverbs) seem to be only peripherally related to it, while others (for example Ecclesiastes) even question its essential features."[1] Even to the average Bible reader, Proverbs appears banal, and Ecclesiastes, disturbing. These books have been largely ignored by contemporary theologians and are rarely preached from in contemporary Western churches. They are loose cannons within the canon. So why bother with Proverbs and Ecclesiastes?

There are at least four reasons why it makes sense to pay new attention to these biblical outliers:

1. Biblical scholars have shown intense new interest in biblical wisdom literature in the last forty years or so, and their work prompts broader ways of thinking about the unity of the biblical message and, by implication, about the task of preaching. (Preaching on Proverbs may seem particularly daunting, and I offer some guidance in this commentary.)
2. Proverbs and Ecclesiastes speak to our context of religious pluralism. They are both the products of a complex

1. John Bright, *The Authority of the Old Testament* (Nashville: Abingdon Press, 1967), 136.

international quest for wisdom in the ancient Near East. The sages of Israel exhibited a willingness to learn from their cultural and religious others. In our own pluralistic context, it is a willingness that we need to cultivate as well.

3. The theological horizon for both Proverbs and Ecclesiastes is creation rather than redemption or consummation. In an age when ecological concerns are raising urgent questions about our identity as creatures and our relationship to the rest of creation, these books deserve closer study.
4. Proverbs and Ecclesiastes seem to have a special appeal for the religiously disaffected. In their different ways, they set forth theology that grapples honestly with the problems of daily life and can serve as an attractive path to (or back to) biblical faith for both skeptics and seekers.

Rethinking the Unity of the Biblical Message

Proverbs and Ecclesiastes are part of biblical wisdom literature. Job and perhaps Song of Songs also belong to this genre, and a majority of the Christian world regards the later wisdom books Sirach and the Wisdom of Solomon as canonical. As Roland Murphy puts it, "The most striking characteristic of this literature is the absence of what one normally considers as typically Israelite and Jewish."[2] Sirach and Wisdom of Solomon are partial exceptions to this pattern. In Sirach 44–50 the figure of Wisdom is identified with Torah and finds her resting place in Israel. In Wisdom of Solomon 11–19, Israel's salvation history is retold as the story of Wisdom's redeeming acts. By contrast, Proverbs and Ecclesiastes are paradigmatic wisdom books. They show little interest in issues of worship and cultic purity. Even more strikingly, the big events in Israel's history—the covenant with Abraham, the exodus from Egypt, the giving of the law, the stories of the kings of Israel, the exile and return—are all missing.

For Christian readers of Scripture, these gaps cause larger problems: Proverbs and Ecclesiastes' lack of attention to "the mighty acts

2. Roland E. Murphy, *The Tree of Life: An Exploration of Biblical Wisdom Literature*, 3rd ed. (Grand Rapids: Eerdmans, 2002), 1.

of God" on Israel's behalf subverts a common theological and homiletical strategy for construing the unity of the whole biblical canon. Appeals to salvation history have not only been a means for unifying the disparate books of the Old Testament but have also supplied the crucial link to the New Testament narratives of Jesus, thus establishing a basis for reading the entire Bible as the story of salvation. It has proved easier for theologians and preachers to ignore the dissonant voices of the wisdom books than to reconsider Christian understandings of canonical unity. Though they have been treasured by both Jews and Christians for centuries, Proverbs and Ecclesiastes have in modern times often been regarded as disconnected from the authentic faith of Israel and irrelevant to the good news of the gospel.

Yet as the author of Hebrews affirms, "God spoke to our ancestors in many and various ways" (Heb. 1:1). Seeking wisdom is an integral part of Israel's faith in God, neither contradicting nor derivative of its other emphases on law, cult, and sacred history. In the Bible, the law is associated with Moses, the psalms with David, and wisdom with Solomon. Proverbs and Ecclesiastes are both ascribed to Solomon, though, as modern biblical scholarship has shown, this ascription should be construed less as a claim about historical authorship and more as a certificate of authenticity. The ascription functions primarily to establish that the wisdom of Proverbs and Ecclesiastes is a bona fide dimension of Israel's faith. Both books, in different ways, reflect Israel's struggle to find its identity in a time of cultural crisis, when the monarchy and the priesthood were no longer sources of authority and stability. They can also speak to contemporary people who search for meaning and purpose in an uncertain world.

Rather than silencing or excluding their voices, we should accept the opportunity Proverbs and Ecclesiastes offer to broaden our understanding of biblical faith. As Eberhard Busch notes, "The witness of Scripture is there for us only in the fullness of the various witnesses, which resists our manipulating grasp. These witnesses need to be seen, each in its own particular color."[3] Once we attend

3. Eberhard Busch, "Reformed Strength in Its Denominational Weakness," in *Reformed Theology: Identity and Ecumenicity*, ed. Wallace Alston and Michael Welker (Grand Rapids: Eerdmans, 2003), 24.

to the particular color of biblical wisdom, we start noticing that its influence reaches far beyond the books usually designated as wisdom literature. It extends into the Law, Psalms, and Prophets, and into the New Testament as well, especially the book of James and the teachings of Jesus. Wisdom is a biblical witness that needs to be better seen—and heard.

Intellectual Ecumenism

Wisdom literature looks at the world through a wide-angle lens. It is concerned with the meaning and purpose of human life in general, not with the story of a particular nation or tribe. Israel's sages probed everyday human experiences of the world. "Just as water reflects the face, so one human heart reflects another" (Prov. 27:19). Or, in a more prosaic vein, "Let your foot be seldom in your neighbor's house, otherwise the neighbor will become weary of you and hate you" (Prov. 25:17). Proverbs sounds the dominant themes of Israel's wisdom traditions: it can be understood as "writing for the majority." Ecclesiastes, by contrast, is "writing for the minority," casting a critical eye over Israel's wisdom traditions. It provides an ironic overview of the mainstream wisdom such as we find in Proverbs: "Again I saw that under the sun the race is not to the swift, nor the battle to the strong, nor bread to the wise, nor riches to the intelligent, nor favor to the skillful; but time and chance happen to them all" (Eccles. 9:11). Despite their differences, both Proverbs and Ecclesiastes speak from within Israel's wisdom traditions. Both model and commend the attempt to discern God's presence in human life without appeal to direct visions or messages from God or to the unique experience of one people.

The wisdom of Proverbs and Ecclesiastes was developed and honed in the company of Israel's ancient Near East neighbors. Egypt and Mesopotamia were the motherlands of this wisdom. It is likely that the influence of their wisdom teaching spread to smaller nations like Israel in part through the phenomenon of second-language instruction. While oral wisdom traditions have deep roots in ordinary Israelite life, biblical wisdom literature *as literature* is closely connected with the international phenomena of scribal formation and education in literacy in the ancient Near East. Sages and scribes in the courts of Israel's kings had at least some hand in the articulation and preservation of Israel's wisdom. Biblical wisdom thus has a pronounced international flavor.

The Ghanaian theologian Mercy Amba Oduyoye tells about how she discovered this feature of the book of Proverbs while still a girl attending a British boarding school in Kumasi, Ghana: "I remember clearly our morning ritual assembly for prayers and announcements. Each girl, in turn, was required to recite a biblical text. It was our tradition to quote from the book of Proverbs, Ecclesiastes, or the Sermon on the Mount; the book of Proverbs was our favourite." That was because proverbs were already part of their culture, and so in a pinch "school girls could easily get away with converting Akan proverbs into King James language and then simply inventing chapter and verse numbers."[4] Both the universality of Proverbs' wisdom and her teachers' lack of familiarity with that biblical book contributed to the success of Oduyoye's scheme!

The idiosyncratic teachings of Ecclesiastes also reflect cross-cultural exchange of some sort, perhaps with currents of Persian or Hellenistic thought, though there is little scholarly consensus about this. The agnosticism of many in the Persian period about conventional expressions of religiosity seems to be echoed in Ecclesiastes. The wisdom of Ecclesiastes is less connected to Israel's larger testimony than that of Proverbs. Ecclesiastes' message speaks to our current cultural context, in which traditional religious certainties have waned for many. The robust communal setting of Proverbs' quest for wisdom is also missing in Ecclesiastes. As William Brown notes, Ecclesiastes "depicts communal institutions, such as the family and government, on the verge of collapse or plagued with the withering effects of indifference."[5] This institutional skepticism is also a feature of our own time.

Wisdom addresses questions that all human beings ask. So it is

4. Mercy Amba Oduyoye, *Beads and Strands: Reflections of an African Woman on Christianity in Africa* (Maryknoll, NY: Orbis Books, 2004), 91.

5. William P. Brown, *Character in Crisis: A Fresh Approach to the Wisdom Literature of the Old Testament* (Grand Rapids: Eerdmans, 1996), 159.

not surprising that every religious community has wisdom traditions—Jewish, Muslim, Hindu, Taoist—and that these traditions are often a promising place to begin interfaith conversations. Like the sages of Proverbs and Ecclesiastes, most of us do not live in a self-sustaining religious society clearly demarcated from others. Our faith survives and flourishes amidst a variety of cultural and religious currents. The theological traditions we have inherited are themselves the result of scavenging and borrowing from the traditions of others. While other parts of the Old Testament strongly admonish Israel *not* to learn from their neighbors, the sages of Proverbs and Ecclesiastes model receptivity to the wisdom of others. Their confident assimilation of the wisdom of other nations is evidence that their devotion to the God of Israel was a devotion to the creator and sustainer of all peoples. All true wisdom, no matter what its proximate human source, ultimately comes from God. As we today confront problems too big for any single religious community to handle—violence, poverty, ecological degradation—searching out the commonalities and connections of our wisdom with those of our religious neighbors is a good place to start.

Our Identity as Creatures

"The profit and pleasures we pursue lay waste the land and pollute the seas." This line in a prayer of confession from the Christian Council of Asia acknowledges our failure to be faithful creatures.[6] From large-scale ecological disasters to the small destructive patterns of our daily lives, we have violated our relationship with our Creator and with our fellow creatures. Attempts to lay all this at the feet of Christian faith, particularly the mandate in Genesis 1:28 for human beings to have dominion over the earth, seem overblown. Yet it is true that Christians have developed ways of reading the Bible that have undermined serious theological attention to our identity as God's creatures. Here too, the wisdom books are valuable resources.

David Kelsey argues that Christian faith tells three interrelated

6. The text of this prayer is available at http://www.cca.org.hk/resource/liturgies/misc/eco20602.htm.

but distinct stories about how God relates to us. The triune God is the One who creates us, who draws us to eschatological consummation, and who reconciles us when we have become estranged from God.[7] Creating us obviously has a kind of logical priority: without creation, there would be no human subjects for consummation and reconciliation. Creation, however, does not imply consummation or reconciliation. God declares the finite creation "very good" (Gen. 1:31). There is no obligation on God's part to bring all or part of it to eschatological consummation. Reconciliation presupposes some sort of estrangement from God, yet God continues to relate to us creatively even in the midst of our estrangement—the sun rises and rain falls on the just and the unjust alike (Matt. 5:45). Kelsey insists that each of these ways of God's relating to us has its own logic and that theological anthropology should be faithful to all of them.

Christian theology and preaching in the West has often focused on the reconciliation story alone, narrowing the rich economy of God's dealings with us. Creaturehood in particular becomes an elaborate scenic backdrop for the salvation story. Whereas the creation stories in Genesis serve as a preface to the story of God's deliverance in Exodus, Proverbs and Ecclesiastes help us consider our relationship to God as creatures in its own right. As Walther Zimmerli notes, canonical "wisdom thinks resolutely within the framework of a theology of creation."[8] The physical and temporal limits of created life are accepted in biblical wisdom. They are not viewed as something human creatures can or need to get out from under. The focus of Proverbs and Ecclesiastes is on finite creaturely life lived before God.

As creator, God gives human creatures a lifelong vocation to pursue wisdom. Human wisdom is patient, attentive discernment of the character and quality of life as God has given it. Human beings flourish not by evading or overcoming the ambiguities of their finite and contingent life as creatures but by recognizing and coming to terms with them and by seeing the opportunities of this creaturely life as God's gracious gift. As David Ford and Graham

7. David H. Kelsey, *Eccentric Existence: A Theological Anthropology* (Louisville, KY: Westminster John Knox Press, 2009), 8.

8. Walther Zimmerli, "The Place and Limit of the Wisdom Literature in the Framework of the Old Testament Theology," in *Studies in Ancient Israelite Wisdom*, ed. James L. Crenshaw (New York: KTAV Publishing, 1976), 316.

Stanton comment, "Wisdom is about trying to integrate knowledge, understanding, critical questioning and good judgment with a view to the flourishing of human life and the whole of creation. Theological wisdom attempts all that before God, alert to God, and in line with the purposes of God."[9]

Proverbs is more confident than Ecclesiastes about the scope and competency of human wisdom. As Proverbs portrays it, the created world is sufficiently stable and reliable to permit human beings to seek the wisdom that will enable them to flourish in it. This is because the created world in all its intricacy and beauty is a reflection of God's wisdom. Wisdom is woven into the fabric of the universe, and God invites us to become wise by paying attention to the patterns of creation. We ignore or flout those patterns at our peril. In our own time, environmentalists are perhaps the voices closest to the sages of Proverbs. They share Proverbs' sense of moral urgency about the communal cultivation of a wise and just way of life. They warn us of the terrible consequences of ecological folly. The stock characters of Proverbs—the wicked, the scoffers, the lazy, the foolish, the wise—all have their counterparts in ecological discussions.

God's gift of wisdom is not confined to human creatures. According to Proverbs, even ants, badgers, locusts, and lizards display wisdom that can aid human creatures in their quest for a wise way of life (Prov. 30:24–28; cf. Job 12:7–9). We human creatures are realizing that we need to spend more time listening to the "speechless voice" (Ps. 19:3–4) of the rest of creation—the glaciers of the Arctic, the ozone layer, the rain forests. As Gerhard von Rad notes, Israel's wisdom shows us that truth about the world and ourselves "can never become the object of our theoretical knowledge; that reliable knowledge can be achieved only through a relationship of trust with things."[10] In a time of ecological crisis, we sorely need to restore that relationship of trust with our fellow creatures.

9. David F. Ford and Graham Stanton, eds., *Reading Texts, Seeking Wisdom: Scripture and Theology* (Grand Rapids: Eerdmans, 2004), 2–3.
10. Gerhard Von Rad, *Wisdom in Israel* (Nashville: Abingdon Press, 1972), 318.

An Invitation to the Religiously Disaffected

Ecclesiastes made it into the canon by the skin of its teeth (see p. 139, "Introduction to Ecclesiastes"). Precisely the features of Ecclesiastes that imperiled its acceptance into the canon—its ambiguities and contradictions, its voicing of radical doubts—have endeared it to many subsequent biblical readers. Qohelet, the renegade wisdom teacher of Ecclesiastes, is not afraid to question received religious commonplaces, not afraid to say out loud that life experience and theological convictions sometimes clash. When sudden disaster makes us feel like "fish taken in a cruel net" (Eccl. 9:12), when the ironies and perplexities of life pile up, Ecclesiastes is a welcome biblical companion, a freethinker within the canon of Scripture. The robust communal setting of Proverbs' quest for wisdom is missing in Ecclesiastes. Qohelet was a seeker and gives voice to the seekers of our own day, who also exhibit a passionate search for wisdom without a confidence in communal structures to guide the way.

In its own way, Proverbs is also a biblical refuge for those who wonder about the plausibility and relevance of faith in God. The philosopher Charles Taylor has described with great learning and at great length what it is like to live in a "secular age."[11] One of his recurring images for our secular age, following Max Weber, is of life in a "disenchanted" world. According to Taylor, humanity since the throes of modernity is consigned to existence in a mechanistic world with no porosity between the realm of ordinary daily experience and a mysterious realm of spiritual powers. This is not the world of Proverbs and Ecclesiastes: biblical wisdom presents an everyday world permeated with God's presence. Yet it is fair to say that if the world of Proverbs is not a disenchanted world, it is in a sense unenchanted. Mesopotamian wisdom texts reflect a keen interest in spells, omens, and sorcery. But Proverbs presents a world devoid of magic, devoid of what Rowan Williams has called "short cuts in the management of reality."[12] Proverbs urges us to work hard, to learn

11. Charles Taylor, *A Secular Age* (Cambridge, MA: Belknap Press of Harvard University Press, 2007).
12. Rowan Williams (sermon, King's College London 175th anniversary service, Westminster Abbey, October 19, 2004).

from others, to control our tempers and our tongues, to be generous and just in all our dealings. Proverbs sees no disconnection between the reality of God's active presence, on the one hand, and the need for human discernment, struggle, and patience, on the other. God is not a superhero who can be called upon to swoop down and solve all our problems. Faith in God is not a matter of believing the right things or saying the right words so that all will go well for us. Nor does Proverbs have a sense of divine powers embedded in certain sacred places or objects. Proverbs is a spiritual guide on the days when, in Ellen Davis's words, "water does not pour forth from rocks and angels do not come for lunch."[13] Most days in the church are like that. The honesty and practicality of Ecclesiastes and Proverbs are appealing to seekers and veteran Christians alike.

Theological Companions

There is an implicit theological perspective at work in every biblical commentary, but a self-proclaimed theological commentary needs to be more explicit about it. A deliberate attempt will be made in this commentary to read Proverbs and Ecclesiastes in conversation with a broadly Augustinian tradition. There are both negative and positive reasons for this theological decision.

The negative reason is to provide some resistance to popular appeals to biblical wisdom as presenting an upbeat, positive alternative to classical Christian views of human nature.[14] According to this view, the wisdom provided by communal teaching and honest self-reflection is enough to turn us from sin and folly and enable us to realize our creaturely wholeness and human potential. In Augustine's time, this view was represented by his opponent Pelagius. In my Augustinian reading of Proverbs and Ecclesiastes, human sin and folly are much more stubborn and tragic than a Pelagian view allows. Both books puzzle over humanity's persistent attempts to live at

13. Ellen F. Davis, *Proverbs, Ecclesiastes, and the Song of Songs*, WBC (Louisville, KY: Westminster John Knox Press, 2000), 12.

14. See, for example, Matthew Fox, *Original Blessing: A Primer in Creation Spirituality in Four Paths, Twenty-six Themes, and Two Questions* (Santa Fe, NM: Bear Press, 1983).

cross purposes to God's intentions and attend to the roles of self-deception and habit in human folly and wickedness. The tragedy of a misdirected heart is never explained in Proverbs and Ecclesiastes, much less resolved. For Israel's sages, being "wise in one's own eyes" is the height of human folly (Prov. 3:7a). Wisdom in any full sense of the term belongs to God, and a central part of human wisdom is to acknowledge "our necessary passivity and neediness in a world that we do not control."[15]

The positive reason for pursuing an Augustinian reading is that it makes sense of the pervasive emphasis in Proverbs and Ecclesiastes on the human heart and its passions.[16] Human beings always act out of love for some good, and sin and folly are the consequences of our disordered pursuit of these goods. Wisdom is finally about ordering our desires aright, and this is to be sought in the context of a trustful acknowledgment of God's transcendent wisdom. Augustine sees no contradiction between the desperate human need for grace and the importance of striving for wisdom, and his writings abound with appeals to biblical wisdom. Indeed, according to Marcus Plested, wisdom emerges as "the alpha and omega" of Augustine's theology.[17]

In my commentary on Proverbs, the Augustinian tradition will be mediated especially through Reinhold and H. Richard Niebuhr, who have some claim to being America's wisdom theologians. Both brothers understood the life of faith as an ongoing communal response to the God who is present and active everywhere. They evinced a keen attention to the texture of the daily life of faith and resolutely rejected deus ex machina solutions to human dilemmas. Their intertwining of personal faith with social ethics and their realism about human sin and self-deception resonate with the perspective of Proverbs. In my commentary on Ecclesiastes, I turn to a more tormented Augustinian soul, Søren Kierkegaard. Like Qohelet's

15. Martha C. Nussbaum, *Upheavals of Thought: The Intelligence of Emotions* (Cambridge: Cambridge University Press, 2003), 530.
16. See Christine Roy Yoder, "The Objects of Our Affections: Emotions and the Moral Life in Proverbs 1–9," in *Shaking Heaven and Earth: Essays in Honor of Walter Brueggemann and Charles Cousar,* ed. C. Roy Yoder, K. M. O'Connor, E. E. Johnson, and S. P. Saunders (Louisville, KY: Westminster John Knox Press, 2005), 73–88.
17. Marcus Plested, "Wisdom in the Fathers: An (Eastern) Orthodox Perspective," in *Encounter between Eastern Orthodoxy and Radical Orthodoxy: Transfiguring the World through the Word,* ed. Adrian Pabst and Christoph Schneider (Farnham, UK: Ashgate, 2009), 243.

wisdom, Kierkegaard's thought is "frequently iconoclastic and rife with tension"; it "subverts tidy explication and defies coherent summarizing."[18] Kierkegaard's disillusionment with the philosophical and religious establishments of his day and his frequent recourse to personal narrative and ironic parables echo Qohelet's approach. Like Qohelet, Kierkegaard found that faith in God created space for joy in the midst of the absurdities of life.

18. William P. Brown, *Ecclesiastes* (Louisville, KY: Westminster John Knox Press, 2000), vii.

PROVERBS

Introduction to Proverbs

The titles scattered across the book of Proverbs suggest that it is an anthology, a collection of collections. There are few clues to the sociohistorical context of its different teachings. Chapters 1–9 and 31:10–31 are seen by most scholars as later additions to Proverbs that are linked thematically with one another and frame the book as a whole. They are usually dated sometime after the return from the Babylonian exile, arguably in what is called the Persian period (roughly 539–337 BCE).

These editorial "bookends" serve as a guide to reading the entire book in two crucial ways. First, they establish the theological context of the quest for wisdom: finding wisdom is inseparable from "fear of the LORD." Proverbs is not a "self-help" book. The wisdom it offers is the fruit of and guidance for life together in the presence of God. Proverbs teaches us how to live with, not against, the grain of the universe that God has made. Second, the two female personifications of wisdom that frame the beginning and end of Proverbs chart a pedagogical journey that extends across the whole book: the reader starts as a child in the parental home and is called to claim Woman Wisdom as sister and friend; the reader finishes as an adult living in a wise woman's household. The theological orientation and pedagogical trajectory of Proverbs will both be central to this commentary. Because of the importance of these editorial bookends for reading and preaching on Proverbs, they will receive closer attention in the commentary than the large central section.

The scholarly consensus is that the large central section of Proverbs (chaps. 10–29) contains the oldest material in the book.

Scholars debate about the relationships among the various original settings of Proverbs' teachings—in homes and villages, in scribal schools and royal courts. It seems likely that these teachings circulated in oral form in ordinary Israelite life, passed on by countless fathers and mothers, and were eventually gathered together and edited by scribes or sages associated with the royal courts (25:1). The discrete proverbial teachings of this section, shelved one after another like library books, seem to defy the commentary genre. There are many possible ways to group the proverbs in these central chapters, none wholly satisfactory. For devotional purposes, Ellen Davis's suggestion is valuable: treat each proverb as a little haiku poem, memorizing and "chewing" on it so as to internalize its wisdom.[1] For the purposes of this commentary, however, loose thematic connections and word repetitions among groups of proverbs will guide the approach, opening out frequently to further reflections that go beyond the particular set of proverbs under consideration.

Immediately following chapters 10–29 are two short units that seem to be attributed to non-Israelites: Agur (30:1–33) and Lemuel's mother (31:1–9). These sections seem to reinforce the international, ecumenical scope of Israel's search for wisdom, a feature that was already in evidence in the main section of Proverbs as well, most notably in 22:17–24:34 (see pp. 105–11, commentary on Prov. 22:17–24:34). Whatever the exact setting for its various teachings, Proverbs is a book that comes out of communal practices of pedagogy. The cohesiveness of 10:1–31:9 is to be found less in the arrangement of its themes than in the pedagogical trajectory of gradually increasing complexity and ambiguity in its wisdom teachings. As these chapters of Proverbs move, gradually and unevenly, from clear antitheses between the wise and foolish to more ambiguous statements about the compromises and uncertainties of wise judgments, from the childhood home to the adult public sphere, and from Israelite to foreign wisdom, the reader is called to progress as well in order to attain a mature, seasoned wisdom. The wisdom of the earlier chapters is not left behind, but it acquires depth and nuance as more of the tensions of human experience unfold throughout the

1. Ellen F. Davis, *Proverbs, Ecclesiastes, and the Song of Songs*, WBC (Louisville, KY: Westminster John Knox Press, 2000), 11–12.

book and as earlier teachings are seen in new light. As noted above, 31:10–31 serves as a final "bookend," mirroring the personification of wisdom in chapters 1–9. Taking the form of an intricate acrostic poem, 31:10–31 serves as an elegant ending to Proverbs.

Proverbial teachings are guardians of tradition, reflecting the foibles and prejudices of their time as well as its enduring insights. Some of the "common sense" of Proverbs on a variety of subjects will not resonate with contemporary readers. Young men were the original audience, and the male perspective of the arrangers and interpreters of the book's teachings is apparent throughout. Learning from Proverbs thus requires careful discernment, not rote acceptance. The genre of wisdom itself, with its multiple, even conflicting, perspectives on what is wise and good and true, invites this critical engagement. Any fool can spout proverbs, but the wise person knows how to draw out of the treasury of human wisdom "a word fitly spoken" (25:11) in a particular situation.

Structural Outline

The superscriptions in the book of Proverbs divide it into the following sections:

1:1–9:18:	"The proverbs of Solomon, the son of David, king of Israel."
10:1–22:16:	"The proverbs of Solomon."
22:17–24:34:	"The words of the wise."
25:1–29:27:	"These also are proverbs of Solomon that the officials of King Hezekiah of Judah copied."
30:1–33:	"The words of Agur son of Jakeh. An Oracle."
31:1–9:	"The words of King Lemuel. An oracle that his mother taught him."

Though Prov. 31:10–31 does not have a superscription, its form as an acrostic poem sets it apart as a distinct section.

1:1–7

The Purpose of the Book of Proverbs

The first seven verses of Proverbs form an introduction to the whole book by announcing its pedagogical purpose: to teach wisdom. The initial verse ascribes the book of Proverbs to Solomon, linking the wisdom it offers to the king of Israel renowned for pursuing wisdom (cf. 1 Kgs. 3:9–28; 4:29–34). Some of the teachings in the central portion of Proverbs (chaps. 11–29) may date back to the period of Israel's monarchy, but the ascription to Solomon is an editorial device certifying the authority of Proverbs' wisdom teaching. Parallel to the law and the prophets and not subsumed under either of them, wisdom has its own integrity.

Following the ascription, the next verses pile up pedagogical terms, variously translated as *instruction, discipline, teaching, skill, knowledge*. These words recur throughout Proverbs, underscoring that wisdom is not innate or intuitive; it must be learned, and learned in community. While the young and simple have a desperate need for wisdom (v. 4), the wise and discerning also need communal instruction for their continued growth (v. 5). It is the mark of fools to resent teaching and discipline (v. 7). Human health and flourishing depend on acquiring wisdom. Becoming wise is not a matter of uncovering the principles of the universe or acquiring technical skill. Wisdom is deeply practical knowledge. As Karl Barth notes, "Human wisdom means the art of living. The wise man as distinct from the fool knows how to make a use of his life and of the whole universe which is in harmony with its creation and preservation by God and therefore meaningful, rich in promise and redemptive."[1]

1. Karl Barth, *Church Dogmatics* II/1, *The Doctrine of God*, trans. G. W. Bromiley, ed. T. F. Torrance (Edinburgh: T. & T. Clark, 1957), 433.

The centerpiece of these introductory verses is a trio of moral terms: *righteousness*, *justice*, and *equity* (v. 3b). These terms echo the language of the biblical prophets and show that the wisdom commended by Proverbs is inseparable from social ethics. Wisdom concerns not simply personal flourishing but the flourishing of the whole society. While the prophets decry particular acts of injustice and oppression, the wisdom of Proverbs focuses mostly on the forming of character, the cultivation of lifelong dispositions and virtues that are conducive to building a just and equitable common life. As Michael Fox asserts, "Wisdom means not only knowing but also *wanting* to do what is right and to avoid sin."[2]

> **To be good is to be good at being human. It is to know how to play out one's part in social life. It is to have the kind of formed and developed character that enables one to enter into a life of friendship, and by so doing become better than one was. "Virtues are dispositions to make choices which will make you better able to make choices." And because our choices express our relationship to the community and to its flourishing, they have an ineliminable political dimension.**
>
> Alasdair MacIntyre, review of *The Good Life: Ethics and the Pursuit of Happiness*, by Herbert McCabe, *Tablet* (10 Sept. 2005): 22.

The last verse of the introduction contains what can be considered the motto of Proverbs as a whole: "The fear of the LORD is the beginning of knowledge." This affirmation is repeated, with close variations, at key points throughout the book of Proverbs: here at the very beginning; in 9:10 at the end of the large section that provides the opening frame for the collections of proverbs in chapters 10–29; in 15:33, at the midpoint of the book; and in 31:30, in the closing frame of the book. The entire wisdom of Proverbs is thus couched in a worldview that acknowledges the sovereignty of the Holy One and the dependence and limitations (both cognitive and moral) of human beings. Acquiring wisdom is not a human self-help project but a creaturely response to the fearsome, gracious, and wise presence of God. God is acknowledged as the source of human wisdom; the futile and deadly alternative to

2. Michael V. Fox, "The Pedagogy of Proverbs 2," *Journal of Biblical Literature* 113 (1994): 243.

fearing the Holy One is trying to be wise in one's own eyes (3:7). God's gift to us as creatures is the space and time to become wise, that is, the opportunity to learn to live in the presence of the just and holy God so as to reflect in our modest creaturely ways God's own wisdom. Following this path of God-fearing wisdom is what Karl Barth calls "the only possible life."[3] Every other kind of human life is delusional and ultimately destructive.

Theology and ethics are never separated in Proverbs. Knowing and fearing God involves a reorientation of one's whole life. What Proverbs calls "the fear of the LORD" is consonant with H. Richard Niebuhr's two-stranded definition of faith: faith in God is "on the one hand an expression of confidence, on the other, an oath of allegiance. In the one sense it means, 'I trust in God'; in the other, 'I will keep faith with him.'"[4] We might think first of corporate worship as the center of the community's faith, but Proverbs is remarkably unconcerned with the worship of God. The focus of faith's expression for Proverbs is not the worshiping assembly but the ordinary settings of home, field, and marketplace. It is in this Monday-to-Friday world that both the trusting acknowledgment of God and loyalty to God's project must be worked out.

3. Barth, *Church Dogmatics* II/1, 433.
4. H. Richard Niebuhr, *Radical Monotheism and Western Culture* (New York: Harper, 1960), 18.

1:8–4:27

The Surpassing Value of Wisdom

1:8–1:19

What follows in the rest of chapters 1–9 is a series of lectures and poems that are all moral exhortations to a youth about the importance of embracing wisdom. These opening chapters constitute a hermeneutical guide to interpreting the book of Proverbs as a whole. Raymond Van Leeuwen refers to the teachings in chapters 1–9 as "threshold speeches" addressed to young men on the verge of adulthood.[1] The primary teacher in this household instruction is the father (mothers are referred to only in 1:8 and 6:20). The male perspective of Proverbs is thus established from the beginning. As Carol Newsom notes, "A casual reader asked to describe Proverbs 1–9 might reply that it was the words of a father talking to his son, mostly about women."[2]

The first of these speeches contains shockingly violent language. The youth is warned against the enticements of rapacious thieves, those who "lie in wait for blood" and "wantonly ambush the innocent" (v. 11). The thieves' lure for participating in their violence is easy wealth and comradery. "Throw in your lot among us," they urge the youth; "we will all have one purse" (v. 14). This vignette makes clear that the path of true wisdom is not obvious; the teachings of fathers and mothers about what makes for human flourishing are in competition with false promises of wealth and friendship.

C. L. Seow notes that the wicked in this passage are described

1. Raymond C. Van Leeuwen, "Liminality and Worldview in Proverbs 1–9," *Semeia* 50 (1990):111–44.
2. Carol A. Newsom, "Woman and the Discourse of Patriarchal Wisdom: A Study of Proverbs 1–9," in *Gender and Difference in Ancient Israel*, ed. Peggy L. Day (Minneapolis: Fortress Press, 1989), 142–60.

in terms reminiscent of personified Death in Canaanite mythology: "Like Sheol let us swallow them alive and whole" (v. 12). The insatiability of Death is used "to describe the insatiability of human oppressors" and the terrible social consequences of their greed for "booty" (v. 13).[3] This dramatic imagery underscores another parental point: wisdom is a matter of life and death. Moreover, it is a matter of life and death not only for the victims of the thieves' plundering but also for the thieves themselves. In the harshly ironic language of verses 18–19, the wicked set an ambush for themselves: the greed that leads them to deadly violence will end up costing them their own lives. It is a common theme in Proverbs: Wickedness is ultimately self-destructive. Living in ways that flout God's righteousness, justice, and equity is finally a dead end. Verse 17 is probably a common proverb but is here given a specifically theological meaning: "The bird" looking on over the schemes of the wicked is God, and the Holy One will not be mocked.

1:20–33

Proverbs in many ways reflects the patriarchal society from which it emerged. The "child" (Heb. *ben*) addressed by its teachings is a young man, and the book's perspective on marriage and family life is decidedly male. Yet all the memorable characters in Proverbs are female, and the most striking of them by far is the figure of Woman Wisdom, who makes repeated appearances in the first nine chapters.

Unlike the thieves in the previous passage who sneak around, lying in wait for their unsuspecting victims, Woman Wisdom makes a dramatic entrance. She raises her voice in the most public places of the city, in the corridors of power and influence. Her authoritative presence is impossible to miss and defies patriarchal conventions about appropriate female social roles. Later on, Proverbs will depict Woman Wisdom in inviting, even alluring ways. But in this first appearance she is a harsh figure, castigating those who have spurned her teaching. She vows to show them no pity, to laugh at their calamity and to mock them when panic strikes (v. 26).

3. C. L. Seow, *Ecclesiastes* (Garden City, NY: Doubleday, 1997), 263.

Though like the parents in the previous passage she urges the young and simple to acquire wisdom, her authority clearly transcends theirs. In her public role, Woman Wisdom is reminiscent of the wise woman in 2 Samuel 20:16–19, who boldly summons King Joab to give him advice in the midst of a crisis. But even more she brings to mind prophetic depictions of God, such as those found in Isaiah 65:2, 12; 66:4; and Jeremiah 7:24–27. As Roland Murphy notes, what is attributed to God in prophetic speeches is here attributed to Woman Wisdom: "It is she who feels rebuffed, and who threatens those who refuse to listen. She has divine authority, and she hands out reward and punishment."[4] The reward and punishment Woman Wisdom promises are not arbitrary or capricious but rather the expectable result of human actions that either respect or defy the justice and order of God's world. The disaster that awaits those who hated knowledge and would have none of Wisdom's reproof (vv. 29–30) is one they have brought on themselves: "They shall eat the fruit of their way and be sated with their own devices" (v. 31). By contrast, to those who listen to her teaching, Woman Wisdom promises security and ease.

> **The Wisdom Woman appears abruptly in . . . all places where crowds gather, where people come together to transact daily commerce and legal dealings in the ancient cities. In the thick of life at its shabbiest and most exciting, in the routine of daily marketing and in the struggles of ordinary people to survive—it is there that the Wisdom Woman extends her invitation.**
>
> Kathleen M. O'Connor, *The Wisdom Literature* (Wilmington, DE: Michael Glazier, 1988), 70.

2:1–22

The second chapter of Proverbs is a twenty-two-line poem, addressed once again to a nameless "child." The first verses urge the hearers to respond to Woman Wisdom's invitation with the same alacrity as she extended it: as she cried out and raised her voice and stretched

4. Roland E. Murphy, *Proverbs* (Nashville: Thomas Nelson, 1998), 12.

out her hand, so they too are to stretch out (NRSV: "incline") their hearts and cry out for insight and raise their voices for understanding (vv. 2–3). They are to seek wisdom as devotedly as they would search for silver and hidden treasures (v. 4). Proverbs sees obtaining wisdom as the central project of human life, and success in this endeavor requires eagerness and diligence.

The theological orientation of wisdom is again affirmed. The wisdom human beings seek is "the fear of the LORD" and "the knowledge of God" (v. 5). God is the source of wisdom, and wisdom is God's gift to us (vv. 6–7). There is no contradiction here with the preceding exhortation for human beings to seek wisdom. Everything important in the life of faith is both a gift and a task. The acknowledgment of wisdom as God's gift goes hand in hand with the eager human pursuit of it. Just as sanctification is both a gift of the Holy Spirit and an intentional forming and disciplining of our lives, so acquiring wisdom is a deliberate living into the gift of creaturehood. As our Creator, God welcomes us into a life-giving and life-sustaining network of relations with the physical world, with various human communities, and with God's own self. Wisdom is both God's gift to us and a lifelong task to pursue. Its goal is the flourishing of creaturely life, both human and nonhuman. Throughout the book of Proverbs, divine agency and human agency are never a "zero-sum game." God is always the giver of wisdom, and we are to be its constant seekers.

The metaphor of the *path* predominates in the second half of the poem (2:11–22). Ellen Davis notes two important features of a path as a metaphor for the pursuit of wisdom. First, the decision to follow a path must be made again and again. It is possible to forsake a path after starting down it (v. 13). Pursuing wisdom requires persistence—what Eugene Peterson (following Friedrich Nietzsche!) has called "a long obedience in the same direction."[5] Second, a path is by definition a communal artifact: "Many feet clear it, over a period of time; repeated use keeps it open."[6] Pursuing wisdom is not a solo

5. Eugene Peterson, *A Long Obedience in the Same Direction: Discipleship in an Instant Society* (Downers Grove, IL: InterVarsity Press, 2000).
6. Ellen F. Davis, *Proverbs, Ecclesiastes, and the Song of Songs*, WBC (Louisville, KY: Westminster John Knox Press, 2000), 36.

endeavor: we depend on those who have walked ahead of us, and our attempts to follow the path of wisdom guide those who will come after us.

To understand wisdom as faithfulness to a communal path cuts sharply against modern Western sensibilities of the freedom and autonomy necessary for authentic human selfhood. Charles Taylor provides an acute description of this modern understanding of self:

> Not only should I not fit my life to the demands of external conformity; I can't even find the model to live by outside myself. I can find it only within. . . . Being true to myself means being true to my own originality, and that is something only I can articulate and discover. In articulating it, I am also defining myself. I am realizing a potentiality that is properly my own. This is the background understanding to the modern ideal of authenticity, and to the goals of self-fulfillment or self-realization in which it is usually couched.[7]

Obviously, this view of what it means to realize one's authentic self rejects the kind of communal formation in wisdom that Proverbs urges and exemplifies. Taylor sides with Proverbs against these modern sensibilities, noting that human beings are inherently dialogical: we become full human beings only through deep and repeated exchange with others. Our authentic identity is forged in interaction, not in isolation. Taylor writes,

> Only if I exist in a world in which history, or the demands of nature, or the needs of my fellow human beings, or the duties of citizenship, or the call of God, or something else of this order *matters* crucially, can I define an identity for myself that is not trivial. Authenticity is not the enemy of demands that emanate from beyond the self; it supposes such demands.[8]

Proverbs simply assumes that we are all confronted with demands that emanate from outside ourselves. These are not to be seen as a distraction from our own self-realization. Negotiating these demands with integrity is what authentic human life is about.

Unquestioning conformity to communal demands is not what

7. Charles Taylor, *The Ethics of Authenticity* (Cambridge, MA: Harvard University Press, 1991), 52.
8. Ibid., 57.

Proverbs advocates. As Kathryn Tanner notes, the acknowledgment that the self is socially constituted does not in itself specify the *kind* of society that *ought* to constitute the self.[9] According to Proverbs, the wicked also follow ways and paths (2:13–15). Not all communal paths deserve to be pursued; some need to be shunned. But even the paths that are deemed good and just (v. 30) can only be followed with effort and discernment. Various wisdom traditions flourished across the ancient Near East, and Proverbs itself reflects the creative appropriation and reworking of wisdom from other cultures. Passing wisdom on across time and space takes imagination and risk as well as diligence. Because the path of wisdom continues into the future, the challenge of staying on it falls to each generation anew. The "common sense" of Proverbs reflects a stable, patriarchal, preindustrial society that differs greatly in many respects from our own. Following the path of wisdom for us will mean discerning the shape of righteousness and justice and equity (v. 9) in our own contexts; faithfulness to the same divine wisdom may require us to do things our forebears in Proverbs could not have imagined.

Our constant endeavor, day and night, is not just to transmit the tradition faithfully, but also to put it in the form we think will prove best.

John Calvin, "Defense against Pighius," quoted in *Tradition and the Modern World: Reformed Theology in the Nineteenth Century*, B. A. Gerrish (Chicago: University of Chicago Press, 1978), 13.

A new character abruptly appears on the scene in 2:16, a dangerous female counterpart to Woman Wisdom who intrudes several times in chapters 1–9 (5:1–23; 6:20–35; 7:1–27; cf. 9:13–18). The NRSV refers to her as a "loose woman" and an "adulteress," but Roland Murphy's translation of verse 16 is more accurate:

> To save you from the women who is a stranger,
> From the outsider whose words are smooth.[10]

Scholars debate the identity of this figure; in any case, as Christine

9. Kathryn Tanner, "The Care That Does Justice: Recent Writings in Feminist Ethics and Theology," *Journal of Religious Ethics* 24 (Spring 1996):171–91.

10. Murphy, *Proverbs*, 13.

Roy Yoder notes, her prominent feature is that she is "someone 'outside' socially accepted categories, whether ethnic, legal, social, or sexual."[11] Like the wicked men of verses 12–15, her ways are evil. Verse 17 can mean either that she has forsaken her marriage partner, breaking the covenant witnessed to by "her God," or, reading marriage as a metaphor for covenant fidelity to God, that she has been faithless to God. Either way, consorting with her is perilous. For the young men who "go to her" (v. 19) (a phrase with sexual overtones), the result is death.

The references to abiding in and being rooted out of the land (vv. 21–22) suggest a link between the opening nine chapters of Proverbs, which most scholars think were composed in the Persian period, and the concerns of the postexilic books Ezra and Nehemiah. In those books anxiety about recovering and holding onto the land after the exile prompted strong warnings against the dangers of exogamous marriage to "strange women" (Neh. 10:27; Ezra 9:12; 10:2, 10–18, 44). The fear that marriage to foreign women threatened both fidelity to God and Israel's prospect of regaining the land may be echoed in Proverbs' warnings in 2:16–19. In the absence of king and temple, marriage and the household were central to the recovery of both economic stability and religious integrity.

FURTHER REFLECTIONS
Strangers

Ancient Israel was a porous, heterogeneous society full of outsiders. Not surprisingly, then, biblical Hebrew has a rather well-developed vocabulary to denote people who were strangers. The Hebrew words used to describe the "strange woman" in Proverbs 2:16–19; 5:1–23; 6:20–35; and 7:1–27 are *zar* and *nokhri*. The first term almost always has a negative valence in Scripture, characterizing persons who are in some way a threat to the community. The term *nokhri* can be used as a more neutral reference to someone foreign. Ruth, for example, refers to herself this way (Ruth 2:10). However, from the

11. Christine Roy Yoder, *Proverbs*, Abingdon Old Testament Commentaries (Nashville: Abingdon Press, 2009), 30.

same root comes the word used to indicate idolatry (literally, the worship of "strange" gods, e.g., Jer. 5:19). This term appears several times in Ezra and Nehemiah to refer negatively to foreign wives who threaten the cohesion and stability of the postexilic community and who are to be banished, along with their children. When *zar* and *nokhri* are paired, as they are in the first nine chapters of Proverbs, they take on an unambiguously hostile tone. The strange woman, the outsider, is someone who threatens the well-being of the whole community. The same word in its masculine form is used in Ecclesiastes 6:2 for one who usurps the family inheritance.

It is important to remember, however, that this is not the whole biblical story on strangers. The most common term for stranger in Scripture is *ger*, a general term referring to those who by virtue of not "belonging" experience social and economic vulnerability. Like orphans and widows, this is a protected group: the duty to welcome and defend the stranger is one of the constant themes of the Torah. Just as the people of Israel were "strangers in the land of Egypt," so they are called by God to "know the heart of the stranger" (Exod. 23:9) and to offer them refuge and protection. The *toshav*, often translated "resident alien," is another group that deserves special communal protection.[12] The biblical narrative abounds with broad injunctions to show hospitality to the stranger and the alien.

Yet at various points Scripture also recognizes that outsiders can pose a grave threat to the children of God. This recognition is especially apparent in the Israelite community after the exile and in the Johannine community of early Christians. In a world of violence and insecurity, the community of faith tends to turn inward, excluding those who threaten its integrity and well-being. The stranger in the community's midst is sent home, and the stranger at the door is denied entry. "Do not receive into the house or welcome anyone who comes to you and does not bring this teaching," 2 John 10–11 counsels, "for to welcome is to participate in the evil deeds of such a person." In circumstances of extreme vulnerability, this may be a necessary stance for people of faith to take. However, they always make the decision to exclude as morally compromised creatures;

12. See the discussion on strangers in Johanna W. H. van Wijk-Bos, *Making Wise the Simple: The Torah in Christian Faith and Practice* (Grand Rapids: Eerdmans, 2005), 29–32, 195–202.

their sense of physical or moral weakness remains a temptation to a sectarian community that recognizes God's faithfulness only to people like themselves. As with the women in Ezra and Nehemiah, often those excluded are among the most vulnerable members of the society to begin with.

It must also be recognized that welcoming the stranger can exacerbate the vulnerability of less-powerful persons in the host community. A flagrant example of this is found in Genesis 19:1–8, where, in an effort to protect his two guests, Lot is willing to sacrifice the well-being of his daughters. Welcoming the stranger can also intensify unjust relations within the host community. Women and servants, for example, often bear most of the burden of hosting strangers. Children of hosts sometimes go hungry so that important guests will be well fed. Welcoming others cannot be pursued at the cost of neglecting or abusing "the least" within the community. The "strange woman" in Proverbs 1–9 and the strange man in Ecclesiastes 6:2 may be non-Israelites or simply marginalized members of Israel's community. In any case, concerns for justice toward the most vulnerable must guide the community's treatment of the stranger.

3:1–12

The references to long life, honor, and wealth make chapter 3 a favorite of contemporary prosperity-gospel preachers. Certainly Proverbs makes connections between acquiring wisdom, on the one hand, and physical, social, and material well-being, on the other. Wisdom seeks a holistic human flourishing. But the connections between wisdom and wealth are not as straightforward as they might appear at first glance. The poem in verses 1–12 urges a life of humble trust in God; the material blessings that may come are by-products of this relationship, not its goal. The center of faith is aligning ourselves with God's love and intentions for the world, not realizing certain spiritual or material blessings for ourselves.

The parental voice again pleads with the child to remember teaching and obey instruction. The promise of long life and flourishing that will result (v. 2) reflects a kind of "natural consequences" parenting

> **Those with experience raising children will have already discovered the inadequacy of libertarian negative freedom (don't tread on me, who are you to tell me what to do) in favor of moralistic intervention: mediate forcefully in the lives of one's offspring in the hope that they will some day grow up to be healthy, law-abiding, thoughtful, generous-spirited, self-conscious about their motives, uninclined to wallow in sloth or self-pity.**
>
> Alain de Botton, *Religion for Atheists: A Non-believer's Guide to the Uses of Religion* (New York: Pantheon, 2012), 74.

style. Health and long life are not the invariable outcome of wise living, but they are an expectable result. The parental instruction is true and life-giving even if obedience to it does not guarantee physical or material benefit. This is quite different from a parent who promises a reward *in exchange* for obedience. When promised rewards are extrinsic to the desired behavior, they threaten to become the goal of it all; obedience becomes simply the means to some independently desirable end like wealth or honor. For Proverbs right relation to God and neighbor *is* the end. Since "the Lord by wisdom founded the earth" (v. 19), it is right to expect that living according to the grain of the universe will make for human flourishing. The sages of Proverbs are hopeful but not naïve about the consequences of wise living.

It is divine, not human, loyalty and faithfulness to which the child is to adhere. Like Deuteronomy's instruction regarding the Torah (Deut. 6:8), Proverbs urges that God's loyalty and faithfulness are to be kept in mind at all times by creating a visible reminder of their constant presence: "Bind them around your neck" (v. 3). The child is likewise instructed to write God's faithfulness "on the tablet of [his] heart," as Jeremiah urged regarding God's law (Jer. 31:33), so that there is a perfect consonance between one's outward appearance and inward reality. Outward actions and inward attitudes are woven together to make a life that is pleasing both to God and to others (v. 4).

The history of Israel, and indeed of all nations, is littered with rulers who did "what was right in their own eyes" rather than "what was right in the sight of the Lord." In the terminology of Proverbs, they relied on their own insight and satisfied themselves with being wise in their own eyes (vv. 5, 7). This is a permanent human temptation, and it is as disastrous for ordinary persons as it is for rulers and their nations. Proverbs calls us back to what Ellen Davis describes as "the deeply sane recognition that I am not God, and when I pretend to be God, I only destroy myself."[13] If pretending to be God destroys us, walking in the paths God has made straight and turning away from evil (vv. 6–7) does us good all the way to our bones (v. 8b).

In verse 9 we find Proverbs' only exhortation to participate in religious observance. Compared to the expressive beauty of the psalms and the detailed injunctions of the law, Proverbs is strikingly unconcerned with worship. However, in its own way, it is just as intent on life lived faithfully in the sight of God. Here the reference is to the offering of the firstfruits of the harvest to God in thanksgiving, which were used to support the Levitical priests as well as resident aliens, widows, and orphans (cf. Deut. 26:12; Neh. 10:35–39). Generosity toward these dependent and vulnerable members of the community will rebound to the giver: their barns and wine vats will be filled. As Kathryn Tanner notes regarding biblical understandings of sacrifice, "Benefits do not come back to the offerer because the conditions of something like a contract have been fulfilled but because the rite trades on God's unbroken faithfulness to a decision to be with those engaged in Temple service."[14] Proverbs makes very few references to worship, but its teachings reflect deep commitment to the piety and social ethics underlying Israel's worship rituals. In their writings, H. Richard and Reinhold Niebuhr likewise advocate a covenantal view of humanity as intrinsically relational and interdependent and argue that this is vital to sustaining a democratic society: "Contractual political arrangements freely entered into for political advantage can just as easily and freely be abandoned; covenantal politics presupposes commitment and a bond among human beings for the sake of which all political advantage must be subordinated."[15]

In contrast to the material abundance of verse 10, the "discipline" of verses 11–12 seems to refer to the suffering or want that the

13. Davis, *Proverbs, Ecclesiastes, and the Song of Songs*, 41.
14. Kathryn Tanner, *Christ the Key* (Cambridge: Cambridge University Press, 2010), 264.
15. H. Richard Niebuhr, *Theology, History, and Culture: Major Unpublished Writings*, ed. William Stacy Johnson (New Haven, CT: Yale University Press, 1996), xxxii–xxxiii.

> **The actual world of human nature and history does not by any means guarantee self-realization through self-sacrifice unless self-realization is conceived in terms quite distinct from the ordinary will-to-survive in physical life. History may bestow immortality of fame upon a martyr, but it certainly does not guarantee that an honest man will prosper because of his honesty or an unselfish man succeed because of his generosity.**
>
> Reinhold Niebuhr, *An Interpretation of Christian Ethics* (San Francisco: Harper and Row, 1963), 33.

faithful may experience. Material blessing is not a guaranteed result of pursuing wisdom. Even in circumstances of hardship, the wise continue to trust in God.

3:13–18

Woman Wisdom reappears in much more alluring guise than in her previous portrayal in 1:20–33. This time she is not the stern prophet but rather the immensely attractive object of human seeking. "Nothing you desire can compare with her" (v. 15). She is a better investment than precious metals and jewels, mediums of exchange of that day. To acquire her promises long life, honor, riches, pleasantness, and peace. There are several linguistic links between this poem and the paean in 31:10–31 to a "woman of substance" (see pp. 133–35, commentary on Prov. 31:10–31). The "woman of substance" is in some ways a real-life incarnation of Woman Wisdom, and, in turn, Proverbs' characterization of Woman Wisdom may owe something to actual successful and prosperous women in the Persian period. There are also similarities between the portrayal of Woman Wisdom in verse 16 ("Long life is in her right hand; in her left hand are riches and honor") and various Egyptian deities, including female ones such as Ma'at, who are depicted as holding the ankh, the symbol of life, in their right hand, and the scepter, the symbol of riches and honor, in their left. Here, as in chapter 1, the figure of Woman Wisdom is associated with divine authority, though in a rather provocative way for Israelite readers.

This paean to wisdom in chapter 3 promises material blessings while at the same time relativizing their significance. Wisdom is to be treasured far more than any earthly riches (vv. 14–15). Prosperity may accompany wisdom, but the happiness wisdom brings (vv. 13, 18) does not depend on it. This happiness, as in Psalm 1, is found in following the way of the righteous. The righteous are like "trees planted by streams of water, which yield their fruit in its season, and their leaves do not wither" (Ps. 1:3a). Similarly, Wisdom is "a tree of life to those who lay hold of her" (v. 18). This phrase also recalls "the tree of life" in the garden of Eden, which Eve saw "was to be desired to make one wise" (Gen. 3:6). Whereas eating from this tree was a source of shame and suffering for Adam and Eve, the tree of life represented by Wisdom is a source of honor and long life (v. 16). Larry Rasmussen notes that every time the Torah is returned to the ark after a Sabbath reading, Jewish congregations recite 3:18 as part of a sung prayer: "It is a tree of life to those who hold fast to it, and its precepts are right. Its paths are paths of pleasantness and all its paths are peace. Return us to thee, LORD, and we shall return. Renew our days as of old."[16] This prayer reflects the explicit identification of Wisdom with Torah found in the deuterocanonical book Sirach but also the deep biblical resonances between wisdom and law about what makes for human flourishing.

3:19–26

Proverbs has already asserted that God is the source and bestower of wisdom (2:6–7), but now the link between wisdom and God's work of creation is affirmed more explicitly and will be elaborated still further in 8:22–31. The earth, heavens, and waters are all founded and established by God's wisdom. Divine wisdom is woven into the fabric of the universe, and we ignore this wisdom at our peril, as our current ecological crisis demonstrates. These verses exhort us to fall in step with the rhyme and reason of God's handiwork. The way to a secure and confident earthly life is found not by trusting in our own wisdom but by keeping to the path of divine wisdom.

The imagery of verses 21–26 is reminiscent of inducements elsewhere in Scripture to follow God's law. But whereas the injunctions

16. Larry L. Rasmussen, *Earth Community, Earth Ethics* (Maryknoll, NY: Orbis Books, 1996), 199.

to follow the law are rooted in God's redemptive act of bringing Israel out of slavery in Egypt (e.g., Exod. 20:2; Deut. 5:6), the appeal to follow wisdom in Proverbs is grounded in God's work of creation. In Proverbs, we find no narratives of God's mighty acts on behalf of Israel.[17] Though 30:1 identifies that chapter as an "oracle," appeals to special visions or signs from God seem out of place. Both Proverbs and Ecclesiastes model and commend the attempt to discern God's presence in human life by paying attention to common human experience and the example of other creatures (e.g., Prov. 30:24–31). Discerning the wisdom by which God founded the cosmos is a project given to all people. It is not the special province of Israel. Yet Israel's pursuit of wisdom was just as much an expression of faith as its obedience to the law. As Gerhard von Rad put it, "The experiences of the world were for [Israel] always divine experiences as well, and the experiences of God were for [Israel] experiences of the world."[18]

3:27–35

The bulk of chapter 3 has focused on relationships with God and with Woman Wisdom. But these are always inseparable from wise living in community, and the rest of the chapter turns to consider relationships with neighbors. The warnings of verses 27–31 chart a progression of wrong relation. The first stage is "passive-aggressive" actions—harming the neighbor by failing to do them the good that is due them (vv. 27–28).

> **Never give a hollow greeting of peace or turn away when someone needs your love. Bind yourself to no oath lest it prove false, but speak the truth with heart and tongue.**
>
> *Rule of St. Benedict,* chap. 4, http://christdesert.org/Detailed/71.html.

The second stage is actively planning harm against unsuspecting neighbors and picking fights with them (vv. 29–30). The third stage is making common cause with the violent, either in our hearts or in our actions (v. 31). Joan Chittister's

17. By contrast, portions of deuterocanonical wisdom deliberately integrate the figure of Wisdom with the history of Israel.
18. Gerhard Von Rad, *Wisdom in Israel* (Nashville: Abingdon Press, 1972), 62.

reflections on *The Rule of Benedict* resonate with Proverbs' drive toward transparency in our relations with others:

> Dissimulation, half answers, vindictive attitudes, a false presentation of self are all barbs in the soul of the monastic. Holiness, this ancient rule says to a culture that has made crafty packaging high art, has something to do with being who we say we are, claiming our truths, opening our hearts, giving ourselves to the other pure and unglossed.[19]

The wise are trustworthy in their words and actions and do not violate the trust of others. They are not tempted by the prosperity of those who thrive by dishonest or violent dealings. They are the humble whom the Lord favors (v. 34), the righteous who enjoy God's confidence (v. 32). First Peter 5:5 quotes verse 34 in exhorting the Christian community to humility: "'God opposes the proud, but gives grace to the humble.'" Humility is the sane recognition of one's good yet finite creaturehood (see pp. 103–4, "Further Reflections: The Vice of Pride and the Virtue of Humility").

By contrast, "the perverse are an abomination to the LORD" (v. 32). The word *abomination* (*toevah*) is often used in Deuteronomy and Leviticus with reference to transgressions in cultic behavior, especially those involving idolatry or participation in foreign rituals. We have already noted Proverbs' lack of attention to matters of worship, and it holds true here as well. The word *abomination* in Proverbs is most often associated with ethical failings, such as using false weights (11:1; 20:10, 23), lying (12:22; 26:25), and other forms of wickedness in neighborly dealings. Concrete instances of failure to love the neighbor are an abomination to God.

These teachings about right relation with the neighbor apply both individually and collectively. Human institutions of all sorts are capable of loveless inaction, malicious intent, and outright violence toward others. The industrial practices and government policies that contribute to environmental degradation are a good example: the welfare of the neighbor, both human and nonhuman, is scorned in favor of convenience and profit. But as Proverbs notes, "Toward the scorners [God] is scornful" (v. 34). The cry of the earth and the cry

19. Joan Chittister, *The Rule of Benedict: Insights for the Ages* (New York: Crossroad, 2009), 51.

of the poor are intimately connected, and God hears them both.[20] The Hebrew word order in verse 35 heightens the contrast described throughout this section: "Glory, the wise inherit; but fools, disgrace."

4:1–27

Three times in this chapter, parents exhort children to listen to their instruction and hear their words (vv. 1, 10, 20). The focus is not on the content of their teaching but on the benefits of adhering to it and the dangers of forsaking it. The father commends his teaching in verse 3 by appealing to his own experience as a youth. He is not exercising arbitrary authority over his child but passing down the time-tested wisdom of the community that he once received from his own parents. Just as he found life in this communal teaching, he now urges his child to do the same.

The core of the parental instruction in verses 5–9 is to "get wisdom." Wisdom is once again personified as a woman, and it is clear that "getting her" is more important than undertaking particular wise actions. The imagery in verses 5–8 is of desire and devotion: the youth is to love, embrace, and prize wisdom, and she in turn will keep, guard, exalt, and honor her beloved. The emphasis is on disposition and character, not on specific acts. If the heart is oriented toward wisdom, everything else in life will fall into place. "A fair garland" and "a beautiful crown" in verse 9 evoke the adorning of a bridegroom (cf. Song 3:11; Isa. 61:10), and the wedding imagery is apt: the youth is to cleave to Woman Wisdom as his lifelong companion.

Like Moses laying before the people of Israel the choice between good and evil, the way of life and the way of death (Deut. 30:15–20), Proverbs presents two communal paths in verses 10–19: the life-giving path of wisdom and the death-dealing path of wickedness. As Richard J. Clifford notes, "One joins a community of people on the same path and shares their fate."[21] Those who join the path of the

20. Leonardo Boff, *Cry of the Earth, Cry of the Poor* (Maryknoll, NY: Orbis Books, 1997).
21. Richard J. Clifford, *Proverbs: A Commentary* (Louisville, KY: Westminster John Knox Press, 1999), 22.

wicked cause others to stumble and eventually stumble themselves (vv. 16, 19); those who take the path of the upright will not stumble even when they run (v. 17). The wicked bumble around in the dark while the path of the upright is lit up like the light of dawn (vv. 18–19). Proverbs does not speculate about why some choose death over life or why "the bread of wickedness" and "the wine of violence" (v. 17) remain perversely and perennially attractive. Instead, it fights fire with fire, appealing to the heart's desires by portraying the delights and benefits of Woman Wisdom. The NRSV translation of verse 13 captures this strategy. Even though the word translated "instruction" is masculine in Hebrew, the second part of the verse switches to the feminine: "Guard her, for she is your life." All the parental instruction, words, precepts, teachings, and commandments are expressions of Woman Wisdom. Following them is not a burdensome duty but the gateway to joy and abundant life.

> **The fault of an evil will begins when one falls from Supreme Being to some being which is less than absolute. Trying to discover causes of such deficiencies—causes which, as I have said, are not efficient but deficient—is like trying to see darkness or hear silence.**
>
> Augustine, *City of God* 12.7, trans. Henry Bettenson (London: Penguin Classics, 1972), 480.

The last unit of instruction in 4:20–27 gives an anatomical inventory: ears, eyes, heart, flesh, mouth, lips, and feet. This inventory is obscured in the NRSV translation: where the NRSV has the words *speech* and *talk* in verse 24, the Hebrew has *mouth* and *lips*. The KJV's rendering of this verse is closer to the original Hebrew: "Put away from thee a froward mouth, and perverse lips put far from thee." The point of this literary device is that following wisdom involves the whole person. At the center of this section is verse 23, with its counsel to "keep your heart with all vigilance, for from it flow the springs of life."

This emphasis on the heart anticipates what will become the core of Augustine's theological anthropology: the disposition of our hearts is the source of all that we are and do. The wisdom advocated by Proverbs is not a cool, detached form of reasoning. While Proverbs praises self-control and warns against giving in to violent and greedy impulses, its counsel is not one of "moderation in all things."

Rather, Proverbs advocates a passionate engagement of the whole person toward what pleases God and makes for human flourishing.

From a heart rightly oriented toward God and neighbor "flow the springs of life." The wise person is to "hate what is evil, hold fast to what is good" (Rom. 12:9). A misdirected heart will lead one's ears, eyes, flesh, mouth, lips, and feet to alienation and death. The Bible presents this contrast in the figure of Solomon. In 1 Kings 3:9–12 God gladly grants Solomon's request for a "listening heart" that is turned toward God and able to discern what is right. But by 1 Kings 11:1–5 Solomon's many wives, whom he "clung to in love," had "turned away his heart" from the true God. The theme of dangerous sexual liaisons, always depicted in terms of male foolishness in response to female seductiveness, also returns in the next chapter of Proverbs.

The citizens of the holy City of God, living in accordance with God in the pilgrimage of this present life, fear and passionately desire, grieve and rejoice, and because their love is right, all these emotions of theirs are right.

Augustine, *City of God* 14.9, trans. Martha Nussbaum, "Augustine and Dante on the Ascent of Love," in *The Augustinian Tradition*, ed. Gareth B. Matthews (Berkeley: University of California Press, 1999), 70.

5:1–7:27

Looking for Love in All the Wrong Places

5:1–25

The strange woman reappears in chapter 5, this time in a more sexually explicit portrayal than in chapter 2. There is an abbreviated recapitulation of the anatomical inventory of the previous section in verses 1–2, with the youth enjoined to keep ears and lips in the path of understanding and knowledge. It is immediately followed by an expanded description of the strange woman, whose lips, palate, and feet lead to Sheol. (Where the NRSV has *speech* in verse 3, the Hebrew has *palate,* suggesting a more intimate contact with the strange woman than simply listening to her words.) Though "in the end" the strange woman is sharp and bitter, she initially appears smooth and sweet: her lips "drip honey," and her palate "is smoother than oil" (vv. 3–4). No wonder the unsuspecting are drawn to her! The strange woman tricks others, but she is also self-deceived: she herself has wandered from the path of life but does not know it (v. 6). Her foolishness fools others.

In the next section, verses 7–14, the parents paint an imaginative picture of the disaster and remorse awaiting the youth who consorts with the strange woman. Wealth, health, and public reputation are all at stake. The warning that "strangers will take their fill of your wealth, and your labors will go to the house of an alien" (v. 10) may echo fears about exogamous marriage in Ezra and Nehemiah, since "within the patrilineal land tenure system women were capable of inheriting and disposing of property"[1] (see pp. 23–27, commentary on Prov. 2:1–22).

1. Harold C. Washington, "The Strange Woman of Proverbs 1–9 and Post-Exilic Judaean Society" in *Second Temple Studies,* vol. 2, *Temple and Community in the Persian Period,* JSOT

True to the parents' larger rhetorical strategy, these harsh warnings are balanced by enticements to embrace the wise path (vv. 15–23). While chapter 4 depicts wisdom as a metaphorical mate, chapter 5 for the first time portrays the youth as actually married. Embracing wisdom and embracing one's wife are drawn together. Eros within marriage is part of wisdom. Folly is not connected with the youth's desire for sexual intimacy but with the temptation to find it in the bosom of another woman (v. 20). The word translated "adulteress" in verse 20, as in 2:16, is more accurately rendered as "stranger," though violation of marriage vows is suggested here. Using language reminiscent of Song of Songs, verses 15–19 describe "the wife of your youth" as a cistern and fountain, as "a lovely deer, a graceful doe." Her ever-flowing love refreshes and delights. "May her breasts drench you at all times" is a more literal translation of verse 19 than that provided by the NRSV.[2] Given the intoxicating pleasure of sex at home, why go elsewhere? The NRSV translation blunts the verbal connections between verses 19 and 23. In contrast to the wise youth who enjoys the "intoxicating" love of his own wife, the one who embraces the strange woman is "intoxicated" by folly and dies for lack of discipline. To embrace one's wife is to embrace Wisdom herself.

Alice Ogden Bellis points out the power of Proverbs' personification of wisdom as a woman. There is an erotic charge that would be missing if all the encouragement to pursue wisdom were made only on an abstract level. But the imagery is not as effective for persons who are not sexually attracted to women. Bellis writes her own version of a parental exhortation to seek wisdom for her teenage daughters:

> Do not be misled by handsome faces, by beautiful bodies, by the right clothes, or the correct manners. Especially do not be deluded by flatterers who tell you that you are beautiful (of course you are!) and then ask you to give them your body or your soul. The pretty boys and jocks will beckon to you. They

Supplement Series 175, ed. Tamara C. Eskenazi and Kent H. Richards (Sheffield: JSOT Press, 1994), 235.

2. Patrick D. Miller, *The Ten Commandments* (Louisville, KY: Westminster John Knox Press, 2009), 308.

> will ask you to go out. Soon, they will ask you to bed. It's a dangerous world. Their ways lead to death, not just moral death, but physical death as well. . . . Do not cavort with folly. Do not consort with the frivolous. Rather spend your time with men of substance and worth. A good man is hard to find, but he is more precious than jewels.[3]

Wisdom in Proverbs is not a solo pursuit. We find wisdom in the intimate company of others.

6:1–19

Obstacles to pursuing wisdom come not only from violent men and seductive women. They also come from one's decisions about work and finances. Poor financial judgment and laziness are repeatedly warned against in the main body of Proverbs' teaching, and they make an appearance here (vv. 1–11). The financial snare of pledging one's own property to guarantee the debt of another is vividly depicted in verses 1–5 (cf. 11:15; 17:18; 20:16; 22:26–27; 27:13). Christine Roy Yoder suggests that this practice, which is not reflected in biblical law codes, might have been more common in the Persian period, when a barter economy shifted to a monetary economy.[4] The temptation to make a little money by intervening with a creditor on behalf of a debtor is strongly warned against here. By a word and a handshake (vv. 1–2) the guarantor becomes financially liable for another's debts. He puts himself "in the hand" of another (v. 3b) as surely as a gazelle is in the hand of a hunter or a bird in the hand of a fowler (v. 5). If the debtor defaults, the guarantor can lose everything, putting everyone in the household at risk. Better to lose face in getting out of this dangerous financial game (v. 3–4) than to lose one's shirt.

The humble ant is held up as a model of industry in 6:6–8. Biblical wisdom literature sees the natural world as permeated with God's

3. Alice Ogden Bellis, "A Letter to My Daughters," in *Wisdom and Psalms,* A Feminist Companion to the Bible, 2nd series, ed. Athalya Brenner and Carole Fontaine (Sheffield: Sheffield Academic Press, 1998), 91.
4. Christine Roy Yoder, *Proverbs*, Abingdon Old Testament Commentaries (Nashville: Abingdon Press, 2009), 72–73.

wisdom and thus a source of revelation for human seekers of wisdom. Just as King Solomon is depicted as speaking of "animals, and birds, and reptiles, and fish" (1 Kgs. 4:33), so the sages of Proverbs appeal to many different creatures as examples for human creatures to emulate and to learn from (cf. 30:25). Harvest typically falls in the summer months in Palestine, so the ant wisely gathers its sustenance then, in preparation for the cooler, wetter months when food is less plentiful. The industrious ant is contrasted with the human lazybones in verses 9–11, who shuns prudent foresight and honest work until overtaken by poverty. Failure to work during harvest time is not simply a failure of personal self-discipline: in agricultural societies this failure has disastrous consequences for the whole community. "The lazy person does not plow in season; harvest comes, and there is nothing to be found" (20:4; see also 10:5). Shirking harvest labor represents a breach of social responsibility.

FURTHER REFLECTIONS
Poverty and Work

Proverbs lauds hard, honest work and repeatedly insists on a connection between laziness and poverty (6:9–11; 13:4; 14:23; 15:19; 19:24; 20:4; 21:25; 24:30–34). But it is important to recognize that the relationship Proverbs posits is one-directional. Laziness invites poverty, but poverty is not always the result of laziness. Sometimes, for example, poverty comes as a result of injustice: "The field of the poor may yield much food, but it is swept away through injustice" (13:23). Likewise, Proverbs recognizes that wealth is not always the result of virtue and hard work: "The getting of treasures by a lying tongue is a fleeting vapor and a snare of death" (21:6). Contemporary Christian reflection on work has recognized the need to raise critical questions about the assumed connections between hard work, economic success, and virtue that are central to the cultural mythology of the United States. In particular, African American theologians and ethicists have reflected on the coercive, exploitative, and alienating work that characterized the period of chattel slavery. The wealth of slave owners was not virtuous: it was the result of sinful exploitation of fellow human beings. The hard work performed by slaves was not good work: it was oppressive and dehumanizing work. As Joan Martin insists, if the way in which economic relations structure human life and work is ignored, there is a danger of "abstracting, mystifying, and romanticizing all forms of work as theologically and morally 'good.'"[5]

In our own time, we need to critique the way in which the economic relations of global capitalism structure the working conditions of millions of poor persons around the world who work to produce consumer goods for the wealthy to enjoy. Proverbs' warnings against laziness also apply to the rich, who prefer not to trouble themselves to find out about the dehumanizing conditions under which their clothing and electronics are manufactured. More broadly, Proverbs calls to account both companies and communities who are heedless about the long-term social and environmental costs of their way of life, choosing the path to wealth and comfort that is easiest in the short run.

Following the mocking portrait of the slacker is the still sharper portrayal of the wicked person in verses 12–15. The wicked person's mouth, eyes, feet, and fingers are all devoted to wrongdoing. The phrase "with perverted mind" in verse 14 is better translated "with perverted heart." Proverbs regards the heart as the most important human organ for learning. As Clifford comments, "The heart is the engine that drives a person and in this case the heart is perverse."[6] We have already noted resonances in Proverbs with what will become Augustine's emphasis on the disposition of the heart as the core of our moral identity (see pp. 36–38, commentary on 4:1–27). According to Proverbs, crime does not pay. Just as the lazy suddenly find themselves overwhelmed by poverty, so the wicked are without warning laid low by calamity.

The numerical list of what the Lord hates in verses 16–19 anticipates the more elaborate play with numbers in 30:18–31. As already

5. Joan Martin, *More Than Chains and Toil: A Christian Work Ethic of Enslaved Women* (Louisville, KY: Westminster John Knox Press, 2000), 128.
6. Richard J. Clifford, *Proverbs: A Commentary* (Louisville, KY: Westminster John Knox Press, 1999), 76.

noted, the word *abomination* in Proverbs is most often associated with ethical failings rather than cultic transgressions. Here too the emphasis is on proud, manipulative, and violent dealings with the neighbor; of the seven abominations listed, "the heart that devises wicked plans" is symbolically at the center. Proverbs shows repeated concern with lying witnesses and false messengers (13:17; 14:5, 25; 19:5, 9; 25:19), whether in court or in everyday conversation. Lying and falsehoods are also at the center of sowing discord "in a family," literally, "between brothers." This can refer to blood relations or to neighbors and fellow citizens more generally. As James, the "wisdom book" of the New Testament, insists, the human tongue can be "a restless evil, full of deadly poison" (Jas. 3:8). It can fuel envy and selfish ambition. But the tongue can also be used for good: "a harvest of righteousness is sown in peace for those who make peace" (Jas. 3:18). Proverbs is intensely concerned with the character of human speech.

6:20–35

The imagery in 6:20–23 and the beginning verses of the next chapter, 7:1–3, echo the foundational commandment of Judaism in Deut. 6:4–9, known as the Shema. This imagery aligns the father's commandment and the mother's "teaching" (*torah*) in verse 20 with God's instruction of Israel in the Torah given through Moses at Sinai. These teachings are to be embraced and kept close, a commandment still reflected visibly in the Orthodox Jewish practice of

Hear, O Israel: The LORD is our God, the LORD alone. You shall love the LORD your God with all your heart, and with all your soul, and with all your might. Keep these words that I am commanding you today in your heart. Recite them to your children and talk about them when you are at home and when you are away, when you lie down and when you rise. Bind them as a sign on your hand, fix them as an emblem on your forehead, and write them on the doorposts of your house and on your gates.

Deut. 6:4–9.

wearing *tefillin*, small boxes with Torah passages inside them, during morning prayers (cf. Deut. 11:18).

The parental teaching is also aligned with Woman Wisdom, though this connection is obscured by the NRSV translation of verse 22. It should read, "When you walk, *she* will lead you; when you lie down, *she* will watch over you; and when you awake, *she* will talk with you." As Ellen Davis avers, the suggestion here is that the youth "might enjoy 'pillow talk' with Wisdom."[7] Given that the content of the parental teaching in this part of chapter 6 concerns the dangers of sexual promiscuity for young men, the appeal to intimate relationship with Woman Wisdom is an important rhetorical strategy.

Whereas 5:15–19 urged faithfulness in marriage by appealing to the sexual pleasures of one's own wife, this chapter appeals to the disastrous consequences of sexual promiscuity. It is better to take this passage as a warning against all kinds of sexual promiscuity, not only against liaisons with a married woman. The identity of the woman in verse 24a is unclear; the Hebrew can be translated either "an evil woman" or "the wife of another." The reference in verse 24b is to "a strange woman," not "an adulteress." Thus verse 24 might best be translated,

> To keep you from an evil woman,
> from the smooth-tongued foreigner.[8]

It is also uncertain whether the point of verse 26 is to contrast the costs of consorting with a prostitute (a loaf of bread) and the costs of consorting with a married woman (one's very life) or to condemn them both. It is possible to translate verse 26 as a parallel construction:

> For the price of a whore is a loaf of bread,
> and the wife of a man will stalk your precious soul.[9]

The teaching in verses 27–35 then moves on to the practical social

7. Ellen F. Davis, *Proverbs, Ecclesiastes, and the Song of Songs*, WBC (Louisville, KY: Westminster John Knox Press, 2000), 58.
8. I am here following an unpublished translation by Johanna W. H. van Wijk-Bos.
9. Ibid.

repercussions of such unwise actions. Adulterous affairs in particular are playing with fire. The penalty for getting caught is beyond the reach of "hush money" and predictably leads to social disgrace and physical harm. As the sages conclude in verse 32, "He who commits adultery has no sense," literally "lacks heart." The result of such misdirected passions is self-destruction.

7:1–27

Chapter 7 begins with Deuteronomistic injunctions to hold fast to parental teachings (cf. 6:20–21). Again the parents urge intimacy with Woman Wisdom: "Say to wisdom, 'You are my sister,' and call insight your intimate friend" (v. 4). *Sister* and *friend* are here terms of romantic endearment (cf. Song 4:9–12). Being enamored with Woman Wisdom will keep the youth safe from the blandishments of the strange woman, the smooth-tongued foreigner (v. 5). The competition between the two female figures for the youth's affections is heating up. Chapter 7 presents the most extensive treatment yet of the lures of the strange woman. In chapter 8, we have Wisdom's majestic self-presentation, and in chapter 9, both Woman Wisdom and the strange woman will set their lavish table and issue enticing invitations to come join them. As we have already noted, being wise in Proverbs is not a matter of tamping down one's emotions in favor of cool reason: it is channeling one's passions toward what is just and life-giving. But passionate love can also lead to disaster, as the rest of chapter 7 demonstrates.

Proverbs 7:6–27 reads like an episode from a romance novel. As evening falls, the anonymous eyewitness (Woman Wisdom?) secretly watches from inside the house as a foolish youth deliberately heads where he has already been warned not to go (5:8–14). There he is approached by a femme fatale "decked out like a prostitute" (v. 10). Though she looks ready for love, her locked and blockaded heart (v. 10) permits no genuine emotional intimacy. She quickly accosts the young man and kisses him. The secret witness overhears her words: " 'I had to offer sacrifices, and today I have paid my vows' " (v. 14). This seems to refer to bringing an animal to the temple to be slaughtered as a "sacrifice of well-being" (cf. Lev. 3:1–19; 7:15–17). After the priests have poured the blood of the animal against the sides of the altar and burned the fat, the meat is returned to the sacrificer for home consumption. The strange woman thus presents herself at once as a model of religious devotion and as one with fresh meat to share. However, as Yoder notes, her summons to a feast also "establishes her capacity to kill, and foreshadows the outcome of their meeting: the youth hastening to his death 'like an ox to the slaughter' (7:22b)."[10] The strange woman further entices the youth with her luxurious and perfumed bed, assuring him that her husband is away for "a long journey," leaving them free to take their "fill of love" without risk of discovery. The gullible youth "bounds like a stag toward the trap" and rushes like a bird "into a snare" (vv. 22–23), becoming one in the long line of her victims (v. 26).

10. Yoder, *Proverbs*, 87.

8:1–9:18

In the Beginning Was Wisdom

8:1–21

Proverbs has so far introduced two arresting female figures who both speak confidently and loudly in public places and compete for the youth's attention and loyalty. Despite prodigious amounts of scholarly discussion, the direction of historical influence between these two figures—how one affected the development of the other—is not clear. Many suspect that Woman Wisdom developed as a literary counterpart to the "strange woman."[1] In any case, what is clear is their opposing moral valence: whereas following the strange woman is a dead end (7:27), following Woman Wisdom leads to life and joy (3:16–18). Carol Newsom rightly points out that Proverbs' pedagogical device of using contrasting female figures to symbolize the extremes of good and evil, wisdom and folly, is not innocent.[2] This device is a male projection that objectifies women and contributes to gender stereotypes that continue to plague women today. The binary characterization of women as either Eve or Mary, either wily seductress or submissive wife, distorts the lives of real women and plays into attempts to disempower them as being either too pure or too morally compromised for positions of authority and leadership.

However, the rhetorical ploy of presenting Wisdom as a compelling and safe alternative to the seductive attractiveness of the strange woman is overwhelmed in Proverbs 8 by the grandeur of Woman Wisdom's authority. Though the youth in Proverbs is encouraged

1. See Joseph Blenkinsopp, "The Social Context of the 'Outsider Woman' in Proverbs 1–9," *Biblica* 72 (1991): 457–73.
2. Carol A. Newsom, "Woman and the Discourse of Patriarchal Wisdom: A Study of Proverbs 1–9," in *Gender and Difference in Ancient Israel*, ed. P. L. Day (Philadelphia: Fortress Press, 1989), 142–60.

to address Woman Wisdom with the affectionate familiarity of "sister" and "friend" (7:4), it is clear right from the start of chapter 8 that Wisdom is far too imposing a persona to fit neatly into a moral lesson about choosing an intimate partner wisely. Her commanding presence explodes the narrow trope of "the good wife" (though this trope will reemerge in 31:10–31). Both Woman Wisdom and the strange woman deviate from the patriarchal social norms of Israelite society, in which appropriate roles for females were restricted to being either a chaste, obedient daughter in her father's house or a loyal, child-bearing wife in her husband's house. The strange woman's adulterous advances obviously violate these norms. But the foil to the illicit excitement offered by the strange woman is not contented domesticity with a model wife. In her own way, Woman Wisdom destabilizes the norms of patriarchal society by emerging in chapter 8 as a figure of cosmic power and authority.

Wisdom and the strange woman are not truly comparable figures in chapters 7–8. The strange woman singles out a gullible youth under the cover of darkness and offers him a secret one-night stand. By contrast, Woman Wisdom boldly addresses "all who live" (v. 4): male and female, young and old, wise and simple alike. She proclaims her righteousness (vv. 6–11), her authority (vv. 12–16), and her benefits (vv. 17–21) in universal terms. Unlike the strange woman's boast of her luxurious bedding (7:16–17), Woman Wisdom promises rewards that are more valuable than any human treasure (8:10–11, 18–19). Unlike the strange woman's ploy to subvert her husband's authority over her (7:19–20), Woman Wisdom claims the authority to guide even the earth's most powerful men: by her, "kings reign, and rulers decree what is just" (8:15). The proper human attitude toward her is love (8:17) but also obedience to her call to listen and take instruction (8:6, 10). This mingling of love and obedience is typical of patriarchal religion's portrayal of the proper relationship of the believer to the male deity. If the figure of the strange woman defies patriarchal gender roles, the figure of Woman Wisdom hardly restabilizes the patriarchal norm of female deference to male authority. Instead, her power and goodness are larger than life, demanding acknowledgment by all people. In a similar way, the person of Jesus will explode the trope of bridegroom in the New Testament:

all people, both married and single, male and female, are to be his bride. In both cases, the marital metaphors, while not losing all their problematic cultural baggage, are stretched to the breaking point.

8:22–36

Theologians over the centuries have given verses 22–31 more attention than any others in Proverbs, and for good reason: they set an exquisite theological frame around all the prosaic teachings about relationships, speech, money, hard work, and so on that make up the bulk of Proverbs' teaching. God's gracious generosity toward creation and creation's utter, continuing dependence on God are the operative background beliefs in the biblical wisdom books. In verses 22–31, these theological background beliefs are foregrounded. It is as if a light shone briefly from behind an opaque scrim, illuminating what is generally hidden from view: the ceaseless, wise, delighted work of God the Creator, whose loving energy is behind every manifestation of life.

These verses insist that God's creating is not a manipulation of some preexisting matter—God is the sole source of all that exists. As medieval theologians would later work out, God is not a kind of thing belonging to a generic category populated by other items on the inventory list of the universe. God does not stand at the top of a great chain of being with some parts of creation in closer ontological relation to God than other parts. Thus God is appropriately portrayed in verses 22–31 as the creator of all—mountains and hills, the fountains of the deep—not just of the bits of reality that we might deem most like God. Furthermore, God creates intimately and directly, not relinquishing this role to some mediating power: in these verses it is God who establishes the heavens and assigns to the sea its limit. There is no "buffer zone" between the Holy One and the world, no need for God to be protected from compromise and corruption when coming into contact with finite reality.

Wisdom's primordial presence at creation, already alluded to in 3:19–20, is elaborated in 8:22–31 in an astonishing self-portrait, one of the most-developed personifications in the Old Testament.

Biblical scholars have looked for parallels in the self-presentation and self-praise of gods and goddesses from neighboring ancient Near East cultures.[3] The stately poetry of these verses will also remind readers of the creation hymn in Genesis 1:1–31. But there are some key differences. The speaker throughout the creation account in Proverbs is Woman Wisdom. As William Brown notes, unlike the remarkably elevated view of humanity in Genesis 1–2, "there is no 'anthropic principle,' at least in any strong sense, at work in Proverbs. Humanity is barely mentioned. The poem's primary focus is on Wisdom."[4] Wisdom's testimony to her presence at God's work of creation in verses 22–31 undergirds her repeated claims in earlier verses to have the authority to guide human beings in their search for creaturely wisdom. As the "I-witness"[5] to creation, she knows and delights in the basic structures and patterns of the entire universe that God has made.

Woman Wisdom begins by declaring her preeminence: she was the firstborn of God's creation, "the first of his acts of long ago" (v. 22). She was brought forth "before the beginning of the earth" (v. 23), before anything else had come into being. Many biblical scholars see maternal imagery in these first verses describing God's relationship to Wisdom. Brown, for example, translates verses 22–25 this way:

> YHWH had me (as) the beginning of his way;
> the earliest of his works of yore.
> Of old I was woven, from the very beginning,
> even before the earth itself.
> When the deeps were not existent, I was birthed.
> When the wellsprings were not yet laden with water,
> when the mountains were not yet anchored,
> before the hills themselves, I was brought forth."[6]

3. For example, Gula, the Mesopotamian goddess of healing, declares herself in a long self-praise poem, asserting, "I bestow life on the one who reveres me. I make straight the path of the one who seeks after my ways." Raymond Van Leeuwen, "The Book of Proverbs," NIB 5 (Nashville: Abingdon Press, 1997), 90.
4. William P. Brown, *The Seven Pillars of Creation: The Bible, Science, and the Ecology of Wonder* (Oxford: Oxford University Press, 2010), 169.
5. Ibid.
6. Ibid., 164. See also Christine Roy Yoder, *Proverbs,* Abingdon Old Testament Commentaries

As Terence Fretheim notes, birthing language is used in Proverbs 8 for Wisdom but not for the other things God produces in this text—hills, mountains, springs, and so forth—so that Wisdom's relationship with God in this passage is established as a unique one.[7] Yet these verses leave Woman Wisdom's precise relationship with God mysterious. As Christine Roy Yoder comments, "It is as though the details of her beginnings lie just beyond her words, that the multiple metaphors she evokes—birthing, establishing, anointing, creating—point variously to what is otherwise ineffable. The effect is certainty about God's initiation of their association before the creation of anything else and absolute wonder as to how."[8] Later christological reflection on 8:22–31 will hinge on this issue of Wisdom's relation to God (see pp. 53–55, "Further Reflections: Jesus Christ and Woman Wisdom").

Regardless of how exactly Wisdom was brought into being, she insists that she precedes the creation of everything else: without her, not one thing came into being—not the watery depths (v. 24), not the mountains (v. 25), not the fields (v. 26). She makes her point again, this time positively: she was at God's side in the creation of "the skies above [and] . . . the fountains of the deep" below (v. 28), and everything in between. She ends by affirming her intimacy with the Holy One: she was daily God's delight, rejoicing before God and in God's creative work and "delighting in the human race" (vv. 30–31).

Wisdom's characterization of her relation to God's creative work in verse 30a hinges on the translation of the Hebrew word *ʾāmôn*. The NRSV translation "master worker" harks back to the compressed cosmogony in 3:19–20: "The LORD by wisdom founded the earth. . . ." This translation highlights Wisdom's intimate knowledge of the overarching structures and patterns of God's creative work. As God's "architect associate"[9] in the creation of the whole world, Wisdom is an authoritative guide to the details of daily human life. Human beings are to continue this "wise building" in their own

---

(Nashville: Abingdon Press, 2009), 94–95; and Claudia V. Camp, *Wisdom and the Feminine in the Book of Proverbs* (Sheffield: Almond Press, 1985), 84.

7. Terence E. Fretheim, *God and World in the New Testament: A Relational Theology of Creation* (Nashville: Abingdon Press, 2005), 211.

8. Yoder, *Proverbs*, 95.

9. Van Leeuwen, "Book of Proverbs," 94.

endeavors (cf. Exod. 31:1–11). This translation also connects well with the imagery of the following chapter, where Wisdom the architect builds a house of seven pillars (9:1–2), creating space for her students to come and be nourished at her table.

On the other hand, the word *ʾāmôn* can also be translated "little child," and this translation too makes theological sense. The translation "little child" or "darling" continues the maternal imagery of Wisdom's creation in 8:23–25 and emphasizes Wisdom's sharing in the delight, even playfulness, of God's creative work. The imagery of play and delight reminds us that God does not need a world in order to be God. Creation is an act of free grace. The whole world reflects the artistry and joyfulness of the Creator, who fashioned the fearsome Leviathan to sport in the sea (Ps. 104:26). Wisdom, there at the very beginning of God's work, exudes a child's delight in God's creative acts, especially the creation of humans. Humans who heed her guidance for living wisely are also promised a sharing in her primordial joy: "Happy are those who keep my ways" (8:32b; cf. 8:34).

FURTHER REFLECTIONS
Jesus Christ and Woman Wisdom

The sages who compiled the book of Proverbs do not seem to have been particularly interested in the metaphysical identity of Woman Wisdom. They were more interested in her rhetorical function in their teachings as a mediating figure between God and humanity. They portray Wisdom as fashioned in a mysterious way by God to be the voice of God to humanity; humanity, in turn, is to embody Wisdom by beholding and following the ways of God in its communal life.

However, metaphysical questions about the figure of Woman Wisdom in Proverbs 8 resurface repeatedly in subsequent Jewish and Christian thought. Ben Witherington notes that, once introduced into the biblical wisdom tradition, personified Wisdom "took on a life of its own and grew in importance, in complexity, and in depth as time went on."[10] The deuterocanonical books Baruch and

10. Ben Witherington, *Jesus the Sage: The Pilgrimage of Wisdom* (Minneapolis: Fortress Press, 1994), 50.

For she is a breath of the
power of God,
and a pure emanation of the
glory of the Almighty;
therefore nothing defiled
gains entrance into her.
For she is a reflection of
eternal light,
a spotless mirror of the
working of God,
and an image of his goodness.
Although she is but one, she
can do all things,
and while remaining in herself,
she renews all things;
in every generation she passes
into holy souls
and makes them friends of
God and prophets.

Wis. 7:25–27.

Sirach use the figure of Wisdom as a way of talking about what later became the central focus of Israelite faith—torah. Wisdom also becomes an important vehicle for talking about the center of Christian faith, Jesus. When early Jewish Christians, steeped in Jewish wisdom traditions, "were looking for exalted language from their heritage that gave adequate expression to their new-found faith in Jesus Christ, they found no language better suited for such praise than the paeans about personified or hypostatized Wisdom found in Proverbs 8," as well as in Sirach and the Wisdom of Solomon.[11]

Christological appropriations of personified Wisdom start already in the New Testament writings and represent perhaps the earliest way Christians attempted to understand the relationship between Jesus and the one he called "Father."[12] Being with God at the beginning, communicating revelation or divine knowledge, offering spiritual food, being accepted by some and rejected by others—these are all attributes of the figure of Woman Wisdom in the first nine chapters of Proverbs that resonate with Christian affirmations about Jesus. The Gospel of John, in particular, with its identification of Jesus Christ with the Logos of God, reflects the influence of the language and motifs of Israelite wisdom tradition.[13]

11. Ibid., 289.
12. James D. G. Dunn, *Christology in the Making* (Grand Rapids: Eerdmans, 1996), 212: "The origin of the doctrine of the incarnation is in a Wisdom Christology."
13. Raymond Brown, in his magisterial commentary on John, notes a dozen wisdom motifs in John's portrayal of Jesus. Raymond E. Brown, *The Gospel according to John* (New York: Doubleday, 1966), 1:cxxii–cxxv.

The fourth-century theologians Athanasius and Arius, in the debates leading up to the Council of Nicea, both employed inherited Christian assumptions about an identity between Jesus Christ and Woman Wisdom. They argued fiercely about how to understand Wisdom's ontological relation to God, particularly her declaration in 8:22 that she "was created at the beginning of God's works." Arius's insistence that Wisdom fell on the creaturely side of the Creator-creature distinction ultimately did not carry the day. Athanasius argued that Jesus Christ is savior, and only God can save us. Therefore Wisdom, incarnate in Jesus Christ, must be of the same being with God. This metaphysical oneness is better conveyed by the sexual imagery of begetting or birthing rather than the language of creating or making. Thus while 8:22–31 freely mixes imagery of creating and birthing to describe Wisdom's relation to God, Athanasius makes a clear distinction between the two. In what becomes standard Trinitarian language, the Son is eternally begotten by God the Father, not made. Unlike Arius, Athanasius reads 8:22 as a reference to the incarnation: the eternally begotten Son is "made flesh" for human salvation. Woman Wisdom in Proverbs 8 is thus at the exegetical center of what becomes the church's Trinitarian doctrine. As Augustine would later put it, "She is sent in one way that she may be with human beings; she has been sent in another way that she herself might be a human being."[14]

Contemporary wisdom Christologies have taken a bewildering variety of forms—Christ as laconic sage, avatar of universal divine wisdom, eternal ordering principle of the universe, female personification of God, to name only a few—and remain a subject of sharp disagreements among biblical scholars and theologians. Yet the conviction that the power of God incarnated in Jesus Christ has been at work throughout all creation from the beginning has been at the center of a long tradition of Christian readings of biblical wisdom. King Solomon had great wisdom, but in Jesus Christ "something greater than Solomon is here" (Matt. 12:42): Jesus Christ is God's Wisdom made flesh.

14. Augustine, *De Trinitate* 4.20.27, "*Sed aliter mittitur ut sit cum homine; aliter missa est ut ipsa sit homo*," http://www.thelatinlibrary.com/augustine/trin4.shtml; my translation.

In 8:32–36, Wisdom resumes her role as teacher, addressing once again her audience in 8:4–5. She mixes exhortations to listen and obey with promises and warnings. In 8:34 she promises blessing to the one who, like a lovesick teenager, is always "hanging around," watching daily at her gates, waiting beside her doors (cf. Song 2:9). To love Wisdom is to find life and divine favor. Wisdom ends her teaching with a sharp warning: to fail to find her is to do violence to oneself. To hate her is to love death. This strong language makes clear, once again, that Wisdom is not calling for a dispassionate reasonableness: she is urging the creaturely flourishing that comes from ordering one's loves aright. As Augustine also insists: what you love finally determines who you are.

9:1–18

Proverbs 9 presents two dinner invitations, one from Woman Wisdom (vv. 1–6) and one from "the foolish woman" (vv. 13–18) who has appeared in various guises throughout chapters 1–9. It is the final showdown between the personifications of wisdom and folly in Proverbs (though the two figures reappear in Eccl. 7:23–29). On the surface, the invitations look very similar: both women call out to the simple from the high places in the town, urging them to "turn in here" (vv. 4, 16). Both offer food and drink. But once again, the outcome of accepting these invitations could not be more different. Those who walk in the way of Woman Wisdom will find their days multiplied in the company of the righteous (v. 11). Those who follow the path of folly will end up in the company of the dead in Sheol (v. 18).

There has been much scholarly speculation on the significance of the seven pillars of Wisdom's house (v. 1). Are they a cosmological reference to the seven heavens or the seven firmaments upholding the universe? Do they suggest instead that Wisdom's house should be regarded as a temple? Do the seven pillars simply indicate a very large and spacious house with room for all? Roland Murphy comments, "A discussion of various theories is like walking through a cemetery; one should leave them all in peace."[15] Whatever the significance of this

15. Roland E. Murphy, *Proverbs* (Nashville: Thomas Nelson, 1998), 58.

poetic detail, it certainly adds to the grandeur of Woman Wisdom's invitation, providing the staging for the rich feast she has prepared. Wisdom's hospitality is lavish: servant girls doing her bidding, and a banquet of meat, wine, and bread on offer. All these details stand in contrast with the invitation of the "foolish woman" that follows in verses 13–18. There we find no descriptions of her house, nor any mention of servants. On offer are only bread and water.

In between the two invitations are verses that seem like an interruption to the dramatic tension created by the contrasting female figures. However, on closer examination, verses 7–12 turn out to have an important rhetorical function by recapitulating the opening themes of 1:1–7 and by anticipating the short sayings about the righteous and the wicked that will dominate the next five chapters of Proverbs. These verses thus set off chapters 1–9 as a distinct unit and at the same time prepare the reader for the big stylistic transition beginning at 10:1. Roughly at the center of verses 7–12 is the repetition in verse 10 of Proverbs' motto from 1:7: "The fear of the LORD is the beginning of wisdom." This is a reminder that the book of Proverbs is not principally a virtue ethics. The guidance it offers about "how to be good at being human" is couched in a way of life that has at its center the acknowledgment of utter dependence on God and of the radical limits of human wisdom. For this reason, the scoffers of verses 7–8 will never be wise. Woman Wisdom's voice chimes in again in verse 11, aligning her teaching with "the knowledge of the Holy One" (v. 10b) and touting its life-giving powers. The whole world is God's creation, and there is no greater folly than to try to "go it alone" in acquiring wisdom for creaturely flourishing (cf. 26:12).

The first three verses of 9:7–12 pick up themes from 1:1–7 about who benefits from instruction in wisdom. The wise and righteous (v. 9) are eminently teachable: part of the wisdom they already possess is to know that they need more. The wicked and the scoffers (vv. 7–8), by contrast, take offense at attempts to teach them; much like the fools of 1:7, they "despise wisdom and instruction." The section closes in verse 12 with an enigmatic verse that returns to the theme of benefits. What effect does absorbing or resisting instruction in wisdom have on a person? The answers given in the two halves of verse 12 are not quite parallel. You are wise "for yourself" (v. 12a), which does not preclude benefitting others with your wisdom, but the burden of scoffing is borne by "you alone" (v. 12b). This last claim does not ring true. The burden caused by arrogant people who cannot tolerate any correction or criticism, particularly when they are in positions of power, rarely falls on them alone. In fact, it is usually others who are hurt most directly. Perhaps, as Ellen Davis suggests, the point of verse 12 is that "wisdom always generates a community, or aims at serving a community," whereas "scoffing proceeds from alienation and serves only to deepen it."[16]

The second dinner invitation follows this short interlude. The foolish woman in verse 13 seems to be an amalgam of the dangerous and seductive female figures who have already made several appearances in Proverbs. She is both brash and self-deceived, but she is also a very good talker, echoing exactly the same invitation that Woman Wisdom extended: "'You who are simple, turn in here!'" (v. 16). Christine Roy Yoder notes that while Woman Wisdom wants her guests to lay aside their immaturity (9:6), the foolish woman aims to capitalize on it.[17] Water imagery often has sexual connotations, as we have already seen in 5:15–18; "'stolen water'" (v. 17) suggests illicit sexual activity. The meal to which Folly is luring her guests is a guilty pleasure, not wholesome nourishment.

In a famous passage from his *Confessions,* Augustine recounts a teenage misdeed of stealing some pears from a vineyard. He ruefully admits that he was not hungry and that the pears were not of good quality—in fact, he had better ones at home. He confesses that he "simply wanted to enjoy the theft for its own sake, and the sin." In that incident, Augustine sees a microcosm of the sinful human condition. "I was in love with my own ruin, in love with decay: not with the thing for which I was falling into decay but with decay itself."[18] Proverbs too stresses the absurdity and self-destructiveness of sin. It makes no sense to give up the better food Woman Wisdom offers and join the foolish woman's guests in Sheol (v. 18). Yet it is perversely

16. Ellen F. Davis, *Proverbs, Ecclesiastes, and the Song of Songs,* WBC (Louisville, KY: Westminster John Knox Press, 2000), 73.

17. Yoder, *Proverbs,* 108.

18. Augustine, *Confessions* 2.9, trans. Maria Boulding (Hyde Park, NY: New City Press, 1997), 68. See also Augustine's reflections on Prov. 9:17 in *Confessions* 3.11

tempting to pursue what is foolish and forbidden, to be in love with sin and even with one's own ruin.

The youth has not yet taken up permanent abode in either wisdom's house or the house of folly. Gaining wisdom is a lifetime's work, not something gained or lost in a single decision. But both virtue and vice are habit forming, so good decisions still matter. Accepting the hospitality of others in Scripture is often a metaphor for moral and spiritual choices. Not every offer of hospitality is life-giving. As the apostle Paul insists, "You cannot drink the cup of the Lord and the cup of demons. You cannot partake of the table of the Lord and the table of demons" (1 Cor. 10:21). Part of wise discernment is to shun the hospitality of those who would lead one astray. Like the prophet Daniel's refusal to eat the king's sumptuous food (Dan. 1:8), some invitations to hospitality must be rejected. But which ones? This question is heightened because the parental figures who have been prominent in the first nine chapters of Proverbs are fading into the background, and the responsibility for wise choices is beginning to center on the youth, who has been silent up until now. One of these dinner invitations must be refused, but it is not always easy to distinguish between them. Wisdom, it turns out, has many counterfeits. As 16:25 says, "Sometimes there is a way that seems to be right, but in the end it is the way to death."

FURTHER REFLECTIONS

Preaching on Proverbs from the Lectionary

Proverbs is largely ignored in contemporary Western preaching. Readings from Proverbs appear only a handful of times in the three-year cycle of the Revised Common Lectionary:

Text	Year	Sunday
1:20–33	B	24th Sunday of Ordinary Time
8:1–4, 22–31	C	Trinity Sunday
8:1–8, 19–21; 9:4b-6	A, B, C	Easter Vigil
9:1–6	B	20th Sunday of Ordinary Time
22:1–2, 8–9, 22–23	B	23rd Sunday of Ordinary Time
25:6–7	C	22nd Sunday of Ordinary Time
31:10–31	B	25th Sunday of Ordinary Time

Note that chapters 10–15 of Proverbs do not appear at all in the Common Lectionary (see pp. 71–73, "Further Reflections: Preaching on Proverbs 10–15 without Sounding Like Job's Friends").

In preaching on Proverbs, it is important to remember its grand, ultimate aim: to make us "friends of God and prophets" (Wis. 7:27), wise lovers of God and neighbor. It aims at personal virtue only insofar as this virtue serves the flourishing of communal life before God. Proverbs pursues its goal not by giving its readers a list of hard and fast rules, a biblical equivalent of "The Seven Habits of Highly Effective People." Rather, Proverbs seeks to evoke wisdom in us by gathering human experience in condensed, poetic form and offering it as grist for our own attempts at living wisely. Proverbs is concerned with what ordinary creaturely faithfulness looks like. This makes it a natural book to draw from during the long stretches of "ordinary" time in the church year, when preachers want to spur reflection on practical discipleship in the Monday-to-Friday world of their hearers. All the lectionary readings except two fall in Ordinary Time.

Proverbs' teachings are designed to be easily memorized and passed on to others in oral form. This can be an edifying congregational exercise as well. For example, someone preaching on the lectionary selections from chapter 22 (Year B, 23rd Sunday of Ordinary Time) could pick one verse for the congregation to practice saying out loud and encourage them to memorize it and reflect on it during the week. Many biblical stories contain proverbs "writ large,"[19] and calling attention to these connections in preaching can help people think more deeply about a particular proverb and its significance in their own lives. For example, the reading from chapter 25 (Year C, 22nd Sunday of Ordinary Time) is linked to the story in Luke 14 about Jesus watching the jockeying for position in the house of a Pharisee. Jesus' teaching frequently reflects Israel's wisdom traditions (see pp. 113–15, "Further Reflections: Jesus as Sage").

The selections from chapter 8 for Trinity Sunday encourage a christological reading of Woman Wisdom (see pp. 53–56, "Further Reflections: Jesus Christ and Woman Wisdom"). In her analysis

19. Van Leeuwen, "Book of Proverbs," 24.

of fourth-century theological controversies over chapter 8, Frances Young has advocated an ethical reading of texts. This means for her that "readers have a responsibility to the text, but also to themselves."[20] Responsible reading thus requires both distance and appropriation. Distance is required to respect the text's own claims and context and to provide critical leverage on far-fetched or over-confident interpretations. Young notes, for example, that Athanasius assumes that his Trinitarian interpretation of 8:22–31 is its timeless, universal meaning, placed there by the Holy Spirit for him as an exegete to uncover. Thus he is not cognizant of how his particular community of interpretation is influencing his textual assumptions about chapter 8. According to Young, recognizing the distance of the interpreter from the text will require allowing multiple readings in different communities across space and time. On the other hand, she insists on "a recognition that a Christian reading of the Bible has to wrestle with issues of its unity and the ways in which it points to a reality beyond itself. . . . A Christian ethical reading also has to do justice to 'ourselves,' and that includes the tradition of reading in which we stand."[21] The figure of Woman Wisdom invites Christians to think about Jesus Christ beyond the familiar categories of salvation from sin.

The Easter Vigil is the one place where readings from Proverbs appear in all three years of the lectionary cycle. This service is in some ways the heart of the church's calendar, with its grand sweep of biblical readings telling the whole story of the church's pilgrimage as those who proclaim the light of Christ breaking through the darkness of suffering and death. The verses from chapters 8 and 9 are nestled in a litany of the "mighty acts of God" in Israel's history. They remind the church that in the midst of the grand story of redemption in Christ, God is still sustaining creaturely life and calling the church to pursue the wisdom that makes for creaturely flourishing.

20. Frances Young, "Proverbs 8 in Interpretation (2): Wisdom Personified," in *Reading Texts, Seeking Wisdom: Scripture and Theology*, ed. David F. Ford and Graham Stanton (Grand Rapids: Eerdmans, 2004), 114.

21. Ibid., 115.

10:1–15:33

Practicing Wisdom's "Regular Verbs"

10:1–8

The superscription "The proverbs of Solomon" alerts the reader to a scene change. The very first proverb in this collection, "A wise child makes a glad father, but a foolish child is a mother's grief" (v. 1) is like a little shove pushing the youth onto a stage for a public performance. The extended and persistent exhortations and explanations from the parents and Woman Wisdom that have dominated chapters 1–9 abruptly come to an end. In their place is a long, jumbled sequence of mostly two-line proverbs, without explicit guidance for how to order and make sense of them. It is as if, after an extended period of explicit instruction, the youth's teachers step back and say, "Now, try it yourself."

While this first Solomonic collection of proverbs stretches from 10:1 to 22:16, the first six chapters, 10:1–15:33, form a stylistically distinct subunit. These chapters are dominated by antithetical proverbs in which the second line reinforces the first line by means of a sharp moral contrast. There is not a lot of gray scale in the repeated oppositions between the righteous and the wicked, the wise and the foolish, and the diligent and the lazy. All three contrasts are given a moral valence. For the sages of Proverbs, there is no such thing as wicked wisdom or righteous sloth. The moral distinctions are sharp and clear-cut, as are the consequences of the human actions that correspond to these distinctions: "The hope of the righteous ends in gladness, but the expectation of the wicked comes to nothing" (10:28). Someone starting to read the book of Proverbs at the beginning of chapter 10 might think they had stumbled upon a theology primer for Job's friends. Is it always true that "misfortune pursues sinners, but prosperity rewards the righteous" (13:21)?

Anthropologist Mary Douglas observes that the main function of exaggerated symbolic contrasts like these is "to impose system on an inherently untidy experience."[1] For the youth emerging from his period of "home schooling" and trying to get his bearings in the confusing terrain of moral life, these clear separations and demarcations of good from evil and of wisdom from folly impose some semblance of order. Moral compromises and complications will increase as the book of Proverbs unfolds, but for now they have to wait. The youth is first presented with something more manageable, with the "regular verbs" of the difficult language of human wisdom. But even they are not presented as universal moralisms. The proverbs are compressed, artful observations, borne out by the experience of many generations, about how, in general, the world works. Their poetic form is meant to engage the imagination. They function not as inviolable axioms but as pedagogical devices whose purpose is to encourage readers to pay attention to what is going on in particular situations so that they might gain wisdom. They invite reflection, not unquestioning acceptance. Even when readers find themselves challenging the sages' formulations, as I did at the end of the last paragraph, the proverbs are achieving their pedagogical function to clarify, complicate, and discipline our moral understandings.[2] They hone readers' efforts to make moral sense of the world so that they can act wisely for the sake of human flourishing.

The *Highlights* children's magazine has a feature that depicts two brothers, Goofus and Gallant, responding to concrete situations. Goofus is predictably foolish, selfish, and careless. Gallant, by contrast, is always wise, virtuous, and conscientious. Goofus and Gallant are offered up in stark relief as moral types. The point is not to suggest that there really are two well-defined groups of children who resemble Goofus and Gallant. Rather, the assumption is that there is a little of both in each of us. By asking young readers to enter imaginatively into particular situations—answering the phone, sitting on the bus, playing ball with a friend—the magazine feature

1. Mary Douglas, *Purity and Danger: An Analysis of the Concepts of Pollution and Taboo* (London: Ark Paperbacks, 1988), 4.
2. Paraphrase of Christine Roy Yoder, *Proverbs*, Abingdon Old Testament Commentaries (Nashville: Abingdon Press, 2009), 9.

aims to increase their awareness of their own moral strengths and foibles and their capacity to recognize the likely consequences of their actions. Similarly, the stark moral contrasts in chapters 10–15 are not predicated on the existence of clearly delineated groups of righteous and wicked persons. As Proverbs will later acknowledge, "Who can say, 'I have made my heart clean; I am pure from my sin'?" (20:9). Pedagogical exercises are important precisely because in every human life the slip into wickedness remains a threat. It is possible to "mislead the upright into evil ways" (28:10). Nor, as we have already seen, is the demarcation between wise and foolish absolute: even the so-called wise are deficient in wisdom. Yet dispositions toward righteousness and wickedness, as well as toward wisdom and folly, are reinforced by practice, so ordinary acts and decisions matter. The weight of wicked and foolish habits can finally set persons and whole communities on a one-way path toward self-destruction. Chapters 10–15 put moral categories in bold relief for pedagogical purposes. These proverbs sketch the plot lines of wise and righteous characters so that readers will be drawn to inhabit those characters and in them find space for creaturely flourishing.

Where is God in all of this? God is explicitly mentioned only occasionally in chapters 10–15, and rarely as the subject of an active verb. The theological framing supplied by the first nine chapters of Proverbs makes clear that God is intimately involved with the created world, a world suffused with God's own wisdom. This is why human beings can be confident that the world displays some degree

[Walter White, the main character in the TV series *Breaking Bad*] is consciously choosing to transform himself from a law-abiding, humble, conscientious man to a power-hungry, pride-driven, stop-at-nothing drug lord. . . . For five seasons we watch Walt make choices, small and large, that fundamentally alter his moral disposition. Watching Walt break bad is like reading a Flannery O'Connor story that runs off the rails: he is offered moment after moment of grace (usually in the form of a way out of the drug business), and each time he stares it squarely in the face and turns away. In each choice, we, as viewers, are offered the chance to reflect on the small ways the moral life is built, sustained and compromised.

Kathryn Reklis, review of *Breaking Bad*, TV series created by Vince Gilligan, *Christian Century* (Oct. 3, 2012), 42–43.

of order and coherence. In wisdom, God has shaped the mountains and assigned to the sea its limit (8:25, 29); the physical world is held in being by God's constant power and care, without which life itself would not be possible. Proverbs also insists that because of this divine providence the *moral world* has some degree of order and coherence. Certain human attitudes and behaviors have predictable and appropriate consequences. Just and wise conduct is rewarded; wicked and foolish people get what they deserve. As the central body of Proverbs' teachings unfolds, there are more and more qualifications to these confident observations. Sometimes the gain of hard work is stripped away by injustice (13:23). Sometimes what seems at first to be a wise path leads to death (14:12). Wicked people often appear to prosper (16:8). But these maxims are not where novice wisdom seekers are to start. In general, according to the book of Proverbs, foolish, cruel, slothful, or dishonest behavior brings its own punishment. Generous, respectful, diligent, and just dealings with others bring their own reward. "Those who are kind reward themselves, but the cruel do themselves harm" (11:17). This is God's creative providence at work.

The theologian Howard Thurman recounts a personal story from his experience as a teacher that reflects the mind-set of Proverbs:

> I have had students who during an entire semester did not pay much attention to the simple, direct, natural operations of the classroom, who fulfilled none of the day-by-day requirements relative to their work. Then, when the day of judgment arrived, they came into the classroom, read the examination questions and expected, by some beyond-the-natural operation, to participate in the complete knowledge and understanding of the questions raised. In other words, they expected a miracle. What they received was what they had rated—failure. It is a terrible truth that life does not have a habit of making exceptions in our case even though we may be good in general, even though our fathers may be great men and our reputations of outstanding merit. Let us not be deceived by the great illusions, but let us see the finger of God moving in the natural unfolding of antecedents and consequences.[3]

3. Howard Thurman, "What Shall I Do with My Life?" in *Callings: Twenty Centuries of Christian Wisdom on Vocation,* ed. William C. Placher (Grand Rapids: Eerdmans, 2005), 387.

The results of God's moral order in Proverbs are seen primarily in "the natural unfolding of antecedents and consequences." God does not mete out punishments that seem extrinsic to sinful human actions, sending plagues of locusts to punish Pharaoh, for example (Exod. 10:3–15). Nor does God vindicate the faithful in dramatic acts of power, as illustrated in Elijah's contest with the prophets of Baal (1 Kgs. 18:17–39). Instead, as we have noted, God's wise and just presence is understood in Proverbs more along the lines of "natural-consequences" parenting: there are expectable outcomes *intrinsic* to both good and bad behavior. "The righteousness of the blameless keeps their ways straight, but the wicked fall by their own wickedness" (11:5). This too is evidence of "the finger of God."

Proverbs 10:1–8 sets forth the basic moral categories of chapters 10–15 and affirms the concurrence of divine and human activity. The contrast between wise and foolish opens and closes this section (10:1, 8). Within this envelope is the opposition between righteous and wicked behavior (vv. 2–3 and 6–7). Wisdom includes righteousness in Proverbs, but wisdom is a larger category, involving discernment about what righteousness looks like in particular contexts. Wisdom always aims at the broad question: What makes for creaturely flourishing, both now and in the long term? The wise child (v. 1), the prudent child (v. 5), and the wise of heart (v. 8) are responsive to their larger creaturely contexts of family, agricultural rhythms, and communal teaching. In the middle verses, 3–5, both divine and human agency are lifted up. The Holy One sees to it that the righteous do not go hungry, but that does not imply or legitimate human passivity: human hard work and planning are fitting because they reflect in finite, human ways the wisdom of God's creation. The youth is urged to take the opportunity for providing material sustenance "in hand" in order to avert hunger and shame, not just for himself but for his whole community (v. 4).

By contrast, the wicked, though adept in gaining treasure (v. 2), will end up with nothing to show for it. God will thwart their craving or, according to another possible translation, drive them toward disaster (v. 3). The mouths of the wicked conceal the violence that is in their hearts (v. 6), but no one is ultimately deceived: after they are gone, their names will rot (v. 7). Greed and subterfuge may work in the short term but are in the end self-defeating.

10:9–11:8

The babbling fool of 10:8 is followed by a group of verses that emphasize the vital importance of appropriate speech. Like the New Testament sage in the book of James, the sages of Proverbs recognize that the tongue, though only "a small member" of the body, has an outsized capacity for both good and evil (Jas. 3:5). The solidarity and well-being of the society depend on wise and trustworthy speech.

Speech is also a diagnostic of moral character, because words reflect the heart. Proverbs 10:13 and 10:21 describe fools as those who lack heart ("sense" in the NSRV). Moral character is finally a matter of the heart's orientation, and fools' attention and energies are misdirected. Fools resist communal formation in wisdom (v. 13b), and so their abundance of words (10:14b, 19a) is not life giving and, indeed, can actively promote evil (v. 19a). Wickedness and folly are correlated in Proverbs with speech that is self-deceived, excessive, and harmful to oneself and others. The wise, by contrast, are teachable. They are measured in their speech (v. 19b), accumulating wisdom and using it for the well-being of others (10:14a, 21a).

> **Trust is a social good just as much as the air we breathe or the water we drink.**
>
> Sissela Bok, *Lying: Moral Choices in Public and Private Life* (New York: Pantheon Books, 1978), 26.

Walking in integrity (10:9a), without dissonance between inward thoughts and outward acts and words, brings peace and security to one's life. By contrast, a perverse or twisted way of life (10:9b), in which there is deep, hidden contradiction, makes it hard to sleep at night and will eventually be found out. Winking the eye (10:10a), associated with crooked speech in 6:12–13, is a form of nonverbal communication that leads to strife. The NRSV follows the Greek text in verse 10b to provide a better contrast to the first line: honest rebuke, given in good will and appropriately heeded, makes for peace. Proverbs is not shy about the importance of verbal rebuke in moral formation. This is one reason why the words of the righteous (10:11a) are a fountain of life: their instruction provides guidance that leads to communal flourishing. Their words are as valuable as precious metals (10: 20a). The wicked, by contrast, are duplicitous, using their words to conceal the violence in their hearts (v. 11b). This is also the point of 10:18, where the contrast is between one who conceals hatred with lying lips and one who foolishly reveals or spreads rumors. In both cases, there is a failure of what the Benedictine monastic tradition calls "keeping a guard upon the tongue," a practice that is vital to community flourishing.

Concealed hatred is destructive, and open hatred stirs up strife (10:12a), but verse 12b advocates concealing or covering the offenses of others, in the sense of forgiving them. This proverb is echoed in 1 Peter 4:8: "Love covers a multitude of sins"; it is also reflected in Paul's hymn about love in 1 Corinthians 13. As John Calvin comments, "Those who love one another conceal many things among themselves, wink at many things, condone many things in one another—not that one man approves of another's faults, but that he tolerates them, and heals them by admonishing instead of aggravating them by reproaches."[4] This teaching in 10:12 softens the repeated and absolute contrasts between the righteous and wicked that dominate chapters 10–15 by teaching that love, not hatred, is the appropriate response to the offenses of others. Forgiving others also opens the way to confession and seeking forgiveness for one's own transgressions (28:13).

Proverbs 10:15 is the first of many proverbs delivering a wry observation on human affairs without an explicit moral valence. The proverb simply notes that wealth serves to protect and fortify the rich, whereas poverty is the source of disaster and ruin for the poor. There is no praise or criticism given of either group or any suggestion that one or both states of affairs is sent by God. Later proverbs, such as 18:10–11, will pick up where this proverb leaves off, developing Proverbs' ambivalence about wealth by giving an explicitly theological elaboration of this theme: the righteous regard God as

4. John Calvin, *Institutes of the Christian Religion* 3.4.36, ed. John T. McNeill, trans. Ford Lewis Battles, LCC (Philadelphia: Westminster Press, 1960), 1:666.

their fortress, their source of security; the rich, on the other hand, foolishly trust their wealth, for "in their imagination it is like a high wall" (18:11b).

Other verses in this section address the outcome of righteous and wicked ways. According to Proverbs, the future belongs to the righteous: their desires will be granted; they will survive tempests and trials; and their days will be long. By contrast, the worst fears of the wicked will come true: they will be taken captive by their own schemes, and their lives will be cut short. The outcome of the struggle between Esther and Haman in the book of Esther is a vivid narrative depiction of the contrast portrayed in these proverbs. The future vindication of the righteous is envisioned as occurring in the historical future, not in some distant immortal realm. Widespread convictions about resurrection and afterlife are a later development in Jewish thought, so references to life and death in Proverbs should be understood in the context of finite creaturehood. "Righteousness delivers from death" (11:4) in that it pursues the way of creaturely flourishing. The life that is prolonged by the fear of the Lord (10:27) is still a finite life. God's judgment on evil can be seen in the premature death of the wicked and the perishing of their earthly hopes (11:7). From within Israel's wisdom corpus, both Job and Ecclesiastes will contest the adequacy of this scheme for making sense of lived experience. Even in Proverbs the future valence of these teachings leaves unspoken the fact that things may look very different in the *present.* For now, the wicked may well seem to be thriving, arrogantly enjoying their prosperity, confident that their schemes will not catch up with them. The righteous may feel beleaguered, discouraged by how little they have to show for their virtue and humble trust in God.

The fourth-century preacher John Chrysostom enters into a lively argument with Proverbs, wrestling with what seem to be its contradictions of human experience. Concerning the material blessings that accrue to the righteous, Chrysostom asks, "What, then: is it true that no righteous person lived in poverty? Far from it; you could not claim that."[5] Regarding the premature death of the wicked, Chryso-

5. St. John Chrysostom, *Commentaries on the Sages*, vol. 2, *Commentary on Proverbs and Commentary on Ecclesiastes,* trans. Robert Charles Hill (Brookline, MA: Holy Cross Orthodox Press, 2006), 108.

stom remarks, "This does not often happen: why does one person reach a ripe old age, while another is snatched from the vestibule of life?"[6] In keeping with Proverbs' pedagogical purpose, Chrysostom turns these contradictions between the proverbs and human experience into a means of moral instruction. He concludes that the abundance of moral incongruities in human life—the suffering of the righteous and the flourishing of the wicked—teaches us "that the practice of virtue is a matter of choice." After all, Chrysostom insists, if God "caused all greedy people to be poor and all generous people rich," everyone would take the virtuous course as a matter of self-interest.[7] As it is, the vagaries and frustrations of human life require us to live by faith, not by sight. These confident proverbs are more about the *hope* of the righteous than about their present reality.

The two possible translations of 10:22b have different theological implications. Either God adds no sorrow to God's gift of material blessing or human toil adds nothing to God's blessing. The first translation resonates with Proverbs' emphasis on the sorrow that follows ill-gotten gain, though it does not reflect Proverbs' overall ambivalence about wealth. The second translation stresses human dependence on God for material sustenance but goes against Proverbs' repeated valorization of hard work (10:4, 26). Both translations are compatible with the general message of Proverbs: God's generosity is the ultimate source of all that sustains human life, as well as the ground and context for all human effort. The vivid imagery in 10:26 returns to Proverbs' warnings against laziness. The word translated "employers" in the NRSV is more literally translated "those who send." The point is not to contrast labor and management but to illustrate the irritation that results when the lazy violate the trust of those who send them to do work. "The wicked will not remain in the *land*" (10:30b, emphasis added) should be read not in covenant terms as "the land of Canaan" but in creation terms as "the earth." Jesus will supply an eschatological corollary of this proverb in the Sermon on the Mount: "The meek shall inherit the earth" (Matt. 5:5).

6. Ibid., 122.
7. Ibid., 121.

FURTHER REFLECTIONS

Preaching on Proverbs 10–15 without Sounding Like Job's Friends

The many proverbs in this section that contrast the futures of the wicked and the righteous are best preached through gritted teeth. This approach follows a long Christian tradition of prophetic preaching that has insisted, against all odds, that justice and mercy will finally prevail in God's creation. What helped the prophetic preacher Desmond Tutu stand firm in his struggle against South African apartheid was the theological conviction, artfully captured in many proverbs in chapters 10–15, that "we inhabit . . . a moral universe, which means that, despite all the evidence that seems to be to the contrary, there is no way that evil and injustice and oppression and lies can have the last word."[8] This conviction gave Tutu the courage to preach hope to suffering people when the empirical evidence decisively contradicted confident pronouncements like 10:28b: "The expectation of the wicked comes to nothing." As Tutu recounts, "During the dark days of the struggle, when the morale of our people was often low in the face of rampant evil, I used to say, 'This is a moral universe—the upholders of apartheid have already lost.' I also used to appeal to our white fellow South Africans: 'We are being nice to you. Join the winning side.'"[9] As 12:3 insists, "No one finds security by wickedness, but the root of the righteous will never be moved."

Tutu's recollection of his experiences at the Truth and Reconciliation Commission hearings can be read as a narrative unpacking of 11:6, "The righteousness of the upright saves them, but the treacherous are taken captive by their schemes."

> We were seeing it unfolding there before our very eyes as we sat in the commission. Those who had strutted about arrogantly in the days of apartheid, dealing out death and injustice and apartheid's excesses with gay abandon, had never imagined in their wildest dreams that their involvement in machinations and abomination hatched out in secret would

8. Desmond Tutu, *No Future without Forgiveness* (New York: Doubleday, 1999), 86.
9. Ibid., 86–87.

> ever see the light of day. They had fondly expected to rule the roost for as long as they wished. Now it was all coming out, . . . how they had abducted people, shot them and burned their bodies or thrown corpses into crocodile-infested rivers. They helped us exhume over fifty corpses of those they had abducted and then killed and buried secretly. The ghastly and macabre secrets might have remained hidden except that this is a moral universe and truth will out.[10]

Tutu was witnessing in these hearings what David Kelsey calls "signs of God's providential righting of the moral balance" of the universe.[11]

The problem, as Kelsey notes, is that these signs of God's providential righting "are not a steady-state feature of the quotidian." Instead, he suggests, "signs of God's providential preservation of a moral order break out in the quotidian like a small rash, patchy, intrusive, and unpredictable."[12] Many who hunger and thirst after righteousness do not find satisfaction within the boundaries of earthly life. When the proverbs of chapters 10–15 are not said through gritted teeth, when they are assumed to point to a steady-state feature of creaturely life, preaching on them runs the risk of reinforcing an unjust status quo and blaming those who suffer for their own misfortune. These "regular-verb" proverbs are dangerous when they tempt preachers to reason backwards from experiences of comfort and wealth to righteousness, or from experiences of trouble and suffering to wickedness. They are also dangerous when they lead preachers to demand from their hearers no more than an internal serenity that tunes out or denies earthly agonies.

To avoid the temptation to preach from Proverbs in a way that inculcates an oppressive cultural order, Alyce McKenzie suggests subverting proverbs that reflect the views of the dominant status quo, what she calls "proverbs of order." She advocates juxtaposing proverbs of order with others that "undercut the traditional tendency to guarantee order as the outcome of wisdom."[13] In particu-

10. Ibid., 87.
11. David H. Kelsey, *Eccentric Existence: A Theological Anthropology* (Louisville, KY: Westminster John Knox Press, 2009), 340.
12. Ibid.
13. Alyce M. McKenzie, *Preaching Proverbs: Wisdom for the Pulpit* (Louisville, KY: Westminster John Knox Press, 1996), 15.

lar, McKenzie lifts up Jesus and Qohelet, the teacher of Ecclesiastes, as subversive sages who "coin aphorisms that subvert complacent, superficial attitudes and behaviors that do not do justice to the complexity of life and the sovereignty of God over human affairs."[14] Thus Proverbs 13:4, "The appetite of the lazy craves, and gets nothing, while the appetite of the diligent is richly supplied," might be juxtaposed with Ecclesiastes 9:11: "Again I saw that under the sun the race is not to the swift, nor the battle to the strong, nor bread to the wise . . . , but time and chance happen to them all."

Juxtaposing proverbs that are in tension with each other can be a good strategy for preaching on Proverbs, and it should be noted that the preacher does not need to go outside the book of Proverbs to find this tension. For example, 13:4, quoted above, could be juxtaposed with 23:4, "Do not wear yourself out to get rich; be wise enough to desist." The pedagogical trajectory of Proverbs, with its gradual increase in moral complexity, can be used to homiletic advantage in this regard.

However, McKenzie's assumption that certain proverbs are intrinsically proverbs of order ignores the contemporary proverb "Words don't mean; people do." The meaning of any proverb changes depending on who is speaking it, in what tone, and to whom. As H. Richard Niebuhr points out, "Any and every idea man holds may be used defensively or it may be used critically and morally."[15] One of Martin Luther King Jr.'s favorite aphorisms threatened the racist status quo in America precisely by reasserting the moral order of God's providence: "The arc of the moral universe is long, but it bends toward justice." So-called proverbs of order can, and often should, be preached as proverbs of protest.

11:9–12:23

The social horizon of Proverbs gradually expands beyond the household into the public sphere of politics and commerce. As William

14. Ibid.
15. H. Richard Niebuhr, *Theology, History, and Culture*, ed. William Stacy Johnson (New Haven, CT: Yale University Press, 1996), 176.

Brown notes, "Productive and responsible citizenship within the life of the community is of central concern to the editors who produced the book of Proverbs."[16] Proverbs 11:9–11 links the concern of the righteous for the welfare of both neighborhoods and larger communities with the terrible damage inflicted by destructive speech on the body politic. The lives of individuals and whole cities can be done in by slander, self-protective falsehoods, betrayal of confidences, or incendiary rhetoric. Wise and trustworthy persons, by contrast, know when to keep quiet (11:12–13). They refrain from belittling others and from gossip, even when the conduct of others is blameworthy. On the other hand, there are situations in which wise words are needed in public life (11:14) as well as in private. Wise persons know what to say and when to say it.

As Daniel Treier comments, "Wisdom focuses on our money and our mouths."[17] Wise spareness about our words is contrasted in 11:24–26 with wise generosity about our wallets. Proverbs warns against a fiscal shrewdness that puts short-term self-interest ahead of larger moral considerations. Enriching oneself through violence or deceit (11:1, 16, 18) or taking advantage of the needs of the vulnerable (11:15, 17, 26) in hopes of making a quick buck will not bring lasting gain. Paradoxically, the way to one's own material security is found in giving freely to others. This giving is not conditional on a proper return being made by the recipients. It is instead a kind of dim reflection of God's own unconditional giving. It is part of the moral coherence of the universe that "those who are kind reward themselves" (11:17a). As the prayer ascribed to Francis of Assisi affirms, "It is in giving that we receive; it is in pardoning that we are pardoned."[18]

The assurance of the eventual punishment of the wicked (11:21, 31) is based more on God's character than on historical precedent. It is because deception and crookedness are a moral abomination to God (11:1, 20) that the wicked will not escape punishment (cf. 16:5). First Peter 4:18 loosely quotes 11:31 to encourage Christians

16. William P. Brown, *Character in Crisis: A Fresh Approach to the Wisdom Literature of the Old Testament* (Grand Rapids: Eerdmans, 1996), 47.

17. Daniel J. Treier, *Proverbs and Ecclesiastes* (Grand Rapids: Brazos Press, 2011), 28.

18. George Appleton, ed., *The Oxford Book of Prayer* (Oxford: Oxford University Press, 1985), 75.

who were undergoing persecution to "entrust themselves to a faithful Creator, while continuing to do good" (1 Pet. 4:19).

Two verses in chapter 11 have been altered in an attempt to wrest meaning from them. Verse 30a makes an expected association between the righteous and "a tree of life," an image already used to describe Woman Wisdom (3:18). The righteous "flourish like green leaves" (v. 28b), and their lives bear "fruit" that feeds others (v. 30a). However, the Hebrew of verse 30b says that "a wise man takes lives," using a verb that usually refers to killing others (the NRSV translates this verb as "violence"; cf. 1:19b). English translations tend to alter either the subject or the verb of this saying, as it is difficult to make sense of it in its present form. Early readers of Proverbs inserted additional lines in an attempt to make sense of verse 16, which the NRSV translates as "a gracious woman gets honor, . . . but the aggressive gain riches." The last sentence, for example, is sometimes translated "aggressive men." Here it is better to wrestle with the original form. This may be another one of Proverbs' wry observations on human affairs: a woman obtains through beauty what men get by violence. Or it can be read as contrasting the honor of a gracious woman with the ruthlessness of greedy men. The simile in verse 22 about a beautiful woman who has turned away from good sense (not someone who lacks intelligence) is a reminder of Proverbs' male point of view. As in the case of Abigail (1 Sam. 25:3), beauty and wisdom are supposed to go together: a beautiful woman who has forsaken wisdom is as unfitting as a filthy animal adorned with something of great value. Overall, however, Proverbs places very little emphasis on female beauty, portraying it as a source of deception (6:25) and vanity (31:30).

Many proverbs in chapter 12 return to the issue of speech, along with the usual cast of characters: the foolish and wicked, on one hand, and the wise and the righteous, on the other. One's character is displayed both in what one says and how one responds to the words of others. Fools are stubborn and quick to take offense. Convinced that they are in the right (v. 15), they will not listen to wise advice or tolerate rebuke (v. 1). When insulted, they flare out in anger (v. 16). Their own words are rash and hurtful (v. 18), displaying their folly for all to see (v. 23). By contrast, the wise abandon anxious efforts at self-preservation and are open to critique. They love discipline (v. 1) for the moral growth it fosters, and they listen to advice (v. 15). When insulted, they are able to brush it off, in keeping with the original context of the nursery rhyme "Sticks and stones can break my bones, but names can never hurt me." Unlike the prophet Elisha's intemperate response to the boys who teased him about his baldness (2 Kgs. 2:23–24), the wise person remains calm and refrains from verbal or physical retaliation. In their own speaking, the wise are restrained, even silent, when discretion requires it (v. 23) but at other times use their words to bring healing in painful or conflictual contexts (vv. 14, 18).

The wicked seem beyond the reach of advice and rebuke from others; the proverbs concerning them pay attention only to the effects of their speech on others, and these effects are pernicious. They give treacherous advice (v. 5) that leads others into a deadly ambush (v. 6). The wicked are liars (vv. 19, 22) who give false witness in court (v. 17). Judicial settings are another adult realm into which the youth must be inducted, and Proverbs will return to the problem of false witness in judicial settings repeatedly. Raymond van Leeuwen notes that "in predominantly oral cultures, legal disputes and criminal cases are decided primarily through the testimony of witnesses."[19] A deceitful witness "mocks at justice" (19:28) and does harm to the neighbor. Those who deceive others, either with false weights or with false words, are an abomination to the Lord (11:1; 12:22). By contrast, the thoughts of the righteous, from which their words flow, are just (v. 5). While the evil are ensnared by their own wicked words (v. 13), the words of the righteous keep them out of trouble (vv. 6, 21) and even bring them joy (v. 20). In judicial settings the righteous give honest evidence (v. 17), and their actions are a delight to God (v. 22).

The NRSV translation of the Hebrew phrase *ʾēšet ḥāyil* in verse 4a as "a good wife" weakens its force and obscures its connection to 31:10–31, in which the phrase recurs in an acrostic poem enumerating the impressive qualities of a "woman of substance" (see pp. 133–35, commentary on Prov. 31:10–31). Such a woman brings honor

19. Raymond Van Leeuwen, "The Book of Proverbs," NIB 5 (Nashville: Abingdon Press, 1997), 127.

and power to her husband, akin to the "crowns" of riches (14:24), old age (16:31), and grandchildren (17:6).[20]

The first "better than" proverb (12:9) is a sign of the gradually increasing complexity of the wisdom teachings in Proverbs: often wisdom presents itself not in sharp contrasts but in trade-offs between competing goods. The translation of this proverb is debated, but it revolves around economic status and the tensions between self-knowledge and social perceptions. It is possible to translate verse 9a "Better to be despised and a servant of oneself." Perhaps the teaching of Sirach, a later wisdom text from the early second century BCE, shows what is at stake: "Better is the worker who has goods in plenty than the boaster who lacks bread" (Sir. 10:27). Humble self-sufficiency is better than a flashy lifestyle that is unsustainable.

This theme of honest work continues in vv. 10–11, which seems to reflect Israel's old economic base of subsistence farming. The wise prosper by diligently tilling their land whereas the foolish fritter away their time. The righteous are devoted to their animals whereas the so-called mercy of the wicked is cruel. Both the righteous and the wicked have power over their animals. In contemporary Christian theology, the concept of power, particularly "power over" others, tends to have a negative valence. Proverbs does not share this automatic suspicion of power that attempts to direct the conduct of others. The pertinent question for the sages—whether it is the power of a farmer, a parent, or a royal figure—is *how* this power is exercised. The righteous "know the needs of their animals" (v. 10a) and use their power on behalf of their animals' sustenance, safety, and general well-being (cf. 27:23–27). The wickeds' attention to their animals, while it may seem outwardly

> **That which they would have pass for compassion, and their pretended kindnesses, are only a cover for intended cruelties. . . . How many are there who pretend to lament others' calamities, whose tears are like those of the crocodile.**
>
> Jonathan Edwards, "The Blank Bible," in *The Works of Jonathan Edwards*, vol. 24, pt. 1, ed. Stephen J. Stein (New Haven, CT: Yale University Press, 2006), 552.

20. Yoder, *Proverbs*, 142.

merciful, lacks this beneficence. The intended consequences of their care are self-serving. Proverbs' teachings on royal authority will also exhibit this contrast between benevolent and malevolent exercises of power.

12:24–13:25

Proverbs 12:24, one of many proverbs contrasting laziness and diligence, can be read as a socially conservative affirmation that the members of the ruling class got there by their hard work, or it can be read subversively, along with proverbs like 17:2 and 21:22, as upending complacent understandings of social status. "Rule" and "forced labor" (cf. 1 Kgs. 5:13–17) were the social extremes of the day, and a subversive reading challenges the assumption that these social stations are forever fixed, immune to the effects of hard work or its opposite. Proverbs 13:4 contrasts the two groups once again, this time with respect to their appetites. Everyone is driven by their desires, but the cravings of the lazy are frustrated, as are those of the wicked in 13:25.

Two psychological observations in 12:25 and 13:12 speak to the common human conditions of anxiously fearing the future and longing for a future reality that is not realized. Proverbs 13:19 develops verse 12, emphasizing the sweetness of a fulfilled desire but recognizing that not everything that human beings desire is good. The observations in 13:7–8 are linked by the contrast between rich and poor, though there are several ways to read them. The Hebrew in 13:7 does not make clear whether the deception regarding economic status is self-deception or the deception of others. The next verse is best read as another wry observation undercutting the supposed benefits of wealth: the rich risk being held for ransom whereas the poor do not have to worry about such threats to their life.

Proverbs 12:28 boldly proclaims that there is no death for those that walk the path of righteousness, in contrast to the extinction, overthrow, misfortunes, and empty bellies of the foolish and wicked (13:6, 9, 20–22, 25). Roland Murphy cautions that the "lapidary style" of Proverbs should not obscure "the tentativeness of wisdom."

The painful contradictions of human life and the keen recognition of the inadequacies of human wisdom (cf. 21:30) are never far below the surface. "The most dogmatic expression of the triumph of wisdom as opposed to folly, with its guarantee of life and prosperity, must be taken more as a matter of trust and hope than of experience."[21] Without this caution, the "regular verbs" of Proverbs, like the teachings of Job's friends, can become "proverbs of ashes" (Job 13:12; see pp. 71–73, "Further Reflections: Preaching on Proverbs 10–15 without Sounding Like Job's Friends").

The subjunctive mood of Proverbs' "regular verbs" becomes clear when they are juxtaposed with the harsh saying in 13:23: "The field of the poor may yield much food, but it is swept away through injustice." Clearly, it is not always true that hard work is rewarded (13:4) or that wicked people end up with empty bellies (13:25). Part of wisdom is to acknowledge that experience often speaks with a forked tongue. The book of Proverbs does not advocate or even imagine a wholesale overturning of social structures in order to make them more just. Yet it is not shy about acknowledging and protesting injustice, especially toward the poor. Later readers of Scripture, both Jewish and Christian, will search for fuller meaning in these proverbs, envisioning an apocalyptic future in which God will bring down the powerful from their thrones and lift up the lowly (cf. Luke 1:52).

Several verses in chapter 13 address the issue of moral formation (vv. 1, 10, 13, 14, 20, 24). This instruction begins at home but continues throughout one's life. Unlike the scoffer (v. 1), the wise of all ages take advice and respect the commandments. They are careful about the company they keep (v. 20). As the Egyptian wisdom text *Instruction of Ankhsheshonq* notes, "The friend of a fool is a fool; the friend of a wise man is a wise man. The friend of an idiot is an idiot."[22] According to Proverbs, "it takes a village" not only to raise a child but also to stay on the path of wisdom as an adult.

Proverbs accepts corporal punishment as a commonsense part of moral formation, both for children and adults (13:24; cf. 10:13;

21. Athalya Brenner and Carole Fontaine, eds., *Wisdom and Psalms* (Sheffield: Sheffield Academic Press, 1998), 38.
22. Quoted in Yoder, *Proverbs*, 155.

20:30; 22:15; 23:13–14; 26:3; 29:15). H. Richard Niebuhr points out that common sense "is exactly what the phrase indicates—the sense of a community—and that every community is a particular thing, the product of its own past and the possessor of a limited culture."[23] Contemporary "common sense" about the realities of parental abuse and the cyclical nature of violence has led to widespread antipathy toward corporal punishment in the West. Yet it is still true that children do not grow up to be wise and decent adults without intensive moral formation, so Proverbs' larger point still holds: to refuse to discipline your children is to "set your heart on their destruction" (19:18). In the experience of most parents, efforts at moral formation do not always meet with sweet reasonableness. Thus appropriate discipline may require some forms of physical coercion, from restraining a toddler who is biting others to taking away the car keys from a rebellious teenager.

14:1–35

Chapter 14 introduces a few more "irregular verbs" into the sequence of proverbs, casting the ongoing contrasts between wisdom and folly in a new light and forcing readers to wrestle with the ambiguities of human experience. Proverbs about a king also make their first appearance (vv. 28, 35), signaling that the youth is on the threshold of a larger moral stage. A king's glory is linked in verse 28 to the well-being of his people, reflecting a pastoral mode in which monarchical power cannot be manifested independently of care for the people (see pp. 73–78, commentary on 11:9–23). The well-being of a nation is also linked to the righteousness of a king's subjects (v. 34). "The king relies on their wisdom, as they do on his,"[24] and he responds decisively to their actions, both wise and shameful (v. 35).

The first half of verse 1 repeats the announcement of 9:1, "Wisdom builds her house," except that here the subject is plural ("wise women,") a shift not reflected in the NRSV translation. This shift signals a movement from the cosmological wisdom that founds the

23. H. Richard Niebuhr, *Meaning of Revelation* (New York: MacMillan, 1941), 11.
24. Yoder, *Proverbs*, 166.

universe, personified in Woman Wisdom, to finite attempts on the part of ordinary women to appropriate that wisdom in their own lives (cf. 24:3–4; 31:10–31). The wise and righteous "build their house" so as to conduce to creaturely flourishing (14:1a, 11b), whereas foolish and wicked attempts to live against the grain of the universe (14:1b, 11a, 19) are self-destructive and end in disaster, both for individuals and for their households. In our own time, these proverbs also invite an ecological interpretation. As Wendell Berry notes, our entire earthly existence should be seen as the endeavor to live wisely in the "Great Economy" that God has established:

> There is no "outside" to the Great Economy, no escape into either specialization or generality, no "time off." Even insignificance is no escape, for in the membership of the Great Economy everything signifies; whatever we do counts. If we do not serve what coheres and endures, we serve what disintegrates and destroys. We can presume that we are outside the membership that includes us, but that presumption only damages the membership—and ourselves, of course, along with it.[25]

Our contemporary practice of "home economics" must include the whole creation in its purview.

> **The "fear of YHWH" is fundamentally different from the panicky anxiety, the trepidation or even terror that human beings can bring about; it is an alternative fear that effectively displaces and excludes fear of human beings.**
>
> Allan Boesak, *The Finger of God: Sermons on Faith and Socio-Political Responsibility* (Maryknoll, NY: Orbis Books, 1982), 59.

The connection between divine and human wisdom is also reflected in proverbs that link one's moral path and one's attitude to God (14:2, 27–28). "Fear of the LORD" is a healthy cognizance of human vulnerability and accountability in the face of God's loving and sovereign wisdom. It is reflected in dispositions of reverence and humility before God (v. 9), in kindness toward fellow creatures (vv. 4, 21, 31), and in hatred of evil (v. 16). Proverbs recognizes that fear is a constant in creaturely life. Fear of God is a "strong confidence" (v. 26a) that drives out other fears that

25. Wendell Berry, *Home Economics* (New York: North Point, 1987), 75.

are endemic to human existence, culminating in the fear of death (v. 27b). As Christine Roy Yoder notes, "without 'fear of the LORD,' all other fears, including the fears of scarcity, ineptitude, irrelevance, and insecurity, run rampant."[26]

Chapter 14, like the others that have preceded it in the Solomonic collection (10:1–22:16), abounds with stark contrasts between the wise and the foolish. Fools spout arrogance (a better translation of verse 3a than the NRSV provides) and spout nonsense (v. 7), mislead themselves and others (v. 8), fail to guard both their consciences and their tempers (vv. 16, 29), and incur wrath for their shameful acts (v. 35). All they get for their folly is folly (vv. 18, 24). But in the midst of these earnest teachings about the high costs of folly and the rich rewards of wisdom is a proverb (14:12) that stops readers in their tracks: "There is a way that seems right to a person, but its end is the way to death."[27] No matter how deliberate and cautious the wise are about choosing their paths (14:8, 15, 33), no matter how successful they are in controlling their tempers and winning the king's favor (14:29, 35), there is no guarantee that human wisdom will be a "fountain of life," contrary to the assurance in the previous chapter (13:14). In fact, there is more than one way in which it may lead to death. Proverbs here signals the drastic limitations of human wisdom, thereby destabilizing all the sharp distinctions between human folly and wisdom that precede and follow this verse. Proverbs 16:25 repeats this teaching, just in case readers missed it the first time. False confidence in one's own wisdom leads to death, not to life. The only true "fountain of life" is fear of God (14:27; cf. 3:7).

On either side of the "irregular verb" in 14:12 come two others that emphasize the incongruities of human experience. For all Proverbs' emphasis on the importance of familial and communal bonds, 14:10 acknowledges the limits of our emotional connections to others. In times of both bitterness and joy, others can become strangers to us. This should not prevent us from offering a "good word" to those who are weighed down (12:25), but it reminds us that the distance between persons is never fully bridged. Our hearts lie wholly open only to God (15:11). In a saying that anticipates the poignant

26. Yoder, *Proverbs*, 6–7.
27. Translation by Roland E. Murphy, *Proverbs* (Nashville: Thomas Nelson, 1998), 100.

reflections of Ecclesiastes (7:2–4), 14:13 notes the intertwining of joy and sorrow in human life. There is a shadow side to the laughter and joy of creaturely life because, like everything else under the sun, it will inevitably end. Moreover, both love and death are sources of sadness. While elsewhere Proverbs distinguishes the joy a wise child brings to her parents from the sorrow caused by a foolish child (10:1; 17:21, 25), parents know that their love for their children often evokes a mixture of joy and sorrow.

Two pairs of proverbs in chapter 14 seem set in tension with each other. The first pair, verses 20–21, starts with a wry observation about how a poor person (the Hebrew is singular) is shunned even by her neighbor, while the rich (plural) have no lack of fawning admirers. This verse is immediately followed by a moral corrective: it is a sin to despise one's neighbors, and blessings come not to those who curry favor with the rich but to those who are kind to the poor. A similar beatitude can be found in Jesus' Sermon on the Mount (Matt. 5:7; see pp. 113–15, "Further Reflections: Jesus as Sage").

The Old Testament is clear regarding the close relationship which exists between God and the neighbor. This relationship is a distinguishing characteristic of the God of the Bible. To despise one's neighbor (Prov. 14:21), to exploit the humble and poor worker, and to delay the payment of wages are to offend God.

Gustavo Gutiérrez, *Theology of Liberation* (Maryknoll, NY: Orbis Books, 1979), 194.

An explicitly theological codicil follows in verse 31: to oppress the poor is to insult God, the Creator of all people (cf. 22:2). The second pair, verses 29–30, starts with one of Proverbs' frequent admonitions to be slow to anger, literally "long of nostrils." When you are tempted to fly into a rage, the sages advise, take a deep breath! But this verse is juxtaposed with an acknowledgment that harboring resentment and anger can be self-destructive. Passion that is bottled up inside can "make the bones rot" (v. 30b). Preserving a "tranquil mind" (v. 30a) is not easy when surrounded by false witnesses (v. 5b), scoffers (v. 6a), and schemers (vv. 17b, 22a). Wisdom is required to know when to exercise self-restraint and when to respond with indignation.

15:1–33

Chapter 15 is a bridge chapter, closing the first Solomonic subsection and anticipating the repeated references to God's character and agency in chapter 16. The antithetical parallelism that dominated the earlier chapters of this section is beginning to give way to more diversity in proverbial genres, also an anticipation of the teachings to follow. Several proverbs in chapter 15 contemplate what it is to have a joyful and cheerful heart (vv. 13, 15, 30). Of special note are the "better than" proverbs in verses 15–16 that highlight the ambivalence of Proverbs toward material prosperity. A life marked by love and fear of God is to be preferred over luxury, especially when the treasure is gained unjustly (v. 27).

Though their voices have not been heard directly since chapter 9, parents remain on the moral stage all the way through the book of Proverbs (15:5, 20). The fool scorns his mother's wise instruction (v. 5) and, shockingly, even his mother herself (v. 20), and this refusal to heed instruction from parents and others finally amounts to scorn for his own soul (v. 32). Guidance from others is crucial because we are often not the best judges even of our own self-interest, and folly can be death dealing. David's son Amnon is reckoned among "the fools of Israel" for scorning his half-sister Tamar's wise counsel and gratifying his lust by raping her. His horrific act of folly leads to his own death (2 Sam. 13:7–19, 32–33). Other proverbs in chapter 15 likewise pick up on the theme of the importance of heeding the advice and rebuke of others (vv. 10, 12, 22, 31).

Chapter 15 also pays attention to how advice is *given*. Harsh and hot-tempered words antagonize others and lead to more strife, whereas soft and gentle words are a "tree of life," calming and healing people in situations of conflict (vv. 1, 4, 18). Paradoxically, hard words only harden others, while soft words soften them.

Good news and words that are appropriate to the situation bring joy to others (vv. 23, 30), while twisted words break their spirits (v. 4b). Other verses in chapter 15 vividly describe the disastrous effects of foolish and wicked speech. Unlike the circumspection of the wise and righteous (vv. 2a, 7a, 28a), the mouths of fools revel in and pour out folly, just as wicked mouths pour out evil (vv. 2b, 14b,

28b). As a later wisdom text will express it, "In the mouth of fools, their heart / In the heart of the wise, their mouth" (Sir. 21:26).[28] Since seeking wisdom is a communal venture, foolish and wicked words do real damage to others, derailing their attempts to stay on the right path (v. 9).

None of this goes unnoticed by God, who keeps watch over all people (v. 3) and to whom alone all hearts are open (v. 11). God is especially concerned for the vulnerable, particularly the poor (vv. 15–16) and the widow (v. 25b). In our contemporary context, the "boundaries of the widow" are often synonymous with the natural limits of the environment. Violating these boundaries out of greed for unjust gain (v. 27a) leads to suffering for both the earth and the poor. Worship is not a central focus of Proverbs, but where it appears, it is hand in hand with righteous conduct. Liturgical acts mean nothing if they are not accompanied by lives that please God. Because the way of the wicked is an abomination to God (vv. 9a, 26a, 29a), so too are their sacrifices (v. 8a). Similar complaints against insincere worship are found in the biblical prophets (Isa. 1:10–15; Amos 5:21–27; Mic. 6:6–8). Conversely, God approves of those who pursue righteousness (v. 9b) and attends to their prayers (vv. 8b, 29b). Chapter 15 ends with a verse that echoes the connection between human wisdom and fear of the Lord at the start of Proverbs (1:7) and marks the halfway point of the Solomonic collection of proverbs that began in 10:1. Fear of God *instructs* in wisdom (v. 33a) by showing us our complete dependence on God. Augustine notes this pedagogical function of fearing God: it guides us "to lead the right kind of life,

> **Nothing in this world**
> **is as soft and yielding as water.**
> **Yet for attacking the hard and strong**
> **none can triumph so easily.**
> **It is weak, yet none can equal it.**
> **It is soft, yet none can damage it.**
> **It is yielding, yet none can wear it away.**
> **Everyone knows that the soft overcomes the hard**
> **and the yielding triumphs over the rigid.**
> **Why then so little faith?**
> **Why can no one practice it?**
>
> Lao Tsu, *Tao Te Ching: The Definitive Edition* (New York: Penguin, 2001), 91.

28. Ibid., 92.

the life that is according to God's will."[29] Humility is a hallmark of this kind of life (v. 33b) whereas the arrogant are an abomination to God (16:5; see pp. 103–4, "Further Reflections: The Vice of Pride and the Virtue of Humility"). Similarly, Augustine links fear of God with the first beatitude in the Sermon on the Mount: "Blessed are the poor in spirit, for they shall inherit the kingdom of God" (Matt. 5:3). Wisdom is accessible only to those who are not puffed up with pride.[30]

29. Augustine, *The City of God* 14.9, trans. Henry Bettenson (London: Penguin Classics, 1972), 565.
30. Augustine, *Sermon on the Mount*, 1.1.3; *On Christian Doctrine* 2.7.9.

16:1–22:16
Deeper Wisdom

16:1–33

Chapter 16 is the hinge of the book of Proverbs in several ways. First, it marks the midpoint of the book as a whole, which, when calculated by verses, falls at v. 17. Second, chapter 16 marks the start of the second half of the Solomonic collection of proverbs (16:1–22:16), which integrates the "regular verbs" of the first half of the collection (chaps. 10–15) into a deeper, more complicated wisdom. Christine Roy Yoder notes that as readers progress through the book of Proverbs they discover that "absent the father's firm mediation, conflict and contradiction exist not only between the wise and foolish, the righteous and wicked, but within wisdom itself."[1] Third, this chapter is the hinge on which a theological reading of the wisdom in the central section (chaps. 10–29) turns because it reminds readers of the primacy of divine wisdom that was established in the opening frame (chaps. 1–9). The emphasis on God's wisdom in chapter 16 undermines all human pretensions to autonomy or adequate self-knowledge in the search for wisdom, and it relativizes the stark contrasts between wise and foolish persons that have dominated the preceding chapters. An Augustinian approach to Proverbs, such as the one being attempted in this commentary, reads chapters 10–15 in the light of ambiguities and complexities introduced in the second half of the book. Even the wise may be fatally mistaken about the right path (16:25).

The first nine verses of chapter 16 form a unit consisting of proverbs about the concurrence of divine and human agency. The

1. Christine Roy Yoder, *Proverbs*, Abingdon Old Testament Commentaries (Nashville: Abingdon Press, 2009), 111.

antithetical proverbs in verses 1, 2, and 9 are by now a familiar form, but this time the contrast is not between the wise and foolish, or the wicked and righteous, but between God and human beings. These are the kind of proverbs that Augustine could have written! They make clear that every detail of our lives, from our smallest outward actions to the deepest orientation of our hearts, is enveloped within God's own agency and concern. While it is possible to read many of Proverbs' individual teachings within a Pelagian framework, one which assumes that God's moral role in human life is merely to provide external guides and goads to our own attempts at wise and righteous behavior, verses 1–9 refute this assumption of human moral self-possession. There is no use pretending that we operate independently as moral agents. Even true perception of our own moral agency eludes us (v. 2). Human wisdom comes only in the heart's orientation toward God. As Augustine confesses in his famous prayer articulating the human condition, "You have made us and drawn us to yourself, and our heart is unquiet until it rests in you."[2]

While Proverbs repeatedly emphasizes the importance of wise human plans, words, and actions, verses 1 and 9 make clear that these are never outside of God's providence. Every human word (v. 1), every human step (v. 9), has its source in God. The deeper wisdom is to know our radical dependency on God, even in the things we consider most within our moral purview, such as "the answer of the tongue" (v. 1a). The letter of James echoes Proverbs' call to acknowledge the precariousness of our plans when our efforts are not "committed to the Lord" (16:3). Instead of confidently going about planning our future as if we were our own makers and keepers, we ought to say, "'If the Lord wishes, we will live and do this or that'" (Jas. 4:15). "As it is," James chides, "you boast in your arrogance; all such boasting is evil" (Jas. 4:16). Proverbs also views arrogant pretensions to self-sufficiency and self-mastery as an abomination to God (16:5a); the punishment these pretensions bring (16:5b, 18) is the expectable result of this moral idiocy.

The bluntness of 16:4 has sent some interpreters running for cover. If God's providential purposes extend even to the wicked,

2. Augustine, *Confessions* 1.1, trans. Maria Boulding (Hyde Park, NY: New City Press, 1997), 39.

does not God share some culpability for their misdeeds? The Augustinian tradition, especially its Reformed branches, has been willing to grasp the nettle on this theological issue. In his treatment of divine providence in the *Institutes*, John Calvin appeals repeatedly to Proverbs 16 to insist that God "directs everything by his incomprehensible wisdom, and disposes it to his own end," even human folly and wickedness. Calvin argues that even the drawing of lots (16:33) is not a matter of chance: "It is not by their own power that pebbles are cast into the lap and drawn out."[3] While it is difficult to trust God's goodness and providence when our lives seem caught in the grip of evil and capricious fortune, Calvin thought that the theological alternative was even more terrifying: to say that wickedness and calamity fall *outside* of God's providence is to leave us utterly at their mercy.

It makes indeed all the difference if a man attempts to live on [his] own ideas, plans and devices and believes them to be the ultimate reality—or if a man realizes that neither his ideas and wishes nor even his highest willpower may destine his life, but that there exists some other unknown, unseen and hidden elements which alone matters, which is behind everything, which makes history of men and nations, which is the ultimate reality—called God Almighty.

Dietrich Bonhoeffer, "Sermon on Prov. 16:9," in *London 1933–1935, DBW* 13 (Minneapolis: Fortress Press, 2007), 398.

It is tempting to find in Proverbs' repeated calls to wisdom and righteousness a route to justifying ourselves before God, but 16:2 and 16:6 deflate this project and the self-deception that accompanies it. Our ways "may be pure in our own eyes" (v. 2a), but as the philosopher Iris Murdoch points out, we do not have an innate ability to see the world accurately: "By opening our eyes, we do not necessarily see what confronts us. . . . Our minds are continually active, fabricating an anxious, usually self-preoccupied, often falsifying veil which partially conceals the world."[4] God, by contrast, "weighs the spirit" (16:2b; cf. 21:2b) and knows our failings. Our iniquity is not atoned for by our redoubled moral efforts but by God's own "loyalty

3. John Calvin, *Institutes of the Christian Religion* 1.16.4, 6, ed. John T. McNeill, trans. Ford Lewis Battles, LCC (Philadelphia: Westminster Press, 1960), 1:202, 205.
4. Iris Murdoch, *The Sovereignty of the Good* (London: Macmillan, 1970), 82.

and faithfulness" (16:6a). This characterization of God recalls God's promises of blessing and forgiveness to Moses at Sinai (Exod. 34:6–7).

Fear and trust in the Lord, as well as attentiveness to God's word (a better translation of the Hebrew than NRSV's "matter" in 16:20a) are linked in verses 6b and 20 with prosperity and the avoidance of evil. But the wise and righteous may still find themselves confronting enemies (v. 7) and poverty (vv. 8, 16, 19). Thus there is no guarantee that "wisdom is a fountain of life to the one who has it" (v. 22), but wise hearts, minds, and words (vv. 21, 23–24) are still better than the destructive alternatives (vv. 27–30).

Nestled among the admonishments to prefer wisdom and righteousness to wealth (vv. 8, 16) and warnings against pride (vv. 5, 18–19) is a cluster of proverbs about a king (vv. 10–15). The idealized account of the king's divine accountability in these verses does not sit comfortably alongside Israel's actual history of kingship, but it does reflect the biblical insistence on God's concern for wisdom and righteousness in political leadership. As Woman Wisdom declares, "By me kings reign, and rulers decree what is just" (8:15). When God is duly consulted (the Hebrew suggests consultation by means of an oracle or by drawing lots), the king's judgments will be true (v. 10). The establishment of the king's throne is not secured through theft, deceit, or other evil means but, like the very throne of God, by righteousness (vv. 11–12; see Ps. 97:2). A conditional form of this proverb about the establishment of a king's throne in 29:14, surrounded by proverbs about the fallibility of human rulers, gives a more guarded picture. Like God and Woman Wisdom, a just king delights in truthful witness (v. 13). Opposing the king's desire for justice leads to death, while earning the king's favor by righteous conduct leads to life (vv. 14–15). Perhaps verse 32, which extols wise self-control over earthly might, can be read as a check on the power of a wrathful king in verse 14. Ecclesiastes 9:13–16 provides an ironic commentary on the contest between wisdom of a humble man and the might of "a great king."

Just as God's wisdom and righteousness are reflected in a king's rule, so "fear of the Lord" (v. 6b) is extended in chapter 16 to fear of a king (v. 14b; see also 24:21–22). However, there are important differences. As Augustine notes, fear of the king by his subjects is servile fear, a fear of punishment. While the servile fear evoked by powerful rulers can restrain human sinfulness and thus make for earthly peace, it is all too easily co-opted by unjust rulers as well, as Proverbs acknowledges (28:15, 16a; 29:2b, 4b, 16). This servile fear, Augustine concludes, is suited only to our earthly existence. It is wrong to appeal to servile fear of God to threaten and coerce others. Genuine fear of God, by contrast, is a "serene fear" that arises from love and will endure forever (cf. 29:25).[5] Serene fear recognizes, with trembling, the immense chasm between creature and Creator, and it leads us to put our faith in "the God whose power does not threaten our true good but sustains it."[6]

FURTHER REFLECTIONS
Divine and Human Agency

Theologians have debated how best to understand the relationship between divine and human agency. Often the debate has been framed in terms of a distinction between coercive and persuasive divine power. Traditional affirmations of divine sovereignty assert God's ability to coerce appropriate human action through the threat of punishment or the active thwarting of human will—a magnified version of sovereign human power, such as that attributed to the king in Proverbs 16. More contemporary, process-oriented theologies portray God's power as persuasive rather than coercive: it lures human persons toward what is good and life giving. The problem with both approaches is that they assume that God has to work from the outside to affect human conduct, just as other creaturely forces do. This tends to set up a "zero-sum game" understanding of divine and human agency: the more God acts, the less freedom there is for human beings to act.

It is a mistake to conceive of divine and creaturely agency as if they were in competition with each other. As Creator of all, God does not act on creatures from the outside. Instead, as John Webster says,

5. Augustine, *The City of God* 14.9, trans. Henry Bettenson (London: Penguin Classics, 1972), 565.
6. Scott Bader-Saye, *Following Jesus in a Culture of Fear* (Grand Rapids: Brazos Press, 2007), 43.

"the more God moves the creature, the more the creature moves itself."[7] The medieval theologian Thomas Aquinas draws out these implications of God's agency for human freedom: "And just as by moving natural causes He does not prevent their actions from being natural, so by moving voluntary causes He does not deprive their actions from being voluntary; but rather is the cause of this very thing in them, for he operates in each thing according to its own nature."[8] God's action is *constitutive* of creaturely action, that which makes creaturely action possible at all. In Rowan Williams's image, God's ceaseless activity is "a sort of white heat at the centre of everything."[9] God's power is constitutive power.

While the coercive power of despots deserves determined human resistance, so too do human attempts at usurping God's constitutive power. Michel Foucault has described "disciplinary" forms of power in the modern West according to which "subjects are gradually, progressively, really, and materially constituted through a multiplicity of organisms, forces, energies, materials, desires, thoughts, etc."[10] This kind of human power works by constituting or producing its subjects so that they habitually act and think in particular ways, even without external prompting. Foucault's famous example is of a prisoner who, because he is always in the sight of a central watch tower, has so internalized the behavior of a model prisoner that the watch tower need never be manned.[11] Foucault's language of training and discipline is uncomfortably close to that of Proverbs. While efforts at communal formation are not intrinsically corrupt (as Foucault sometimes suggests), they certainly are intrinsically *corruptible*. No one, not even parents and religious leaders, can be trusted with absolute disciplinary power. All abuses of human power, whether those of tyrants or of families and institutional regimes, must be resisted as part of faithfulness to God.

7. John Webster, *Word and Church: Essays in Church Dogmatics* (Edinburgh: T. & T. Clark, 2006), 214.
8. Thomas Aquinas, *Summa Theologica*, q.83, a.1, ad 3.
9. Rowan Williams, *Tokens of Trust: An Introduction to Christian Belief* (Louisville, KY: Westminster John Knox Press, 2007), 35.
10. Michel Foucault, *Power/Knowledge: Selected Interviews and Other Writings, 1972–1977* (New York: Pantheon Books, 1980), 97.
11. Michel Foucault, *Discipline and Punish: The Birth of the Prison*, trans. Alan Sheridan (New York: Vintage Books, 1995), pt. 3, chap. 3.

17:1–18:24

Some of the proverbs in this section achieve their pedagogical aim through vivid imagery, surprise, and exaggeration. The "better than" proverb in 17:1 upends the frequent association of wealth with righteousness, especially since the Hebrew translated as "house full of feasting" has connotations of religious sacrifice. The peace of the poor who have only dry bread is to be preferred to the acrimony of the rich and pious. Another surprising proverb follows in 17:2, which upends the conventions of familial inheritance. This proverb can be read either as subversive encouragement to slaves or as admonishment to misbehaving sons. Accenting a familiar theme of the wisdom of avoiding verbosity (17:27), verse 28 slyly suggests that even quiet fools can masquerade as wise. A proverb variously attributed to Abraham Lincoln and Mark Twain twists the associations between folly and silence but makes a similar point: "It is better to remain silent and be thought a fool than to speak out and remove all doubt." Hyperbole characterizes 17:10, 12 and 18:9. One hundred blows (v. 10b) is far in excess of the forty permitted by law (Deut. 25:3) and serves to highlight the resistance of a fool to correction. The ironic question in 17:16 also makes this point—buying wisdom is futile for a fool who has "no mind to learn" (v. 16b). An enraged mother bear robbed of her cubs (17:12a), a metaphor used to describe the fierceness of David and his army (2 Sam. 17:8), is deemed less fearsome than a fool immersed in folly. A slacker is declared to be "close kin to a vandal" (18:9). The words of a gossip are described as "delicious morsels," eagerly consumed and internalized (18:8); the playful imagery continues in 18:20. The literary flair of these proverbs assumes growing competency in wisdom; reading them in a flat-footed, literal way is to misunderstand them. The New Testament Gospels likewise portray Jesus as regularly employing vivid imagery, exaggeration, and surprise in his teaching. The Gospel of John frequently exploits the ironic potential of literalist misunderstandings of Jesus' words (e.g., John 2:19; 3:4, 11; see pp. 113–15, "Further Reflections: Jesus as Sage").

The pair of proverbs in 18:10–11 makes an ironic contrast: God is "a strong tower" for the righteous, but the rich instead trust their wealth to be a "strong city" and "high wall," though the security it provides is only a figment of their imagination. This proverb pair leads directly into a reiteration of the dangers of pride (18:13; see 15:33b; 16:18). Reinhold Niebuhr observes that the wealthy and prominent are particularly susceptible to this prideful self-deception:

> There is a pride of power in which the human ego assumes its self-sufficiency and self-mastery and imagines itself secure against all vicissitudes. It does not recognize the contingent and dependent character of its life and believes itself to be the author of its own existence, the judge of its own values and the master of its own destiny. This proud pretension is present in an inchoate form in all human life but it rises to greater heights among those individuals and classes who have a more than ordinary degree of social power.[12]

There are several examples in chapters 17–18 (cf. chapters 28–29) of the arrogant abuse of power by those in authority, perhaps reflecting an awareness that the pious righteousness attributed to a king in chapter 16 is not to be counted on. Rulers can be a source of "false speech" (17:7) as well as "inspired decisions" (16:10).

Bribes are a principal illustration of the abuse of power in this section. The sense of 17:8 depends on which half of the proverb is emphasized. If stress is placed on verse 8b, the proverb may be read as a wry observation about how bribes "work like a charm" for the unscrupulous. This seems to be the meaning of 18:16 as well, since the line between gift and bribe is often thin when the goal is "access to the great" (v. 16b). If the stress is placed instead on 17:8a, the power of a bribe is only "in the eyes of those who give it," and their perception may well be as deluded as that of the rich in 18:11b. In that case their prosperity, noted in 17:8b, will be as ephemeral as that of the "crooked of mind" in 17:20a. Bribes are also used to subvert justice in judicial settings, a danger noted in 17:23 and perhaps contributing to the perversion of justice condemned in 17:15, 26 and 18:5. As Ecclesiastes 7:7 notes, "a bribe corrupts the heart." Isaiah

12. Reinhold Niebuhr, *The Nature and Destiny of Man* (New York: Charles Scribner's Sons, 1964), 1:188–89.

also laments Judah's failure to defend the orphan and the widow because "everyone loves a bribe and runs after gifts" (Isa. 1:23).

The abuse of power by the rich is also evident in the way they mock the poor (17:5a), rejoicing in their calamities (17:5b) and giving rough answers to their entreaties (18:23). But God, who "tests the heart" (17:3b), is insulted by this behavior (17:5a) and does not let it go unpunished (17:5b). Commenting on 17:5, John Chrysostom recounts a common refrain he has heard from rich people concerning the poor: "Why is there need to have pity on the poor? If God loved them, he would not have made them poor." Chrysostom indignantly responds, "Whom did [God] love, Lazarus or the rich man?"[13] Proverbs 29:14 makes the establishment of a king's throne contingent on his just treatment of the poor.

Two proverbs in this section, 17:21 and 17:25, address the grief and bitterness caused by foolish children. A literary illustration is seen in Shakespeare's King Lear, no stranger to the sorrow of children gone astray, who lashes out against his daughter Goneril, vengefully hoping that Goneril's own child will

> turn all her mother's pains and benefits
> To laughter and contempt, that she may feel
> How sharper than a serpent's tooth it is
> To have a thankless child.[14]

Two other proverbs, 17:22 and 18:14, address more generally the pain and physical harm of a broken or downcast spirit (the same Hebrew word is used). A balm for this brokenness is suggested by proverbs on close friendship in 17:17 and 18:24, especially in times of adversity. That it is necessary to pick your friends wisely, however, is suggested by the warning in 17:18 not to entrust your money to a friend (the word translated "neighbor" in v. 18 is the same word translated "friend" in v. 17). Other proverbs on friendship counsel forgiving an offense rather than harping on the

13. John Chrysostom, *St. John Chrysostom Commentaries on the Sages*, vol.2, *Commentary on Proverbs and Commentary on Ecclesiastes* (Brookline, MA: Holy Cross Orthodox Press, 2006), 138–39.
14. William Shakespeare, *King Lear*, act 1, scene 4, lines 288–91, in *The Complete Signet Classic Shakespeare* (New York: Harcourt Brace Jovanovich, 1972), 1192.

matter (17:9; cf. 10:12) and refraining from initiating a quarrel (17:14; 17:19 and 18:19 seem also to bear on this, though the Hebrew is obscure). Hearing each other out (18:13) and listening to both sides before rendering a judgment (18:17) help one avoid the isolation of the fool and the wicked, who show contempt for others by their speech and earn the contempt of others in return (18:2–3).

Ellen Davis's retranslation of 18:1 gets to the point of the proverb and shows its wider applicability: "The one who isolates himself seeks his own pleasure; he breaks out against all sound judgment."[15] The issue is not "one who lives alone," but rather isolation as a way of life—a problem for communities and nations as well as for individuals. (The same word in Hebrew is translated "friendless" in 19:4.) The arrogance of narrow self-seeking, indifference toward the suffering of others, and the refusal to heed wise counsel are all too common examples of folly writ large on an international scale.

The dangers of careless or malevolent speech (17:4, 7, 20b; 18:2b, 6–8), a common theme in Proverbs, is recognized by the Benedictine tradition. Joan Chittister notes that the Benedictine emphasis on "a guard upon the tongue" is in the interests of communal flourishing: "When talk is unrestrained, when gossip becomes the food of the soul [see Prov. 18:8], then the destruction of others can't be far behind."[16] Conversely, the nourishment provided by wise speech (12:14a; 13:2a; 18:4, 20) is given special emphasis in 18:20–22 by the personification of the word *tongue* (18:21a), a feminine noun in Hebrew. The tongue is portrayed as a woman with lovers, and in her fruits (v. 20) these lovers will find either life or death, a reminder of the life-and-death consequences of the youth's choice of female consort in chapters 1–9. Finding a wife (v. 22) and finding wisdom are linked metaphorically in Proverbs (3:13; 8:35; 19:8b, 14; 31:10), another reflection of Proverbs' male point of view.

15. Ellen F. Davis, *Proverbs, Ecclesiastes, and the Song of Songs*, WBC (Louisville, KY: Westminster John Knox Press, 2000), 110.

16. Joan Chittister, *The Rule of Benedict: Insights for the Ages* (New York: Crossroad, 2009), 60–61.

19:1–20:30

The link between human flourishing and acquiring wisdom continues in this section. Raymond Van Leeuwen provides a literal translation of 19:8, a proverb that echoes the exhortations in chapters 1–9 to seek out Woman Wisdom: "He who gets heart loves himself; he who keeps understanding tends to find good."[17] To *get heart* and *keep understanding* are synonyms for sticking close to personified Wisdom. The love of self in 19:8a is a healthy disposition, one that takes appropriate heed for one's own creaturely flourishing. The Augustinian counsel is not to reject self-love but rather to love all things, including oneself, within a properly ordered love of God. When "fear of the Lord" governs one's life, then everything else falls into place (19:23). However, when desire outruns understanding (19:2) or when disordered desire leads a person astray (19:3, 16b, 22a;[18] 20:1), the outcome is disastrous. This section provides several illustrations of human desire run amok. Laziness (19:15, 24; 20:4, 13a) and false witness (19:5, 9, 22b, 28), driven by a misplaced desire for ease or personal gain, have already been criticized in Proverbs (on laziness, see pp. 42–43, "Further Reflections: Poverty and Work"). Chapter 20 introduces a new temptation: abuse of alcohol; more warnings will follow in 23:19–21, 29–35; 31:4–5. Alcohol, like dangerous women, is bad company: using the rhetorical device of synecdoche, strong drink is described as a "mocker" and a "brawler" (20:1a); "brawler" is a translation of the same Hebrew word used in 7:11 and 9:13 to describe treacherous and foolish women. The importance of good company, surrounding oneself with those who can give wise counsel, is stressed in 19:20, 25 and 20:18. One of the most basic tenets of Proverbs is that the teachings of family and community can help us order our desires and keep us on the right way (19:18, 27; 20:7). Sometimes, however, the "school of hard knocks" is the most effective teacher: 19:19 and 20:16 recognize the danger of enabling foolish behavior by rescuing persons from the consequences of their actions. The ironic imperatives of 20:16 (cf.

17. Raymond Van Leeuwen, "The Book of Proverbs," NIB 5 (Nashville: Abingdon Press, 1997), 179.
18. The alternate NIV translation of 19:22a is preferable to the NRSV: "A man's greed is his shame."

27:13) assume that strangers will almost certainly renege on their loans, putting at risk whatever was pledged by another as surety.

God has made both the ear and the eye (20:12), and they can each be put to wise or foolish use. The ear can be used to hear advice and gain wisdom (19:20, 25; 20:18) or to listen to gossip (20:19). The eye can winnow evil (20:8b) and direct our industrious efforts (20:13b) or confirm us in our folly (17:24; 26:12). We are accountable to God to use both organs well. The mouth is the organ that receives the most attention in Proverbs, as an instrument of both wisdom and folly. "Biting one's tongue" when one is tempted to quarrel or give an angry response (19:11; 20:3) is a sign of wisdom. Proverbs slyly puts teachings about the anger of a king on either side of these verses (19:12; 20:2), suggesting the limits of royal wisdom. In contrast to God's gift of a wise wife (19:14), a quarreling wife is "a continual dripping of rain" (19:13). Foolish use of the mouth in speech to God is the focus in 19:3 and 20:25. Casually or hastily dedicating something to God (20:25) reflects lack of proper attention and respect to God and to one's fellow creatures. A flagrant example of this is Jephthah's foolish vow to God in Judges 11:30 that results in the tragic death of his daughter. Proverbs 19:3 notes the self-deception that leads persons to rage against God for the ruin brought on by their own folly.

The force of habit that fought against me had grown fiercer by my own doing, because I had come willingly to this point where I now wished not to be. And who has any right to object, when just punishment catches up with a sinner?

Augustine, *Confessions*, 8.11.193.

Alongside these teachings about personal accountability are other proverbs that emphasize our lack of understanding and our dependence in a world we do not control, and the consequent need to trust in God (19:21; 20:22, 24). Proverbs 20:22 discourages vigilante justice, an attempt to settle scores on one's own, and provides support to nonviolent responses to evil (cf. 24:29). This proverb sums up the theology behind Martin Luther King Jr.'s call to resist the temptation to retaliatory violence: "I believe that unarmed truth and unconditional love will have the final word in reality. This is why right temporarily defeated is stronger than evil triumphant."[19] Proverbs 19:21 and 20:24 express the hope that God's good intentions for us will ultimately trump all our efforts at self-determination. The repeated juxtaposition of calls to creaturely accountability and acknowledgments of our creaturely ignorance and vulnerability permits no easy resolution: the book of Proverbs asserts both the vital importance of nurturing the human capacity for wisdom and human wisdom's severe limits. Proverbs 20:27 can be read as affirming both sides of this paradox. God our Creator is present and at work in our inmost being and acts, but we are to claim as well our own capacity for self-reflection that God has given us.

The paradox of striving to "get wisdom" yet avoiding the temptation to be "wise in one's own eyes" (3:7; 26:5, 12; 28:26) is paralleled by the paradox of striving for righteousness without succumbing to the deception of being "pure in one's own eyes" (16:2; 21:2; 30:12). The question posed in 20:9 expects the answer, "No one." No one can claim a pure heart and freedom from sin. The reader has not left behind the "regular verbs" of chapters 10–15 that clearly contrast the way of the righteous and the way of the wicked (cf. 19:16), but the deeper wisdom of 20:9 recognizes that, in the presence of the righteous God, even those who strive for human righteousness are called to repentance. A powerful Jewish prayer of confession for the annual celebration of Yom Kippur, the Day of Atonement, contains a litany of all the vices Proverbs warns against:

> **To repent and be converted cannot mean to achieve perfect honesty. It must mean to achieve the honesty of knowing that we are not honest.**
>
> Reinhold Niebuhr, *Beyond Tragedy: Essays on the Christian Interpretation of History* (New York: Charles Scribner's Sons, 1937), 142.

> We have trespassed, we have dealt treacherously, we have robbed, we have spoken slander, we have acted perversely, and we have done wrong; we have acted presumptuously, we have done violence, we have practiced deceit, we have counseled

19. Martin Luther King Jr.'s acceptance speech on the occasion of the award of the Nobel Peace Prize in Oslo, December 10, 1964. Available at http://www.nobelprize.org/nobel_prizes/peace/laureates/1964/king-acceptance.html.

> evil, and we have spoken falsehood; we have scoffed, we have revolted, we have blasphemed, we have rebelled, we have committed iniquity, we have transgressed, and we have oppressed, we have been stiff necked, we have acted wickedly, we have dealt corruptly, we have committed abomination, we have gone astray, we have led others astray.[20]

In this prayer, the covenant people of God abandon their pretense to perfect faithfulness (*ḥesed*) (Prov. 20:6) and put their reliance instead on God's unwavering faithfulness.

Though the links between poverty and laziness are reinforced (20:13) in these verses, the confident linkages among wisdom, righteousness, and prosperity that appeared earlier in Proverbs (cf. 3:16; 8:18; 13:21–2) continue to fray. Fools, liars, and cheats sometimes enjoy wealth (19:10; 20:10, 14, 23; cf. 28:6), while those who walk in integrity are sometimes poor (19:1a, 22b). Wise words are worth even more than gold and costly stones (20:15). Within families, distorted desire for wealth can motivate violence and abandonment of its most vulnerable members (19:26). Reading 20:20 and 20:21 together, Ellen Davis suggests that what is condemned as cursing in verse 20 "is any behavior by which a child seeks to appropriate parents' property prematurely"[21] (cf. 28:24). King Lear is again a vivid literary illustration of this familial tragedy (see pp. 93–96, commentary on 17:1–18:24). A cluster of verses (19:4, 6–7) acknowledges the isolation and neglect faced by the poor, in contrast to the undeserved adulation enjoyed by the rich. The divine response to the plight of the poor is given in 19:17 (cf. 2 Cor. 9:6–7) and is echoed in Jesus' insistence that "just as you did it to one of the least of these . . . , you did it to me" (Matt. 25:40). Concern for the poor in Proverbs is not an example of spiritual virtuosity, as it is sometimes portrayed in contemporary Western Christianity: instead, it is simply part of creaturely wisdom about what is required of us for the sake of living well in society with others. Care for the poor is wise, not just good.

20. *High Holiday Prayer Book for Rosh Hashanah and Yom Kippur* (Marlboro, NJ: Marlboro Jewish Center Congregation Ohev Shalom, 2006), 112.
21. Davis, *Proverbs, Ecclesiastes, and the Song of Songs*, 117.

21:1–22:16

In this last section of the Solomonic collection of 10:1–22:16, the opposition between wickedness and righteousness is again prominent, buttressed by appeals to God's providence over human affairs. Even the richest and most powerful members of society are not in control of their earthly lives. The king's own heart is directed by God (21:1), and military victory does not depend on the strength of horses (21:31; cf. Ps. 20:6–8) or other material advantages. On either side of these verses, the appeals to God's perfect righteousness and wisdom in 21:2 and 21:30 drastically relativize human pretensions to the same, including the pretensions of the king and others in power.

The "rod of anger" in 22:8b can be read as a reference to the king's royal scepter (cf. Isa. 14:5–6). Like horses, it too will fail if used in the service of injustice (22:8a). A wise and righteous king will instead befriend those who "love a pure heart" (22:11a). That power and wisdom are not always correlated is seen by the story in 21:22 of a single wise person who went up against the fortress of the mighty and prevailed (cf. Eccl. 9:13–18).

> **If only it were all so simple! If only there were evil people somewhere insidiously committing evil deeds, and it were necessary only to separate them from the rest of us and destroy them. But the line dividing good and evil cuts through the heart of every human being. And who is willing to destroy a piece of his own heart?**
>
> Aleksandr I. Solzhenitsyn, *The Gulag Archipelago 1918–1956,* (San Francisco: HarperCollins, 1974), 168.

The wealthy are also put on notice in this section. "A good name" is better than "great riches" (22:1). Getting rich by unjust means (21:6a; 22:16a) is a "fleeting vapor" (21:6b), the same word translated "vanity" in Ecclesiastes. Those who use wealth to bribe others (21:14), ingratiate themselves with the rich (22:16b), or lord it over the poor (22:7) will see no lasting gain. Their pretensions to social superiority are relativized by the God who is the creator of all people, rich and poor alike (22:2). Those who will enjoy God's mercy and material blessing are not those craving their own pleasure (21:17) or selfishly looking to "make a quick buck" (21:5b) but rather those who are generous and attentive to the poor (21:13, 26b; 22:9).

Familiar warnings against laziness and familial discord are treated with comic hyperbole. Life on a rooftop, alone and exposed to the elements, is preferable to life with "a contentious wife" (21:9). The next time the subject comes up, the sages up the ante: it is better to live in the desert wilderness than with such a wife (21:19).

The "strange woman" of chapters 1–9 makes a cameo appearance in 22:14 (cf. 23:27; 30:20), demonstrating that there are indeed worse things than staying at home with "a "contentious and fretful wife" (21:19b). Similarly, the vignette about the lazy person in 22:13 (cf. 26:13) paints an improbable scenario of "the sluggard curled up inside and pointing outside, stammering about an imaginary lion wandering the streets."[22] Laziness and love of ease are given more serious treatment in 21:25–26. The NRSV supplies the subject "the wicked" in verse 26a, since there is no noun in that clause, but it is better to read verse 26a as an extension of the description of the lazy in verse 25. The lazy person craves and covets for herself what she is not willing to work for, while the righteous (and presumably diligent) person gives freely to others (21:26b). In her disordered desires, the lazy person thus resembles the violent who hate what is just (21:7) and the wicked who passionately embrace what is crooked and evil (21:8a, 10). The tragedy of a misdirected heart, one that hates what is good and holds fast to what is evil (contra Rom. 12:9) is witnessed to repeatedly in Proverbs without any attempt at explanation (see pp. 36–38, commentary on 4:1–27). As Reinhold Niebuhr notes, there is "something more stubborn and

Throughout Africa, proverbs emphasize the negative aspects of marriage for the man who might be caught or trapped by a wife who is an irritant or a problem—at best, a necessary evil. Reversing these proverbs to have them apply to husbands does not even enter the thought pattern.

Mercy Amba Oduyoye, *Daughters of Anowa: African Women and Patriarchy* (Maryknoll, NY: Orbis Books, 1995), 65.

22. Yoder, *Proverbs*, 226.

mysterious in human wrongdoing than some easily corrected sloth or malice."[23]

"It is pathetic to hear mosquitoes cough." This Swedish aphorism, a favorite of Krister Stendahl,[24] sums up Proverbs' attitude to haughty, prideful persons (21:4, 11, 24; 22:10) and to those who think God can be deceived or bought off with sacrifices (21:3, 27). In contemporary times, the latter includes proponents of a "prosperity gospel" who use financial sacrifices to the church as an investment strategy for getting rich. Both the haughty and the manipulative betray a pathetic misunderstanding of their identity as neighbor to others and as creature before God. The same goes for those who try to secure themselves by wickedness (21:7, 10, 12, 18; 22:8, 12, 16). True security does not come by denying our vulnerability, attempting to manipulate God, or protecting ourselves at the expense of our neighbors. Instead, the path to creaturely flourishing is humility and "fear of the LORD" (22:4). To pursue wisdom and righteousness is to set oneself in right relation with the riches and honor that the foolish and wicked misguidedly strive after (21:16–17, 20–21, 25–26).

FURTHER REFLECTIONS

The Vice of Pride and the Virtue of Humility

Proverbs consistently portrays human pride as foolish and wicked, a disposition utterly incompatible with a life of trust in God (cf. Prov. 3:5–8). As Augustine comments, "What is pride but a craving for perverse elevation? For it is perverse elevation to forsake the ground in which the mind ought to be rooted and to become, and to be, grounded in oneself."[25] The ultimate expression of arrogance in Proverbs is the human pretension "to be wise in one's own eyes" (Prov. 3:7a). Growing ecological awareness has uncovered "perverse elevation" on the part of human beings regarding their place in

23. Reinhold Niebuhr, *Beyond Tragedy: Essays on the Christian Interpretation of History* (New York: Charles Scribner's Sons, 1937), 141.
24. Krister Stendahl, "Why I Love the Bible," *Harvard Divinity Bulletin* 35, no. 1 (Winter 2007), http://bulletin.hds.harvard.edu/articles/winter2007/why-i-love-bible.
25. Augustine, *City of God* 14.13, 571.

the cosmos—surely greater humility is called for here, alongside a greater sense of responsibility toward all of life.

However, because of human inequalities and abuse of power (cf. 22:7, 16), the effective history of traditional calls to forsake pride and embrace humility shows how morally dangerous this tradition can be. As Neal Plantinga notes, Christian versions of this tradition have "often been dominated by whites who have preached humility to blacks, by men who have preached submissiveness to women, by rigid and unimaginative persons who have regarded every creative impulse, every struggle for personal dignity as a shameful show of arrogance."[26] Proverbs, with its rather undeveloped sense of the dangers of human authoritarianism (e.g., 19:10; 22:15; 23:13–14; 24:21) does not reflect adequate awareness of how easy it is for those in power to love the virtue of humility in *other* people.

Those who preach humility, therefore, need to be clear that it is particularly the powerful who need to cultivate this virtue. As Reinhold Niebuhr notes, "The more man establishes himself in power and glory, the greater is the fear of tumbling from his eminence, or losing his treasure, or being discovered in his pretension."[27] Humility in social relations does not encourage cowering subservience or abusive self-denigration. It is compatible with determined resistance to all forms of injustice. Humility means being secure in the knowledge of who you are, before the God who made you and sustains you, and before your neighbors, who, like you, are created in love by God. In an age of ecological concern, humility is a fitting virtue for human earthlings, earth's most powerful creatures, to cultivate. God has called humanity to live out their creaturely identity in the company of their fellow creatures. Ecological arrogance leads to death. To choose humility is to choose life (22:4).

26. Cornelius Plantinga Jr., *Not the Way It's Supposed to Be: A Breviary of Sin* (Grand Rapids: Eerdmans, 1995), 86.
27. Reinhold Niebuhr, *Nature and Destiny of Man*, 1:193.

22:17–24:34
Words of the Wise

The NRSV follows the Greek text in pulling out "the words of the wise" from the body of 22:17 to serve as the title for this new section (22:17–24:22). More "sayings of the wise" are introduced in 24:23 and continue through the end of chapter 24. The NRSV's title alerts the reader that the lengthy first collection of Solomonic teachings that began in 10:1 has come to an end. A second, shorter Solomonic collection begins in 25:1. In this interlude between Solomonic teachings there is a change of pedagogical form. Antithetical proverbs, the "regular verbs" of chapters 10–15, almost completely disappear. In their place are direct admonitions, harking back to the form of the instructions in chapters 1–9, along with some rhetorical questions. However, this section is not simply a reversion to the "home schooling" of these beginning chapters, under the watchful eye of parents and Woman Wisdom. The wider social horizon of 10:1–22:16 extends to these words to the wise, and the direct admonitory form brings this broader horizon much closer to the reader: the reader is addressed not just as a youth, as in chapters 1–9, but also as a parent (23:13–14), householder (24:27), military leader (24:5–6), and member of a royal court (23:1–3).

Egypt and Mesopotamia were the motherlands of wisdom in the ancient Near East, and there is general agreement that Proverbs' wisdom is internationally inspired. The sages of Israel exhibited what biblical scholar Carole Fontaine calls an "intellectual ecumenism," a willingness to share resources across boundaries of culture and religion. She notes that Israel's sages "were wise precisely because they honed their thought on the words of the sages and the experience of the cultures that preceded and surrounded them."[1] In the "The Words of the Wise" section of Proverbs, scholars have discovered direct literary dependence on the Egyptian wisdom text known as *Instruction of Amenemope*, written late in the second millennium BCE.[2] Dependence on this text is reflected earlier in Proverbs (cf. 15:16; 17:1), but not in such a concentrated way as in 22:17–23:11. In light of the literary parallels between the Egyptian text and this section of Proverbs, many translators emend the text of 22:20 to read "thirty sayings," because *Amenemope* is written in thirty chapters.[3] (The NIV's attempt to divide the text of 22:17–24:22 into "thirty sayings" is not very convincing, however.) The dependence on *Amenemope* is not slavish: the sages of Proverbs felt free to edit, expound upon, and rearrange the Egyptian material.

There is no scholarly consensus about exactly how this literary contact between Egypt and Israel was made, but it is likely that the royal courts in both countries played a role. Carol Newsom posits that the phenomenon of second-language instruction could have been a vehicle for this cross-cultural sharing. Perhaps an Israelite scribe learning Egyptian learned it in part by memorizing and copying *Amenemope*—and then, wanting to construct a comparable curriculum for teaching Hebrew literacy, he adapted this text for his own purposes.[4] However it happened, this dependence has interesting theological implications for both interfaith concerns and the Christian doctrine of revelation (see pp. 109–11, "Further Reflections: Biblical Revelation and the Universal Search for Wisdom").

The parental calls to a youth to embrace wisdom, sprinkled throughout this section (23:15–16, 19, 22–26; 24:13–14, 21–22), are familiar to readers of chapters 1–9. The parallels between the exhortation to "buy" wisdom, instruction, and understanding in 23:23 and the exhortation to "get" wisdom and insight in 4:5, 7 are obscured by the NRSV translation: in both cases the Hebrew verb

1. Carole R. Fontaine, *Smooth Words: Women, Proverbs and Performance in Biblical Wisdom*, JSOT Supplement 356 (Sheffield: Sheffield Academic Press, 2002), 19–20.
2. See James B. Pritchard, ed. *The Ancient Near East: An Anthology of Texts and Pictures* (Princeton, NJ: Princeton University Press, 1958), 237–43.
3. The last chapter of *Instruction of Amenemope* begins this way: "See thou these thirty chapters: / They entertain; they instruct; / They are the foremost of all books," 247.
4. Carol Newsom, personal correspondence, Sept. 24, 2009.

is *qanah*. Similar exhortations to acquire wisdom without an explicit addressee are found in 22:17–21 and 23:12. Wisdom, as always, is firmly aligned with righteousness: the goal of this instruction is for the youth to be a righteous and wise son (23:24).

However, the moral terrain in which this wisdom and righteousness are to be enacted has become more challenging than in chapters 1–9. Wickedness seems ascendant. Three times in this section the wise are counseled not to "envy" evildoers, presumably because the latter seem to be flourishing (23:17; 24:1–2, 19). Nor are they to gloat over the temporary misfortunes of the wicked (24:17–18): God is the Creator of all, wicked and (relatively) righteous alike, and divine mercy is God's alone to bestow. Instead, the righteous are exhorted to put their hope in God (23:18), to remember that wickedness has no long-term future (24:20), and to quell their desire for retribution (24:29).

These three responses have long been linked in Christian calls for nonviolent resistance. Trust in God's justice and confidence about the self-defeating character of evil make possible an asymmetrical response to violence and injustice. While it is tempting to "get even" (24:29a) and seek "payback" (24:29b), retaliatory violence only begets more violence. As Martin Luther King insisted, "We must meet the forces of hate with the power of love."[5]

King was clear, however, that evil must still be actively engaged. It is morally unacceptable to keep aloof from neighbors in mortal danger (24:10–11) or to feign ignorance about their plight (24:12). Nonviolent resistance is still a form of determined resistance. King wrote scathingly about white ministers who in response to systemic violence and injustice directed at African Americans "have been more cautious than courageous and have remained silent

> **If we are going to move on and build a new kind of world community there must be a way in which we can deal with a sordid past. . . . We cannot go on nursing grudges even vicariously for those who cannot speak for themselves any longer. True forgiveness deals with the past, all of the past, to make the future possible.**
>
> Desmond Tutu, *No Future Without Forgiveness* (New York: Doubleday, 1999), 278–79.

5. Martin Luther King Jr., *Stride Toward Freedom: The Montgomery Story* (Boston: Beacon Press, 2010), 87.

behind the anesthetizing security of stained-glass windows."[6] Proverbs reminds the reader that this cowardly behavior does not go unnoticed by the God who weighs the heart and "keeps watch over your soul" (24:12).

Even more insistent than the calls not to envy evildoers are the exhortations to refrain from doing evil oneself. In shockingly direct language, readers are warned in 22:22 not to take advantage of their social power and privilege. Robbing the poor because they are poor and defenseless and abusing one's public status to crush the afflicted in the gate will not bring one advantage, because the poor are not really defenseless after all: God is on their side and will forcefully vindicate them (22:23). In another vivid phrase, the reader is warned not to "lie in wait like an outlaw" against the righteous (24:15). (In keeping with the male perspective of Proverbs, a prostitute, likewise, is said to "lie in wait like a robber" against gullible men (23:27–28). The implication is that this ambush of the unsuspecting may bring initial, even repeated, success. However, because of the moral order that God has established, the righteous will not be ultimately defeated, and the number of the faithless will not always be on the rise (24:16a; 23:28). There are two warnings not to remove ancient landmarks (22:28; 23:10). These were boundary markers designating the land belonging to each of Israel's families (cf. Deut. 19:14). To violate these boundaries was to put at risk the vulnerable who depended on the yield of their land (23:10). Giving false witness, thereby exonerating the wicked (24:24) or condemning the innocent neighbor (24:28), is likewise repudiated. Throughout these words of the wise God appears as a redeemer (23:11) who acts on behalf of the oppressed to bring justice and punish wickedness. Those who fear the Holy One (24:21) embrace God's zeal for righteousness. By contrast, those who foolishly fall into the company of the wicked and scoffers (24:1–2, 8–9) and wear themselves out in pursuit of wealth (23:4–6) will end up empty-handed (24:22). The promise of the violent thugs in 1:11–14 to "find all kinds of costly things; and fill [their] houses with booty" (v. 13) is paralleled in 24:4, in which "rooms are filled with all precious and pleasant riches," but this time it is wisdom that bestows this abundance.

6. Martin Luther King Jr., "Letter from a Birmingham Jail," in *Why We Can't Wait* (Boston: Beacon Press, 2010), 103.

Common themes return in this section. Wisdom is mightier than physical strength (24:5–6; cf. 21:22; Eccles. 9:13–18). The fiscal foolishness of providing surety for the debts of another is again warned against, this time with a sharp question: Why risk having "your bed taken from under you?" (22:27; cf. 6:1; 17:8; 20:16; 27:13). Financial stability is better secured by hard work (24:27). Those who are too lazy to tend their own fields and property will be "attacked" by poverty (24:30–34; cf. 15:19; 20:4; 21:25). Proverbs 23:13–14 assures that beating children "with a rod," a common practice in Egypt as well as Israel, will not kill them and in fact "will save their lives from Sheol" (on corporal punishment, see pp. 78–80, commentary on 12:24–13:25).

Along with God, the king is also to be feared (24:22), though the emphasis falls on gaining the king's favor through skills and shrewd table manners (22:29–23:3) rather than through righteousness. Proverbs 29:25–26 rejects the parallelism between fear of the king and fear of God that is implied by 24:21–22. The dangers of excessive food and drink (23:20) receive rather comic attention. Eating and drinking to excess lead to a stupor that will clothe the indulgent in rags (23:21). Not all invitations to "eat and drink" are sincere, and the bread of the stingy sticks in the throat, only to be vomited up again (23:6–8). The artful riddle about drinking in 23:29–35 starts with six questions, only the last of which, "Who has redness of eyes?" (v. 29b), hints at the cause of all the trouble. The deceptive pleasure of drinking to excess (v. 31) and its debauched results (vv. 33–35) both encourage another drinking binge (v. 35b).

FURTHER REFLECTIONS

Biblical Revelation and the Universal Search for Wisdom

It is fair to say that Christian theologians have generally *not* had Proverbs in mind when constructing their understandings of biblical revelation.[7] Two themes have dominated Christian accounts

7. An exception is John Barton, *People of the Book: The Authority of the Bible in Christianity* (London: SPCK, 1988), who argues that biblical wisdom literature provides the best general paradigm for understanding the revelation contained in the Bible.

about how God is revealed in the Old Testament. First, God is revealed through great acts in history, such as the exodus from Egypt and the giving of the law. Second, God is revealed through prophetic messengers who receive a "word of the Lord" addressed to a particular situation. The understanding of revelation as what God does in history (through both acts and words) on behalf of a particular people is linked to theological perspectives on Israel's relation to the other nations of the world. Being the beneficiary of God's revelatory acts and words privileges Israel and sets her apart from her neighbors: Israel is not like other nations who have not enjoyed this divine favor and guidance. The dire warnings in the Torah and the Prophets against adopting the beliefs and practices of other peoples reinforce this theological perspective and then are extended to serve as a theological model for how Christians are to live in the world as the guardians of biblical revelation. This model has sometimes encouraged a triumphalist and exclusivist approach to other religious traditions, as if the church had nothing to receive from others.

As we have seen, Proverbs turns these understandings of God's revelatory dealings with Israel upside down. There is no "Thus sayeth the Lord" in Proverbs: God never speaks. Proverbs makes no mention of the "mighty acts" of God on Israel's behalf. It is concerned not with acts of divine deliverance for Israel but with God's ongoing sustenance of *all* creaturely life. As Claus Westermann notes, "The sayings of Proverbs 10–31 referring to God testify to the fact that speaking about God and his universal operation must have been far more extensive in ancient Israel than has been assumed in traditional interpretation of salvation history."[8]

Proverbs' approach to knowing God through God's "universal operation" in creation in turn suggests a different theological model of Israel's relations to other peoples. Instead of calling Israel to separate itself from and reject the ways of its neighbors, Proverbs models a critical acceptance of the insights and teachings of other nations. What God intends Israel to learn about creaturely life binds them to people from other cultures and religious traditions,

8. Claus Westermann, *Roots of Wisdom: The Oldest Proverbs of Israel and Other Peoples* (Louisville, KY: Westminster John Knox Press, 1995), 130.

making Israel their debtor in her search for wisdom. This becomes even more explicit in the teachings ascribed to the non-Israelite figures Agur and King Lemuel's mother in the last two chapters of Proverbs. As John Collins observes, "This international character is a very important aspect of proverbial wisdom. The fact that the sages could speak of their God in such an international idiom was a confident affirmation that their God was not the God of Israel alone, but of all humanity, and was in principle accessible to all."[9] Gathering the wisdom of other nations is integral to Israel's quest to know and be faithful to God's wisdom.

The people of God, whether in ancient Israel or today, have never existed in political, religious, or intellectual isolation from their neighbors. Proverbs' appropriation of Egyptian wisdom reflects better than the rhetoric of passages like Deuteronomy 7:1–6 what scholars suspect is the real history of ancient Israel's relations with its neighbors—not a total and violent separation but a complex mix of cultural assimilation and differentiation. Proverbs also models a better approach to living in a religiously pluralistic world today. The search for wisdom is a constant in human life, and the wisdom found within any particular religious tradition can never claim to be fully "homegrown." It is always, to a degree that is impossible to measure precisely, imported from or at least genetically modified by the traditions and teachings of other communities.

Indeed, this section of the book of Proverbs can be seen as a parable of the church's existence. The church lives its life in dependence on others, even when it is unaware of or loath to acknowledge its cultural and religious debts. When the church is flourishing, it borrows wisely from others, shapes what it receives, and shares what it has. The church's vocation to creaturely wisdom is a vocation it shares with God's other creatures, both human and nonhuman (cf. 30:24–28). In giving our distinctive testimony as Christians, part of the "gentleness and reverence" toward others that 1 Peter 3:16 enjoins comes from the conviction that God may also be speaking to us through them.

9. John J. Collins, *Proverbs, Ecclesiastes* (Atlanta: John Knox Press, 1980), 7.

25:1–29:27

Political Wisdom

25:1–27:27

Proverbs 25:1 marks the beginning of a second collection of Solomonic proverbs. This time the collection and editing of the proverbs is ascribed to "officials of King Hezekiah of Judah" (25:1), a sign of the importance of royal courts as a source for proverbial wisdom. While the proverbs gathered by royal officials do not necessarily have their source in court life, it is also true that the wisdom of 25:1–28 reflects a court setting. The second Solomonic collection may extend as far as the end of chapter 29, until the start of an oracle by "Agur son of Jakeh" in 30:1. If so, there is a stylistic break in the middle of this second collection, at 28:1, just as there was in the first Solomonic collection (10:1–22:16, with a stylistic divide at 16:1). A different theme predominates in each chapter of Proverbs 25–27. Chapter 25 focuses on the king and appropriate courtly behavior; chapter 26 portrays the plight of the foolish and lazy; and chapter 27 reflects on friendship. All three themes reflect the growing maturity and adult responsibilities of the implied reader. Apart from 27:11, the parental voice has faded into the background.

The king is depicted as a mediating figure between God and humanity in 25:2–3. The king is a searcher for the wisdom that God has hidden in reality who functions as a royal representative for all human searchers. Yet the king's mind, like God's, is so high and deep as to be unsearchable (cf. Job 5:9; 9:10). When the king's reign is purified of wickedness, just as a metal smith purifies silver (25:4), then his throne will be secure in righteousness (25:5; cf. 16:12; 29:14). However, a check on the power of the king is folded into a passage on care for animals and the rhythms of the natural world (27:23–27). Human political and financial success (27:24) is fleeting: whereas the pattern of the seasons continues without interruption, the king's crown does not last "for all generations" (27:24b). Chapters 28–29 consider the reality of wicked and unjust rulers (cf. 28:3, 15–16a; 29:2b, 4b, 12, 16).

The counsel to younger members of the court who are angling for higher status is one of prudence and self-control, a repeated theme in these chapters (25:6–7b; cf. 25:16, 27–28; 27:1–2, 20–21). When surrounded by social superiors, one should not reach too high and risk "being put in one's place" (25:6–7). Instead of boasting about one's plans for advancement (27:1; cf. Jas. 4:13–14) or one's past successes (27:2), it is better to be patient and wait for others to praise you and invite you to ascend the social ladder. Patience is also the key for "softening" up one's social superiors to bring them around to one's own point of view (25:15). Jesus, observing the same jockeying for position in the house of a Pharisee, turns this counsel into a parable of the kingdom of heaven, where "all who exalt themselves will be humbled, and those who humble themselves will be exalted" (Luke 14:11).

FURTHER REFLECTIONS
Jesus as Sage

We have already noted how the first followers of Jesus, steeped in Jewish wisdom traditions, drew on the exalted descriptions of Woman Wisdom in Proverbs 1–9 and in the deuterocanonical writings to give expression to their faith in him. This wisdom trajectory is especially evident in John's Gospel and the Pauline letters (see pp. 53–55, "Further Reflections: Jesus Christ and Woman Wisdom"). Jesus was himself steeped in Israel's wisdom traditions, and accounts of his teaching in the Synoptic Gospels frequently reflect both the form and content of proverbial wisdom. As Claus Westermann declares, "It was unnecessary for Jesus to adapt himself to these sayings since he was familiar with them from early on, inasmuch as he grew up with them. . . . Before his public appearance, they were his possession intellectually and remained so throughout the period of his ministry."[1]

Jesus' pedagogical style of evoking wise reflection and his persistent attention to ordinary creaturely flourishing mark him as a bearer of Israel's wisdom. Two scenes from Jesus' teaching, chosen almost at random from the Synoptic accounts, will illustrate this.

The first example is from Luke 12:13–21. Jesus sandwiches a parable about a rich fool in between two proverbial teachings (vv. 15 and 21) about appropriate attitudes toward wealth. The first teaching cautions that "'one's life does not consist in the abundance of possessions'" (v. 15b), a sentiment that echoes Proverbs' teachings about the superiority of wisdom to material wealth (Prov. 3:13–18) and the folly of wearing oneself out to get rich (Prov. 23:4–5). The second teaching points to the calamity awaiting "'those who store up treasures for themselves but are not rich toward God'" (Luke 12:21). The Lukan teaching echoes Proverbs' contrasts between the righteous who find security in God (Prov. 14:26) and the deluded trust of the rich in their wealth (Prov. 18:11). As James will later teach, "in the midst of a busy life, [the rich] will wither away" (Jas. 1:11) whereas the poor who are "rich in faith" (2:5) will be heirs of God's kingdom.

In between these two proverbial teachings from Luke sits a parable (Luke 12:16–20) that provides a vivid portrayal of one of Proverbs' stock characters, the fool, who is "wise in his own eyes" (Prov. 3:7a). The reflections of Luke's fool are entirely self-absorbed, with no thought of God or neighbor (vv. 17–19). Like Qohelet, the teacher of Ecclesiastes, the rich fool in Luke tells his soul to eat, drink, and be merry (v. 19; cf. Eccl. 9:7). But that attitude is wise only when one has accepted the true terms of creaturely life: that all one has is a gift from God's hand (Eccl. 2:24b–25), here today and gone tomorrow (Prov. 23:5). By contrast, Luke's rich fool has no sense that his land's produce and his life itself are divine gifts and that his wealth is not for hoarding. He thinks that he can find security and happiness by his own efforts, without trust in God and without concern for others, especially the poor (cf. Prov. 23:9). However, the fool

1. Claus Westermann, *Roots of Wisdom: The Oldest Proverbs of Israel and Other Peoples* (Louisville, KY: Westminster John Knox Press, 1995), 112.

learns the truth of Proverbs 11:4a, "Riches do not profit in the day of wrath," when he hears God's sharp words (Luke: 12:20). Death is the ultimate equalizer, revealing the rich man's lack of control over his life and possessions.

The second illustration of Jesus' pedagogical style is from Mark 7:24–30 (//Matt. 15:21–28), the story of the Syrophoenician woman who comes to Jesus seeking healing for her daughter. Richard Clifford remarks that "the encounter between Jesus and the woman reminds one of two peasants hurling proverbs at each other."[2] Jesus' proverb, "'It is not fair to take the children's food and throw it to the dogs'" (v. 27), is harsh and offensive, despite the efforts of many interpreters to soften it. As Sharon Ringe puts it, Jesus seems to have been "caught with his compassion down."[3] However, the Syrophoenician woman is uncowed and fires back her own proverb: "'Even the dogs under the table eat the children's crumbs'" (v. 28). Of the two of them, the Gentile woman has found the "word fitly spoken" (Prov. 25:11a) for that situation, delivering "a wise rebuke" to Jesus' "listening ear" (Prov. 25:12b). "'For saying that,'" Jesus responds, "'you may go—the demon has left your daughter'" (Mark 7:29). Matthew's Gospel interprets the woman's reply as a sign of her great faith (Matt. 15:28), but Mark leaves open the possibility that it is also her great wisdom that won Jesus over. As Proverbs would say, "Iron sharpens iron, and one person sharpens the wits of another" (27:17). Given the international inspiration of Israel's wisdom and the prominence of female figures as its exemplars in Proverbs, it is fitting that the voice of wisdom in this story is that of a Gentile woman. Yet Jesus' humility and his willingness to learn are also central marks of wisdom: "Give instruction to the wise, and they will become wiser still" (Prov. 9:9a).

The sweetness of social honor and success, when they do come, must be savored in small doses (25:16): it is possible to have "too much of a good thing." This self-control is difficult, given the

2. Richard J. Clifford, *The Book of Proverbs and Our Search for Wisdom* (Milwaukee: Marquette University Press, 1995), 46.
3. Sharon H. Ringe, "A Gentile Woman's Story," in *Feminist Interpretation of the Bible*, ed. Letty Russell (Philadelphia: Westminster Press, 1984), 69.

insatiability of human desire. To the ravenous, "even the bitter is sweet" (27:7). In comparing human desire to rapacious appetites of Sheol and Abaddon (27:20; cf. 30:15–16), Proverbs plays on the imagery of personified Death in Canaanite mythology (see pp. 21–22, commentary on 1:8–19). Receiving honor is thus the true test of a person's humility (27:21). As Jonathan Edwards notes, "To find humility with honor is to find a phoenix. Let an obscure person be lifted up to honor, and how steady and well-composed soever he was before, 'tis a thousand to one but his eyes will dazzle and his head run round when he is upon the lofty pinnacle of praise and honor"[4] (see pp. 103–4, "Further Reflections: The Vice of Pride and the Virtue of Humility").

The importance of verbal artistry is introduced in 25:11–12 and further reinforced with a cascade of vivid comparative proverbs that exhibit verbal artistry themselves (25:11–15, 18– 20, 25, 26; 26:1–2, 6, 8–11, 17–19, 21, 23), despite a number of textual corruptions. Besides evoking delight, beautiful turns of phrase and arresting images are pedagogically effective: they draw the hearer's attention and are not soon forgotten. For example, Yoder points to the aptness of the image of a gold ornament in 25:12: "The rebuke is made for the ear and the ear that receives it is made beautiful."[5] However, the larger point being made through the verbal artistry of these proverbs is that verbal artistry on its own is insufficient. "More matter with less art," the Queen Mother curtly requests of the windbag Polonius in Shakespeare's *Hamlet*.[6] As David Kelsey notes, what Polonius "says so ponderously never relates to the concrete particularities of his

We need to take our cue here from Proverbs, where wise speech is not a simple set of rules but a habit of mind and action whose acquisition takes ongoing practice and discipline.

Shane Berg, "Body Language," *Princeton Seminary Bulletin* 28, no. 1 (New Series 2007): 12–13.

4. Jonathan Edwards, *The Works of Jonathan Edwards*, vol. 24, *The "Blank Bible,"* ed. Stephen J. Stein (New Haven, CT: Yale University Press, 2006), 578.
5. Christine Roy Yoder, *Proverbs*, Abingdon Old Testament Commentaries (Nashville: Abingdon Press, 2009), 250.
6. William Shakespeare, *Hamlet*, act 2, scene 2, line 95, in *The Complete Signet Classic Shakespeare* (New York: Harcourt Brace Jovanovich, 1972), 930.

world. His remarks always seem to flow above the specific details of the immediate situation, or are connected to them only in ironic and unintended ways."[7] By contrast, what makes a proverb as exquisitely crafted as "apples of gold in a setting of silver" is being "fitly spoken" in a particular context (25:11).

Proverbs "fitly spoken" have "performative force to elicit wisdom in concrete situations."[8] The word translated "fitly" in 25:11 may be derived from the Hebrew word for "wheel" (cf. 20:26). "A word fitly spoken" glides; it goes the distance. By contrast, "a proverb in the mouth of a fool" goes nowhere; it has no legs (26:7). Even worse, it is liable to hurt people, like a thorn bush flailed by a drunkard (26:9). Images involving weapons also dramatize the dangers of wicked and foolish speech in other proverbs in this section (25:18; 26:10, 18).

Nowhere in the book of Proverbs is the performative dimension of proverbial speech more explicit than in 26:4–5, where two opposing proverbs are set side by side. The decision about whether "to answer fools according to their folly" depends on wise discernment of the situation at hand. This direct juxtaposition shows the importance of what Susan Niditch has termed the "reoralization" of proverbs in concrete moments of experience so as to guide wise action.[9] Even common English proverbs show the need for this discernment. Confronted with a particular situation, do we say, "Many hands make light work" or "Too many cooks spoil the broth"? Do we say, "Look before you leap" or "The one who hesitates is lost"?

Proverbs are, properly speaking, not universal rules; rather, they are situationally oriented, open-ended sayings, designed to exercise one's mental and moral faculties and thereby enable the moral agent to size up ethically demanding situations and to act appropriately.

William P. Brown, *Character in Crisis: A Fresh Approach to the Wisdom Literature of the Old Testament* (Grand Rapids: Eerdmans, 1996), 13–14.

These tensions are inherent to the genre of wisdom literature, and the book of Proverbs is full

7. David H. Kelsey, *Eccentric Existence: A Theological Anthropology* (Louisville, KY: Westminster John Knox Press, 2009), 223.
8. Ibid.
9. Susan Niditch, *Oral World and Written Word* (Louisville, KY: Westminster John Knox Press, 1996), 39–77.

of them. Proverbs 26:26, for example, depicts the righteous being forced to "give way" to the power of the wicked, a teaching that clashes with the confident statement in 10:30 that the righteous will never be moved. Proverbs 26:26 also stands in tension with the reassurance of 26:27 that the wicked will reap the same mischief that they sow. Proverbs are not universal rules: they address what Thomas Aquinas called the "disputed questions" of a community.[10]

Weather images tie together verses 13–14. The empty promise of clouds and wind that bring no rain is compared to a boaster who never follows through on a promised gift (25:14); in contemporary parlance, she is "full of hot air." By contrast, faithful messengers refresh their senders like cold snow on the brow of those toiling away in the heat of the harvest (25:13). Van Leeuwen notes the practice of hiring runners to bring down mountain snow to refresh the wealthy.[11] A similar image is used in 25:25: the good news of a messenger is "like cold water to a thirsty soul." Weather images of wind and rain are also used to evoke the misery of household bickering, specified, as usual, in terms of a contentious wife (25:23–24; 27:15–16). Quarreling more generally is also treated in several other vivid proverbs: jumping into someone else's quarrel is like grabbing a stray dog by the ears (26:17); whispers by a quarrelsome person fan the flames of a dispute (26:20–21) and slide down into the gut, where they cause trouble (26:22; cf. 18:8). "Undeserved curses" may not go anywhere (26:2), but attempts to make light of one's own deceptive words leave lasting wounds (26:18).

The inclination of wise men to imagine that their wisdom has exhausted the infinite possibilities of God's power and wisdom is merely one aspect of the general character of human sin. Human reason is made the servant and slave of human pride.

Reinhold Niebuhr, *Reinhold Niebuhr: Theologian of Public Life*, ed. Larry Rasmussen (Minneapolis: Fortress Press, 1991), 107.

The intractability of folly is addressed by a familiar call to corporal punishment (26:3) and by two new images: a dog returning

10. Thomas Aquinas, *Disputed Questions on Virtue*, trans. Ralph McInerny (South Bend, IN: St. Augustine's Press, 1999).
11. Raymond Van Leeuwen, "The Book of Proverbs," NIB 5 (Nashville: Abingdon Press, 1997), 218.

to its vomit (26:11) and grain being crushed by a mortar and pestle (27:22). In another arresting image, 26:6 compares sending a message by a fool to "drinking down violence" or "cutting off one's foot." Lest the group of sharp proverbs on fools in 26:1–11 lull the so-called wise into prideful self-satisfaction, the section ends with a piercing question in verse 12 about those who are "wise in their own eyes."

A group of proverbs on the lazy (26:13–16) follows immediately afterward and ends with an ironic observation about the lazy being overly wise "in self-esteem" (v. 16). There is a humorous progression in the lazy person's plight: first he gives the absurd excuse that there is a lion outside to explain why he is unable to get out of the house (v. 13); next he is unable even to get out of bed (v. 14); finally he is too tired even to eat (v. 15). As Van Leeuwen notes, "'fool' and 'sluggard' occupy similar semantic positions" in Proverbs.[12]

The cognate words for *enemy* and *hatred* occur seven times in this section (25:17, 21; 26:24–26, 28; 27:6). The first time the verb *hate* is used hyperbolically to warn against wearing out one's welcome with a neighbor (25:17; cf. 27:14), but the other occasions are more morally serious. Again, wisdom requires an asymmetrical response (see pp. 105–11, commentary on 22:17–24:34). While the wise should not be fooled by the deceptive words and gestures of enemies (26:24–26, 28; 27:6), neither should they respond in kind. Instead, the wise are to treat their enemies mercifully, giving them bread to eat and water to drink (25:21–22). Jesus and the apostle Paul will give the same advice (Luke 6:35; Rom. 12:20a). The motive clause in 25:22, which Paul picks up in Romans 12:20b, is interpreted variously. Commenting on the Romans passage, Krister Stendahl observes that within an apocalyptic framework, heaping coals of fire on your enemy's head seems to have more to do with the perfection of hatred than with self-giving love: "With the Day of Vengeance at hand, the proper and reasonable attitude is to forego one's own vengeance and to leave vengeance to God. Why walk around with a little shotgun if the atomic blast is imminent?"[13] Psalm 140:10 also uses the image of

12. Ibid., 225.
13. Krister Stendahl, "Hate, Non-Retaliation, and Love: 1QS X, 17–20 and Rom. 12:19:19–21," *Harvard Theological Review* 55 (1962):344–45.

burning coals to express a desire for vengeance. By contrast, Ellen Davis suggests that the image of burning coals in Proverbs "stems from an Egyptian penitential rite, in which live coals were placed on the head of a penitent" as a sign of shame and remorse.[14] On this interpretation, showing kindness toward enemies may move them toward repentance. In any case, trust in God's reward makes it possible to avoid escalating present conflicts.

Friends and flocks are the two main subjects of chapter 27. The intimacy of friendship is such that "one human heart reflects another" (v. 19). However, friendship sometimes requires candid criticism (vv. 5–6) so that one's rough and dull edges can be honed (v. 17). The NRSV follows the LXX reading for verse 9b, but the Hebrew also makes sense in this context: the sweet [counsel] of a friend is better than one's own advice. Loyalty and respect toward one's friends and kindred are stressed in verse 10. In their trials, they must not be forsaken; but in one's own day of calamity, it is important to avoid overreliance on kin, especially if they are far away. The emotions of verses 3–4 escalate from a fool's heavy provocation to cruel wrath, overwhelming anger, and unbearable jealousy or envy. Jealousy, in the sense of exclusive love betrayed (cf. 6:34–35), has a more positive moral valence than envy, which is desire for what belongs to someone else (cf. 3:31), though both can be deadly. According to the book of James (cf. Jas. 3:16–4:2), envy puts "human beings in irresolvable competition with each other, leading inexorably to murder, the elimination of rivals."[15] In the face of this murderous envy, no one can stand (Prov. 27:4).

The theme of friendship extends to care of flocks and herds in 27:23–27. As H. Richard Niebuhr comments, trust in God requires "that all beings, not only our friends but also our enemies, not only men but also animals and the inanimate, be met with reverence, for all are friends in the friendship of the one to whom we are reconciled in faith."[16] These verses urge an attentive wisdom about "how the world works as an ordered, food-producing system that sustains

14. Ellen F. Davis, *Proverbs, Ecclesiastes, and the Song of Songs*, WBC (Louisville, KY: Westminster John Knox Press, 2000), 133.

15. William P. Brown, *Character in Crisis: A Fresh Approach to the Wisdom Literature of the Old Testament* (Grand Rapids: Eerdmans, 1996), 161.

16. H. Richard Niebuhr, *Radical Monotheism and Western Culture* (New York: Harper, 1960), 126.

life."[17] Living according to the grain of God's creative purposes means abandoning human tendencies to exploitation and acquisitiveness and finding sustainable patterns of creaturely life. This involves awareness of larger seasonal rhythms (27:25) as well as sensitive attention to particular plants and animals (27:18, 23). The result of this sustainable way of life is not fabulous wealth or power (27:24) but "enough" (27:27): enough clothing, land, and food to supply the needs of the household (27:26–27; cf. pp. 125–32, commentary on 30:1–31:9). The "woman of strength" in 31:19–31 is likewise a wise provider of clothing, land, and food for her household (note the close textual parallel between 27:27b and 31:15b).

28:1–29:27

Antithetical proverbs, so prominent in chapters 10–15, return in the second half of the second Solomonic collection. This section has two dominant themes: government and torah. The word *tôrâ* has appeared before in Proverbs but always in connection with parental teaching (1:8; 3:1; 4:2; 7:2; probably also 6:23, by extension from 6:20). However, in chapters 28–29 *tôrâ* seems to refer primarily to God's teaching and so is translated "the law" in the NRSV (28:4, 7, 9; 29:18). Proverbs 29:18 juxtaposes this term with the Hebrew word for prophecy or prophetic vision. This may be a deliberate reference to two sections of the Hebrew canon—the Law and the Prophets—or it may simply refer to the kind of wise guidance that is entrusted to individuals such as Agur (30:1–33) and King Lemuel's mother (31:1–9). In any case the repeated use of *tôrâ* is a reminder of the larger theological framework of these chapters: God's concern for justice and the welfare of the poor. The NIV is thus right to specify *fear* in 28:14a as "fear of the LORD."

Readers who have been chafing under the glowing descriptions of kings as God's vicegerents of wisdom and righteousness (cf. 16:10, 12–13; 24:21–22) will appreciate the strong dose of political realism in chapters 28–29, with their straightforward acknowledgment of

17. Walter Brueggemann, "The Creatures Know!" in *The Wisdom of Creation*, ed. Edward Foley and Robert Schreiter (Collegeville, MN: Liturgical Press, 2004), 1.

the reality of wicked rulers. Four times in these two chapters the fortunes of the people under wicked and righteous rulers are vividly contrasted (28:12, 28; 29:2, 16). Wicked rulers are like roaring lions or charging bears (28:15a) who trample the poor; who cruelly oppress the people, whether out of incompetence (28:16a) or greed (29:4b); and who let evil run rampant in government ranks (29:12, 16a). The righteous have little recourse but to groan and go into hiding as they wait for the rulers' downfall (28:12b, 28; 29:2b, 16b). Yet waiting it out is not always a political option; other verses point to the struggle and loathing between the forces of the righteous and the wicked (28:4; 29:10, 27).

No society, not even a democratic one, is great enough or good enough to make itself the final end of human existence.

Reinhold Niebuhr, *The Children of Light and the Children of Darkness* (New York: Charles Scribner's Sons, 1960), 133.

Rulers are not invariably wicked and foolish, of course. Wise and just rulers can bring order to chaotic societies (28:2; 29:4a, 14a), and when they are in power, the land prospers and the righteous rejoice (28:12a; 29:2a). Yet the overall effect of chapters 28–29 is to relativize human power and justice. Fear of God and fear of the king are clearly distinguished after being elided in 24:21. While it is natural to fear those in power and to seek their favor (29:25a, 26a), true security and justice are found with God, not with human rulers (29:25b, 26b). As Augustine notes, the servile fear of earthly rulers must give way to a "serene fear" of God that arises from love and will endure forever (see pp. 87–91, commentary on 16:1–33).[18]

The NRSV has altered the text of 28:3 to attribute the oppression of the poor to "a ruler." While this fits with a dominant theme of chapters 28–29, the Hebrew is better reflected in the *New American Standard Bible* translation: "A poor man who oppresses the lowly is like a driving rain which leaves no food." Wickedness is not confined to the rich and powerful: the poor also prey on each other. Many of the contrasts between the righteous and the wicked in this section apply to all people, regardless of social rank. The wicked are

18. Augustine, *City of God* 14.9, trans. Henry Bettenson (London: Penguin Classics, 1972).

skittish, perhaps because they have an uneasy conscience, while the righteous are "as bold as a lion" (28:1). The wicked create mayhem, lead the upright into their evil ways, and arrogantly resist the discipline and instruction of others, trusting instead in their own wits (28:2, 10, 26a; 29:1, 8, 18a). They murder (28:17) and steal from their neighbors and even from their own parents (28:24; 29:24). More fundamentally, the wicked flout God's law, failing to seek and fear God, even as they feign piety and virtue (28:4a, 5a, 9, 13–14). As Reinhold Niebuhr insists, the first step toward righteousness is "to achieve the honesty of knowing that we are not honest."[19] The refusal to confess and renounce our sins is a stiff-necked and self-destructive denial of the truth about ourselves before God (28:13–14; cf. 1 John 1:8).

Clearly, there is plenty of wickedness to go around, and the poor are not exempt from general human failings. Yet these chapters also reflect a particular concern for the wickedness of the rich and powerful. In a reminder that God is creator of all people, 29:13 contrasts the poor not with the rich, as one would expect (cf. 22:2), but with "the oppressor." Wealth is no sure marker of righteousness and wisdom because it is sometimes obtained by crooked and oppressive means (28:6b, 8a, 16b) and can delude the rich into an arrogant and foolish self-centeredness (28:11, 25, 27; 29:7b, 23a). In these instances, it is the poor who exhibit humility, wisdom, and integrity (28:6a, 11b, 23b). It is sometimes only the desperation of poverty that drives the poor to dishonesty (28:21); as Yoder notes regarding this verse, "That the bribe is a single crust of bread, a scrap of food basic for survival, highlights how tenuous justice can be."[20] Proverbs extends

> **The church can and must leave us all without excuses but bring us to the acknowledgment of our wrongness. It requires us to measure our faithfulness against the faithfulness of God and not against the faithlessness of our enemies.**
>
> H. Richard Niebuhr, *Theology, History, and Culture*, ed. William Stacy Johnson (New Haven, CT: Yale University Press, 1996), 172.

19. Reinhold Niebuhr, *Beyond Tragedy: Essays on the Christian Interpretation of History* (New York: Charles Scribner's Sons, 1937), 142.
20. Yoder, *Proverbs*, 270.

less clemency to the miser who is preoccupied with accumulating wealth when it is rather generosity to those in need that brings blessing and security (28:8b, 20b, 22, 27a; 29:14). No one is free from transgressions (28:13), but the rich and powerful are in a position to inflict greater social damage through their wrongdoing.

Most of the antithetical proverbs that dominate this section contrast wickedness and righteousness (as signified by the bookends 28:1 and 29:27). But in between there are also teachings that contrast wisdom and folly, especially with regard to speech. Flattery, perhaps in an attempt to curry favor, is discouraged (28:23; 29:5), especially when a wise reproof is what is needed (28:23a). The ambiguity in the Hebrew of 29:5 about *whose* feet are caught in the net of flattery is retained in the NIV translation, and this links it nicely to 29:6, where the flatterer himself is caught in a snare. Hot-headed, contemptuous, and hasty speech is also warned against (29:8, 11, 20, 22). Another cluster of verses return to the theme of appropriate child rearing. A (grown) child who is unable to control his passions for food, money, or sex (28:7b, 24; 29:3b) has not been adequately disciplined (29:15, 17a); a child who has been raised well keeps the law, loves wisdom, and is a delight to his parents (28:7a; 29:3a, 17b).

30:1–31:9

The Limits of Wisdom

The main body of Proverbs' teaching (chaps. 10–29) has reached its end. It was preceded by an extended unit (chaps. 1–9) celebrating the surpassing value of wisdom and exhorting readers to acquire it for themselves. It is followed by an oracle (30:1–33) that expresses the difficulty of obtaining wisdom and exemplifies the appropriate humility of its human seekers. The theological framework of the whole human enterprise of gaining wisdom is highlighted in both bookends of Proverbs but in different ways. Chapters 1–9 emphasize that because God has imbued the whole created world with wisdom (cf. 3:19–20; 8:22–31), the search for it by human creatures will not be futile. By contrast, chapter 30 stresses the enormous chasm between God's wisdom and human wisdom and therefore the radical inadequacy of all human understanding (30:2–3), a theme also found in the wisdom books Job and Ecclesiastes. Thus the beginning and ending of Proverbs reinforce the Augustinian dialectic we have found throughout the book: the creaturely mandate to strive for wisdom and reject folly, on one hand, and the acknowledgment of our creaturely limitations and radical dependence on God in the search for wisdom, on the other.

Agur and Jakeh are not Israelite names, leading many scholars to suggest that this oracle is another example of Israel's "intellectual ecumenism"[1] in seeking wisdom. Another indication of possible foreign origin is the use of the word "God" in verses 1, 5, and 9, otherwise rare in Proverbs (cf. 2:5; 3:4; 25:2), and "holy ones"

1. Carole R. Fontaine, *Smooth Words: Women, Proverbs, and Performance in Biblical Wisdom* (London: Sheffield Academic, 2002), 19–20.

in verse 3, probably another divine epithet. "The LORD," the usual circumlocution for God in Proverbs, occurs only in verse 9. There is no consensus on how to translate 30:1b; the NRSV obtains its result by some creative tweaking of the Hebrew text.

In verses1–3 Agur adopts the language of first-person confession, a dramatic switch from the more neutral third-person rhetoric of chapters 10–29, to declare the elusiveness of wisdom. His lament that he is "too stupid to be human" (v. 2a; cf. Ps. 73:22) suggests an animal lack of understanding. Despite Agur's presumably earnest attempts, he has not "learned wisdom" (v. 3). Job expresses similar dismay about the inaccessibility of wisdom to human understanding (Job 28:12–13, 20–21). Agur follows this confession of human adequacy with six searching questions (v. 4; cf. Job 38–41; Isa. 40:12–14). The answer to the first five questions can only be "God."

Starting in the heavens and moving down to the earth, stretching from one end of the earth to the other, encompassing the forces of wind and water, God's wisdom knows no bounds. "One after another Agur's questions recall God's activity, stir amazement, and compel humility: only God."[2] The answer to the last question, "What is the name of the person's child?" is probably Agur himself, the student of wisdom. The last phrase of the poem, "Surely you know," ironically echoes Agur's lament in verse 2 that he does *not* know. Yet Agur's confession of "not knowing" is actually a sign of wisdom. As Karl Barth notes regarding this passage, "There can be no doubt that it is a wise man who puts these questions," precisely because "with these questions concerning God he ranges himself with the fool, acknowledging himself to be a fool."[3] By avoiding

Who is so tall as to ascend to
the heavens?
Who is so broad as to compass
the underworld?

Mesopotamian *Dialogue of Pessimism*, c. 1000 BCE, quoted in Leo G. Perdue, *Wisdom and Creation: The Theology of Wisdom Literature* (Nashville: Abingdon Press, 1994), 118.

2. Christine Roy Yoder, *Proverbs*, Abingdon Old Testament Commentaries (Nashville: Abingdon Press, 2009), 281.
3. Karl Barth, *Church Dogmatics* IV/2, *The Doctrine of Reconciliation*, trans. G. W. Bromiley, ed. T. F. Torrance (Edinburgh: T. & T. Clark, 1958), 426.

the hubris of "being wise in his own eyes" (26:12), Agur opens himself up to the wisdom God has indeed provided.

The form of this divinely given wisdom is suggested by the next two verses (vv. 5–6), which probably come from the final editing of Proverbs. The two verses are variants on 2 Samuel 22:31 and Deuteronomy 4:2. The text from Samuel is part of King David's song of thanksgiving for God's deliverance from his enemies: "The promise of the LORD proves true; he is a shield for all who take refuge in him." The text from Deuteronomy is part of Moses' reminder to Israel of God's "statutes and ordinances" before they cross the Jordan into the promised land: "You must neither add anything to what I command you nor take away anything from it, but keep the commandments of the LORD your God with which I am charging you." The Deuteronomy text suggests a written word, though the form of God's word is not specified in Proverbs 30:5–6. Taken together, verses 5–6 call human seekers of wisdom to take refuge in God's word. There is much they do not and cannot know, but they should rest content with what God has supplied, not presuming to "add" to it.

The next three verses (vv. 7–9) constitute the only prayer in the book of Proverbs. Agur has two petitions: to be kept from falsehood and lying (v. 8a) and from poverty and riches (v. 8b). He has just warned against being "found a liar" (v. 6c) by claiming divine authority for one's own words; Proverbs also rebukes liars who bear false witness against a neighbor (19:5, 9). The second petition reflects the culmination of Proverbs' gradual drift away from any tight connections between wealth and righteousness (cf. pp. 29–32, commentary on 3:1–12). Agur sees moral dangers in both financial extremes. The rich are so sated with their own power and possessions that they are tempted to deny God. Significantly, verse 9 is the one place in Agur's oracle where God is referred to as "the LORD," the bestower of Israel's covenant blessings. As an African student of mine once asked, "How can you trust God when you are so rich?" On the other hand, poverty brings its own moral dangers. The poor are tempted to steal and then to blame God for the predicament that drove them to crime. Agur's request is simply "for the food that I need" (v. 8c), his daily bread (cf. Matt. 6:11).

Agur's prayer ends in verse 9, but his concerns about truthfulness and the welfare of the poor continue in verses 10–17. A vulnerable servant has no recourse in the case of a slanderous master but to bring her complaint to God, who will hold the lying master accountable (v. 10). In the litany of verses 11–14, Agur repeatedly laments the failings of his "generation," a term whose breadth is not captured in the NRSV translation. Unlike the cursing servant of verse 10, those who curse their parents are guilty of arrogant ingratitude (v. 11). Those who regard themselves as morally pure while smeared with their own filth, and those who think of themselves more highly than they ought (cf. Rom. 12:3), are caught up in self-deception and falsehood (vv. 12–13). The rich, who like Pharaoh say, "Who is the LORD?" (v. 9; cf. Exod. 5:2) exhibit their denial of God by their vicious oppression of the poor. The couplet in verses 15–16 repeats Agur's call for moderation against those who never have "enough." The first of five numerical proverbs in this chapter (30:15b–16, 18–19, 21–23, 24–28, 29–31), this couplet lists four things that are never satisfied, breaking with the anthropocentric focus of verses 7–15 by placing the yearning of a barren womb alongside much larger realities: Sheol's insatiable appetite for death (cf. pp. 21–22, commentary on 1:8–19), the parched earth's thirst for water, and a fire's demand for fuel. The pattern of putting human concerns within a larger creaturely context will recur in the last three numerical proverbs of this chapter. In verse 17, the retribution for human misdeeds is carried out by nonhuman creatures. Revelation 19:17–21 has a similarly horrific image of carrion birds gorging on the flesh of human sinners. The cumulative message of this chapter is that human beings live in interdependence with God's other creatures, sharing in a more general vocation to seek creaturely wisdom.

I believe Christian discipleship for twenty-first-century North American Christians means "cruciform living," an alternative notion of the abundant life, which will involve a philosophy of "enoughness," limitations on energy use, and sacrifice for the sake of others.

Sallie McFague, *Life Abundant: Rethinking Theology and Economy for a Planet in Peril* (Minneapolis: Fortress Press, 2001), 14.

The tone of Agur's oracle changes from forbidding to delighted in verses 18–19. His lack of understanding, no longer a reason for grief and lament, now supports a sense of amazed wonder at the natural world. The scene moves from the sky to the earth to the seas before settling on the wonder of human love. ("Young woman" is preferable to the NRSV translation "girl"). "The way" of an eagle, a snake, and a ship culminate in "the way" of a man and woman toward each other. This celebration of love between a man and a woman is cut short, however, by verse 20, which illustrates "a way" that abuses and distorts human sexuality. While the NRSV translation has used the word *adulteress* several times already in Proverbs (cf. 2:16; 5:20; 6:24; 7:5; 23:27), this is the first time it corresponds directly to the Hebrew. Despite the limitations of Proverbs' male perspective, the vignette captures the brazenness of adulterers who regard sex as merely a "quick meal"[4] with no moral consequences.

The next numerical proverb, verses 21–23, seems a bit hyperbolic. Every society views some things as "out of line," but does the earth really "tremble" under the four social reversals listed here? In the second example (v. 22b), the fool's "worthless pursuits" have left him with "plenty of bread" instead of "plenty of poverty" (28:19). The third example (v. 23a) may refer to a "disliked" woman in a polygamous household who then gains favor (cf. Deut. 21:15–17). The first and last examples (vv. 22a, 23b) reflect Proverbs' sense that it is not "fitting" for slaves and servants to usurp the positions of their social superiors (19:10b; cf. Eccl.10:7). As Christine Roy Yoder notes, the wisdom of Proverbs, "which may at first appear generally applicable due to its anonymity, has a particular upper-class and patriarchal worldview."[5] Social revolution is not part of Proverbs' cultural DNA, and its complacency about hierarchical social structures chafes against contemporary democratic sensibilities. Yet social upheavals often turn ugly. Our own time has witnessed "the earth trembling" under violent, large-scale social revolutions in Mao's

4. Yoder, *Proverbs*, 285.
5. Christine Roy Yoder, "Proverbs," in *Women's Bible Commentary*, ed. Carol Newsom et al. (Louisville, KY: Westminster John Knox Press, 2012), 234.

China and Pol Pot's Cambodia, in which masses of educated and professional people were either driven into the countryside to perform manual labor or simply slaughtered. The horrors of the Khmer Rouge regime can be glimpsed in one of its proverbs: "To spare you is no profit; to destroy you is no loss."[6]

The two charming numerical proverbs that follow (vv. 24–28, 29–31) have a sharp edge to them in our time of ecological crisis. They remind us that human beings have no monopoly on creaturely wisdom and dignity. Agur's lament about his subhuman stupidity (30:2) here stands corrected: he should rather confess his *human* stupidity.

> **"But ask the animals, and they will teach you;**
> **the birds of the air, and they will tell you;**
> **ask the plants of the earth, and they will teach you;**
> **and the fish of the sea will declare to you.**
> **Who among all these does not know**
> **that the hand of the LORD has done this?**
> **In his hand is the life of every living thing**
> **and the breath of every human being."**
>
> Job 12:7–10.

Ants, badgers, locusts, and lizards are small creatures with "exceedingly" great wisdom—providing for their own needs, ordering their societies, and moving freely. Their resourcefulness is a lesson to human creatures, who also depend on these social goods to flourish. In 30:29–31, the king takes his place alongside three other creatures who move with a stately gait. As Ellen Davis notes, "In the last analysis, they are more alike than they are different, for they owe every moment of their existence to their One Maker. Even the king looks remarkably like the strutting rooster, if you squint."[7] The "word of God" (30:5) that humans are to heed includes the speechless voice and wordless words that pour forth from one end of God's creation to the other (Ps. 19:1–4). Biblical wisdom insists that the *knowing* that Israel is called to is not exhausted in the Torah. As Walter Brueggemann insists, there is "a creaturely knowledge

6. Peace Pledge Union website: http://www.ppu.org.uk/genocide/g_cambodia1.html.
7. Ellen F. Davis, *Proverbs, Ecclesiastes, and the Song of Songs*, WBC (Louisville, KY: Westminster John Knox Press, 2000), 148.

that is God-given and available to all creatures. That is the premise of being a workable creature of God. This knowledge is not 'primitive' or 'savage,' but it is the premise of responsive creatureliness that adheres to the uncompromising reality of the creator."[8]

Proverbs 30:24–31 reminds us that our human creaturehood does not set the terms for God's relation to the rest of creation. Indeed, the rest of creation—from ants and roosters to the glaciers of the Arctic and the ozone layer—can be our teacher in our quest to become responsive creatures. Agur ends by urging self-restraint, "putting a lid" on tendencies to pride and wicked plans (30:32–33). Van Leeuwen notes the puns in verse 33: in Hebrew, "the word for 'anger' is the dual form of the word for 'nose'!"[9] Rather than giving into foolish and wicked desires that make for strife, the wise are to learn "the things that make for peace" (Luke 19:42).

Another oracle follows Agur's, this one by a King Lemuel, otherwise unknown in Scripture (31:1–9). Scholars suspect that this unit, like the preceding one, is of non-Israelite origin. Fittingly, given Proverbs' emphasis on intergenerational learning, Lemuel's oracle was taught to him by his mother, and her voice is heard throughout. She begins with a rebuke, addressing him with terms that indicate her intimate, lifelong relationship with him. Christine Roy Yoder suggests that the threefold "What" ("No" in the NRSV translation) in verse 2 is elliptical for "What is it with you?"[10] Lemuel's mother warns him against two familiar pitfalls: women and alcohol (vv. 3–5). The stories of King Solomon and King David bear out the first warning (1 Kgs. 11:1–13; 2 Sam. 11:1–12:5), and the story of King Ahasuerus (Esth. 1:7–12) bears out the second. The warning against alcohol is elaborated in verses 5–7. A drunken ruler is in danger of neglecting or reversing the laws that

> **If there was something to be gained from promiscuity, then the goat would be king.**
>
> Akan proverb, quoted in Mercy Ambe Oduyoye, *Daughters of Anowa: African Women and Patriarchy* (Maryknoll, NY: Orbis Books, 1995), 56.

8. Walter Brueggemann, "The Creatures Know!" in *The Wisdom of Creation*, ed. Edward Foley and Robert Schreiter (Collegeville, MN: Liturgical Press, 2004), 10.
9. Raymond Van Leeuwen, "The Book of Proverbs," NIB 5 (Nashville: Abingdon Press, 1997), 255.
10. Yoder, *Proverbs*, 291.

protect the weak (v. 5). The king must not forget the needs of his most vulnerable subjects. A tongue-in-cheek counsel follows to save strong drink for the poor and miserable, since they are better off forgetting their own plight (vv. 6–7). The ravages of alcoholism among the poor suggest otherwise.

The heart of her teaching comes in the two positive commands in verses 8–9. Whereas Agur counseled "putting a hand on your mouth" (30:32c) to silence foolish and wicked thoughts, Lemuel's mother exhorts her son twice to "open your mouth" (31:8a, 9a) on behalf of the poor and oppressed. The king is to speak out for those who have been silenced, acting boldly to defend the rights of the vulnerable. Dietrich Bonhoeffer had verses 8–9 heavily underlined in his Luther Bible and appealed to them frequently in calling others to be involved in the political struggle against Hitler on behalf of the Jews. In a letter to a Swiss friend, Bonhoeffer wrote,

> It is also time for a final break with our theologically grounded reserve about whatever is being done by the state—which really only comes down to fear. "Speak out for those who cannot speak" [Prov. 31:8]—who in the church today still remembers that this is the very least the Bible asks of us in such times as these?[11]

Contemporary feminist theologians likewise recognize the importance of speaking out for those whose voices have been silenced. As Bonhoeffer insists, that is the "very least" that justice requires. Following Nelle Morton, however, feminists have also insisted on the practice of "hearing others to speech."[12] It is not enough to listen to and then speak on behalf of the oppressed. The oppressed need the support and encouragement that will enable them to speak out themselves. A wise political leader "defends the rights of the poor and needy" (31:9) by making space for their own voices to be heard.

11. Letter to Erwin Sutz, Sept. 11, 1934, in Dietrich Bonhoeffer, *London, 1933–1935, DBW* 13 (Minneapolis: Fortress Press, 2007), 217.

12. Nelle Morton, *The Journey Is Home* (Boston: Beacon Press, 1985), 127–28.

31:10–31

The Domestication of Transcendence

The book of Proverbs ends in chapter 31 with an intricate acrostic poem about a wise woman. There are so many literary and thematic parallels between her and the figure of Woman Wisdom in chapters 1–9 that, in Christine Roy Yoder's view, "the two women who frame the book essentially coalesce as one."[1] The poem depicts the paragon of human wisdom and fear of the Holy One as a married woman who "surpasses" (v. 29b) all others in hard work, business acumen, generosity, and piety. The NRSV calls her "a capable wife," a colorless translation that lends itself to Mothers' Day platitudes but does not reflect the power and capacity indicated by the adjective *ḥāyil*. Even worse is the NRSV translation of the phrase as "good wife" in 12:4. Better alternatives include "woman of substance" and "woman of strength"—or "worthy woman," as the NRSV translates the same phrase in Ruth 3:11. In verse 30 the phrase "a woman who fears the LORD" eclipses the stronger identification between the woman and God fearing that the Hebrew text makes by setting them in apposition to each other: "a woman, fear of the LORD."

The attention to economic detail in this short poem is quite astonishing. According to Yoder, the Woman of Substance is "a composite figure of real—albeit exceptional—women in the Persian period."[2] Like Woman Wisdom, the Woman of Substance is described in financial terms as "far more precious than jewels" (v. 10b; cf. 3:15;

1. Christine Roy Yoder, *Proverbs*, Abingdon Old Testament Commentaries (Nashville: Abingdon Press, 2009), 290.
2. Christine Roy Yoder, *Wisdom as a Woman of Substance: A Socioeconomic Reading of Proverbs 1–9 and 31:10–31* (Berlin/New York: Walter de Gruyter, 2001), 90.

8:11). The KJV translation of verse 10b is more apt, however: "Her price is far above rubies." This description reflects the socioeconomic realities of the dowry system for marriageable women in Persian-period Palestine (539–332 BCE). As Yoder affirms, "the Woman of Substance is a desirable spouse because she guarantees the financial well-being of her husband. As a bride of high 'price,' she makes it possible for him to live as a wealthy man."[3] Her tireless work, entrepreneurship, and wise management of her household mean that her husband will not "lack booty"—a better translation of verse 11b than "lack of gain." The whole family eats fine food (v. 14), dresses in garments fit for royalty (vv. 21b, 22b), and sleeps in luxurious bedding (v. 22a). Through her, they also stretch out their hands to the poor (v. 20). Like Woman Wisdom (9:1–3), the Woman of Substance presides over a large and prosperous house, with servant girls to do her bidding (v. 15). The effect of 31:10–31 is to reaffirm the connections drawn in chapters 1–9 between wisdom and wealth (cf. 3:16b; 8:18, 21)—connections that had sometimes been called into question in the intervening chapters of Proverbs (cf. 18:10–11; 23:4–5).

However, the Woman of Substance is hardly a figure of cosmic authority and power like Woman Wisdom (1:22–31; 8:15–16, 22–31, 35–36). She never even utters a word. Nor does she appear in Woman Wisdom's other guise, that of an alluring young woman seeking lovers who are eager to receive the gifts she has to offer (cf. 4:5–9; 6:22; 7:4; 8:17–21; see pp. 44–46, commentary on 6:20–35). Life with the Woman of Substance seems devoid of the marital passion advertised in 5:15–20. Her husband hardly seems "intoxicated always by her love" (5:19a). Indeed, she seems to have little time for him. As Roland Murphy notes regarding 31:10–31, "the Song of Songs extols the beauty of the woman and lingers over the attractiveness of her body, while in this poem all is businesslike. Arms, hands, and palms are mentioned, but only in a frenzy of activity."[4]

Unlike Woman Wisdom, the Woman of Substance is truly a counterpart to the "strange woman" of chapters 1–9 (see pp. 48–50,

3. Ibid., 78. I am indebted to Yoder's excellent analysis of the socioeconomic context of Prov. 31:10–31.
4. Roland E. Murphy, *Proverbs* (Nashville: Thomas Nelson, 1998), 249.

commentary on 8:1–21). In his marriage to her, the husband forfeits the passion and adventure promised by the beautiful strange woman (6:25; 7:6–20) for the sake of stability, wealth, and social reputation. His trust in her (v. 11a) is rooted not in affection but in how lavishly she provides for him (v. 11b). His praise for her (v. 28b) is rooted not in her charm and beauty (v. 30a) but in her works (v. 31b) and the public honor they bring him (vv. 23–24). The Woman of Substance is the female Gallant writ large (see pp. 62–67, commentary on 10:1–8). William Brown notes, "The book of Proverbs began with a silent son, instructed in the responsibilities of communal life and family fidelity, and ends with an adult male who has successfully fulfilled them."[5] The wife who was hard to find (v. 10a) and expensive to obtain (v. 10b) has become his crown (12:4). He now resides in wisdom's household. When compared to his wife, however, the husband in 31:10–31 appears quite idle and inconsequential. If his life represents the successful fulfillment of the search for wisdom, the reader may well be having doubts about the whole enterprise. Having the paragon of wisdom appear as a heterosexual wife and mother who commanded a high price in the marriage marketplace is likewise disturbing and limiting. Can this be all the lifelong quest for wisdom comes to? Qohelet, the teacher of Ecclesiastes, stands ready to share the reader's perplexity and disillusionment.

5. William P. Brown, *Character in Crisis: A Fresh Approach to the Wisdom Literature of the Old Testament* (Grand Rapids: Eerdmans, 1996), 48.

ECCLESIASTES

Introduction to Ecclesiastes

Like Proverbs, the book of Ecclesiastes is also postexilic and is considered by many scholars to be one of the latest books in the Old Testament, though there is no consensus about its exact dating. Choon-Leong Seow, a prominent interpreter of Ecclesiastes, proposes an early-fourth-century date for Ecclesiastes, but most scholars suggest a later date, sometime in the third century BCE, when Jerusalem had become a sophisticated international city.[1] In any case, the book reflects the cultural disorientation that characterized the Persian period, a time when economic and religious certainties were fading away. Ecclesiastes voices both disillusionment with the past and uncertainty about the future.

Ecclesiastes' signature word is *hebel,* often translated "vanity," which occurs an astonishing thirty-eight times in this short book. There is also a concentration of economic and financial terms in Ecclesiastes, reflecting large economic changes during the Persian period. Starting in the fifth century BCE, the economy became increasingly commercialized, and new monetary and taxation systems were introduced. As William Brown notes, "A new market-driven economy of global proportions emerged, complete with myriad entrepreneurial opportunities."[2] There were both winners and losers in this new economic context, and Ecclesiastes reflects the radical economic insecurity felt by ordinary people. The book

1. Ellen F. Davis, *Proverbs, Ecclesiastes, and the Song of Songs,* WBC (Louisville, KY: Westminster John Knox Press, 2000), 160.
2. William P. Brown, *Ecclesiastes,* Interpretation: A Bible Commentary for Teaching and Preaching (Louisville, KY: Westminster John Knox Press, 2000), 9.

repeatedly notes the oppressive character of relentless work and the dangers of an obsession with wealth.

Ecclesiastes barely made it into the canon of Scripture. Its untidy structure, its assaults on commonplaces of Israel's wisdom, and its internal contradictions all raised doubts about the book's status. There was a debate among the rabbis about the book during the so-called Council of Jamnia, convened around 90 CE. The more conservative House of Shammai rejected the book, while the House of Hillel approved it. The House of Hillel prevailed at that council, though doubts about Ecclesiastes continued. Ellen Davis cites the Talmud's conclusions about the book's status: "The sages sought to withdraw the book of Koheleth because its words are mutually contradictory. Why then did they not withdraw it? Because it begins with words of Torah and it ends with words of Torah".[3] We can be glad that the wisdom teachings of this renegade sage received a canonical seal of approval and thus survived as an authoritative text for both Jews and Christians.

Structural Outline

The structure of Ecclesiastes has been a subject of scholarly debate. The contradictions and abrupt changes of tone in Ecclesiastes have led some scholars to hypothesize the existence of multiple voices in the book. However, none of these scholarly reconstructions has won widespread support, and they all hinge on (rather modern) assumptions about the degree of coherence that a text needs to exhibit to be considered a compositional whole.[4] This commentary considers 12:9–14 to be the product of a later editorial hand but otherwise tries to make sense of the text as it stands as Qohelet's extended internal dialogue with tradition. As Michael Fox suggests, contradictions are part and parcel of the book's message: "Qohelet is not so much contradicting himself as *observing* contradictions in the world."[5]

3. Davis, *Proverbs, Ecclesiastes, and the Song of Songs* , 165.

4. See John Barton, "An Example: Ecclesiastes," in *Reading the Old Testament: Method in Biblical Study*, rev. and exp. ed. (Louisville, KY: Westminster John Knox Press, 1997), 61–76.

5. Michael V. Fox, *A Time to Tear Down and A Time to Build Up: A Rereading of Ecclesiastes* (Grand Rapids: Eerdmans, 1999), 3.

Unlike Proverbs, Ecclesiastes has no superscriptions, beyond the initial one in 1:1, to suggest distinct sections of the text. There is a prologue (1:1–11) and an epilogue (12:9–14), the latter clearly a later addition. The midpoint of the book occurs at 6:9, with the repeat of "vanity" and "chasing after wind," which have appeared several times in the first half of the book. The second major section begins at 6:10 and concludes with a poem about youth and old age in 11:7–12:8. These features suggest the following outline:

1:1–11	Prologue: "The words of the Teacher, the son of David, king in Jerusalem"
1:12–6:9	Reflections on vanity: the first half
6:10–12:8	Reflections on vanity: the second half
12:9–14	Epilogue: The wisdom of Qohelet

1:1
The Words of Qohelet

Even though the book of Proverbs begins with the superscription "The proverbs of Solomon, son of David, king of Israel" (Prov. 1:1), King Solomon is never presented as speaking directly. The voice of Solomon is instead mediated through many voices—nameless fathers and mothers, Woman Wisdom, King Hezekiah's officials, and even non-Israelites. In Proverbs, Solomon's voice sounds through the voices of a broad communal wisdom. Ecclesiastes also begins with a superscription attributing its words to "the son of David, king in Jerusalem." By verse 2 the character of the king begins to speak, and by verse 12, the king is already speaking in the first person. The assumed royal identity is soon set aside, but the autobiographical style continues. Only in the epilogue at the very end of the book, after the solo speaker has already signed off by repeating the opening refrain (1:2; 12:8), does the anonymous voice of communal wisdom assert itself directly (12:9–14). Clearly, the wisdom of Ecclesiastes, while drawing on larger wisdom traditions, is from the start more individual and more idiosyncratic than what we find in Proverbs.

As already noted, the superscriptions to Solomon in Proverbs and Ecclesiastes (and Song of Songs) function more as imprimaturs than as historical information about the books' authorship. The declaration, unique to Ecclesiastes, that it contains "the words of the Teacher" (1:1) only increases the enigma of Ecclesiastes' authorship. The word translated as "Teacher," *qōhelet,* is a feminine participle of the common verb *qāhāl,* meaning to gather or assemble, so a straightforward translation would be "she who assembles." This word is also the title of the book in Hebrew. (*Ecclesiastes* is the Latin transliteration of the Greek for "member of the assembly.") Masculine participles in Hebrew are commonly used as nouns referring to persons; thus the ordinary word for *shepherd* in Hebrew is "he who shepherds." Few commentators even consider the possibility that Qohelet, "she who assembles," might be a woman speaking under an assumed male persona. A common argument is that the feminine participle is a way of referring to an office, not to a female person, and that it eventually becomes a personal name for the male office-holder. But the example often used to bolster this argument, the feminine participle *sōperet* in Ezra 2:55 and Nehemiah 7:57, from the word *scribe,* only begs the question. Could this not instead be taken as evidence for the existence of female scribes in Israel?[1] In any case, it is an interesting exercise to read Ecclesiastes *as if it were* composed by a woman and see whether it makes any difference to the reader's perceptions (see pp. 46–47, commentary on 7:1–27). This commentary attempts to leave the question open.

1. See Wilda C. Gafney, *Daughters of Miriam: Women Prophets in Ancient Israel* (Minneapolis: Fortress Press, 2008), 123–30.

1:2–11
All Is Vanity

The word translated "vanity," *hebel,* occurs a remarkable thirty-eight times in Ecclesiastes. Appearing in an emphatic form at the opening and closing verses of Qohelet's reflections (1:2; 12:8), it is clearly the leitmotif of the book. For a word meaning vapor, breath, or mist, it is not surprising that the significance of the word *hebel* is hard to pin down in Ecclesiastes. It can connote something empty, futile, fleeting, unsubstantial, or incongruous. By the time Qohelet is done, almost everything that human beings strive for and seek meaning in will be declared *hebel.*

> **When [*hebel*] is translated into the Thai Bible, a Buddhist term *anitjung* is used. When this term is used by Thais it usually refers to things that are unstable, impermanent, and cannot be relied on. Buddhists are taught to think that everything in this world is *anitjung*. If Ecclesiastes was separated from the Christian Bible and handed to Thai Buddhists to read, they might consider it to be a Buddhist book.**
>
> Seree Lorgunpai, "The Book of Ecclesiastes and Thai Buddhism," in *Voices from the Margins: Interpreting the Bible in the Third World,* ed. R. S. Sugirtharajah (Maryknoll, NY: Orbis Books, 2006), 349.

The rhetorical question in 1:3 about the lasting gain achieved by human toil expects the answer "nothing." This answer finally becomes explicit in 2:11: "There is nothing to be gained under the sun." Qohelet's skepticism about the profit from human toil reflects the economic volatility of the Persian-era context (see pp. 1–12, "Introduction: Why Proverbs and Ecclesiastes? Why Now?"), in which diligent labor was no guarantee of financial security. It also strikes a chord with those in our own time caught up in corporate downsizing and the uncertainties of capitalist markets, or those simply numbed by the repetitiveness of daily routines.

Not only is there no certain financial gain from hard work in the present, there is no solace to be had in the reputation and legacy one's work will leave behind. "A generation goes, and a generation comes" (1:4), each one as forgettable as the next. Human lives are a mere flicker on the screen of the cosmos. All the effort of a lifetime vanishes without a trace: the dead are already forgotten, and those still to come can expect nothing better (1:11). Only a few verses into the book, the clash with the sincere and earnest teachings of Proverbs regarding the lasting value of hard work and a good name is evident (cf. Prov. 10:7; 14:23).

The microcosm of useless human effort in Ecclesiastes 1:3, 11 forms an envelope around a larger vision of cosmic futility. The efforts of all creation are for nothing as well. Sun, wind, and water are in constant motion (1:5–7), but their labor gets them nowhere. Round and round they go, ceaselessly returning to where they started and beginning another pointless cycle. Qohelet's ironic refrain about human endeavors is that they are "a chasing after wind" (1:14, 17; 2:11, 17, 26; 4:4, 6; 5:16; 6:9). The problem is not simply that human beings will never catch the wind, but that the wind itself is aimlessly chasing its own tail. For Qohelet, the cosmos exhibits a kind of "frenetic inertia."[1] Despite its perpetual motion, the earth remains the same (1:4). The futility of human effort mimics the futility of larger cosmic forces. Just as there is no lasting gain from human toil,

Like the animals who labor and sweat in a mill with their eyes blindfolded, we go about the mill of life always going through the same motions and always coming back to the same place again. I mean that round of hunger, satiety, going to bed, getting up, emptying ourselves and filling ourselves—one thing constantly follows the other, and we never stop going round in circles until we get out of the mill.

Gregory of Nyssa, *From Glory to Glory: Texts from Gregory of Nyssa's Mystical Writings*, ed. Jean Daniélou, trans. Herbert Musurille (Crestwood, NY: St. Vladimir's Seminary Press, 1995), 50.

1. William P. Brown, *The Seven Pillars of Creation: The Bible, Science, and the Ecology of Wonder* (Oxford: Oxford University Press, 2010), 179.

so there seems to be no ultimate end or purpose to the movements of the cosmos.

Some ultimate end or purpose has often been seen by Christian theologians as a necessary part of the doctrine of creation. To borrow Jonathan Edwards's title, theologians have been intent on determining "the end for which God created the world."[2] It is precisely this intelligible end that is missing in Qohelet's account. Indeed, God is altogether absent from the description of the cosmos in 1:4–7. It seems to be running on automatic pilot. Yet the book of Ecclesiastes as a whole does contain a doctrine of creation, though the questions of the cosmos's origin and its ultimate redemptive or eschatological end are left unanswered. Rather, the emphasis is on creaturely finitude and dependence in the face of God's sovereignty and freedom. God is the Creator, the One "who makes everything" (11:5), though God's creative ways transcend human understanding. The circumstances of creaturely life, both good and bad (7:14), come from God. These circumstances can only be accepted, as it is not within creaturely power to change them. Just as Qohelet calls into question "purpose-driven" human lives—lives that are always on task, always in pursuit of some overarching goal—so Qohelet also asks us to relinquish a "purpose-driven" vision of God the Creator. We do not know God's overarching goal in the creation of the world and the movements of the cosmos—if indeed there is one. Instead, we are to accept the terms that God has set for creaturely life and receive gratefully what comes to us from God's hand (2:24) for as many days under the sun as God gives us (5:18; see pp. 155–56, "Further Reflections: Qohelet and the Missional Church").

Accepting God's terms for creaturely life is not something that humanity finds easy. The wearisome repetition of the cosmos also finds an echo in the insatiability of human desire: just as the sea is never filled by the water flowing from the streams, so human yearning is never fulfilled by what flows to the eye and ear (1:8b). For those looking for something genuinely new (1:10a), for clear signs of progress or lasting accomplishment, the world is a frustrating

2. Jonathan Edwards, "Two Dissertations: I. Concerning the End for Which God Created the World and II. On the Nature of True Virtue," in *The Works of Jonathan Edwards*, vol. 8, *Ethical Writings*, ed. Paul Ramsey (New Haven, CT: Yale University Press, 1989).

place. It cannot deliver what human beings seek. The best recourse is perhaps to keep silent. However, just as the eye and the ear can never get enough, so the mouth cannot stop talking, though it has nothing new or meaningful to say. According to the alternate NRSV translation of 1:8a, "All words are wearisome." Like the toilsome revolutions of the cosmos, human discourse only contributes to "the tedious cycle of nonachievement."[3] Qohelet retains the traditional wisdom bias against the babbling of fools (5:3; 10:12b–14). Even the words of the wise, though they are of some value (9:17; 10:12a), have no guaranteed efficacy (9:16).

3. Sibley Towner, "The Book of Ecclesiastes," NIB 5 (Nashville: Abingdon Press, 1997), 292.

1:12–2:26

The Royal Search for Wisdom

1:12–1:18

In verse 12 Qohelet begins speaking in the first person and assumes the authority of the royal mantle. If *anyone* can "search out by wisdom" everything that happens in earthly life, it would surely be Solomon, the king of Israel who "was wiser than anyone else" and whose breadth of understanding was "as vast as the sand on the seashore" (1 Kgs. 4:29, 31). However, the initial report is not promising. Qohelet declares that it is "an unhappy business" that God has laid upon human beings (v. 13). The human search to understand the totality of existence appears headed toward frustration because it seems that only God's wisdom is adequate to the challenge. In Søren Kierkegaard's imaginative portrayal, "world history is the royal stage where God is spectator, where he, not accidentally but essentially, is the only spectator, because he is the only one who *can* be that." Human beings are barred from "admission to this theater"—they are merely actors in God's "royal drama."[1] Qohelet, in royal guise, boldly claims to be equal to the monumental task of observing "all the deeds that are done under the sun" (v. 14a) but soon declares the whole business to be vanity, as useless as "chasing after wind" (v. 14b).

Qohelet's appeal to proverbial wisdom in verse 15 reinforces this conclusion. An Egyptian wisdom text, *The Instruction of Anii*, stresses the effectiveness of communal instruction by using the image of straightening a crooked stick.[2] Qohelet declares the opposite: it is

1. Søren Kierkegaard, *Concluding Unscientific Postscript, KW* 12, pt. 1 (Princeton, NJ: Princeton University Press, 1992), 158.
2. C. L. Seow, *Ecclesiastes: A New Translation with Introduction and Commentary* (New York: Doubleday, 1997), 122.

impossible to straighten what is crooked (v. 15a). The world, like a recalcitrant student, refuses to be conformed to a human sense of order and coherence. That it is the Creator God who makes things crooked becomes clear a few chapters later (7:13). Likewise, a profit can be counted, but it is impossible to count what is not there (v. 15b). Even the vast wisdom of the king cannot make things "add up." Once again, the human search for understanding and profit comes up empty.

Verse 13 contains the first mention of God in the book, and it is another indication of the differences between Ecclesiastes and Proverbs. The name used regularly for God in Proverbs is "the LORD," Israel's circumlocution for the sacred name of God given to Moses. So whenever Proverbs commends "the fear of the LORD," it is creating a link to the particulars of Israel's narrative, to the story of the exodus, the giving of the law, and the promises and warnings of the prophets, even when it does not mention them explicitly. By contrast, Qohelet always uses the name *Elohim*, the most generic name for God available. This probably reflects Qohelet's pluralistic religious context. It also reflects a modesty about what we can know about God—what Dawn DeVries commends as "pious agnosticism."[3] Qohelet does not claim to know what God is up to in the world, or even what God's disposition is toward the righteous and wise (9:1). Many questions about God remain unanswered and unanswerable. Qohelet does not plead with God for deliverance like the psalmist or argue with God like Job. As Walther Zimmerli notes, "fear of God" for Qohelet means "walking

I've never caught
The Unknown God at leisure in
His rooms.
Nor spied Him in the middle of
His labors,
Although my bruise-bewildered
brain would like to.
Whether or not He makes the
crooked paths straight,
I've had to hack mine out as
sorry-best
I might.

Vassar Miller, "An Athenian Reminisces," in *If I Had Wheels or Love: Collected Poems of Vassar Miller* (Dallas: Southern Methodist University Press, 1991), 221.

3. Dawn DeVries, "The Living God: The Problem of Divine Personality in Reformed Theology," in *Reformed Theology for the Third Christian Millennium*, ed. B. A. Gerrish (Louisville, KY: Westminster John Knox Press, 2003), 72.

under a heaven that is mysteriously closed, walking without the assurance that lightning might not suddenly shoot out and strike you as you go—at every step relying upon the free gift of God, but with every step also summoned to suffer the riddle and oppression that God can inflict."[4]

Tongue in cheek, the confident royal reflection resumes in verse 16, with the king reminding himself of his unparalleled success in acquiring wisdom. His previous inquiry into the totality of human deeds was a bust, but now the king "applies his mind" to wisdom itself, as well as to its polar opposite, folly (v. 17). His scandalous conclusion is that there is not much difference between the two. While traditional wisdom, as represented in Proverbs, insists that folly leads to vexation and sorrow (cf. Prov. 10:1; 17:25), the king finds that wisdom leads to the very same misfortunes! Certainly, this has been his own experience so far: the one whose wisdom "surpass[ed] all who were over Jerusalem before [him]" (v. 16) has found surpassing vexation and sorrow in both the pursuit and the results of wisdom.

2:1–26

Undaunted, the king tries once again. He applies his mighty wisdom to "make a test of pleasure" (v. 1), and this time the irony is applied with an even thicker brush. Before the test has even begun, the results are announced: "This also was vanity" (v. 1). The king subverts conventional wisdom by using it to pursue activities deemed inimical to wisdom: indulging the pleasures of wine and tightening his grasp on folly (v. 3; cf. Prov. 15:21; 20:1). This is only the beginning of the king's exploration of "what is good for mortals to do" during their short lives (v. 3). Sounding like some ancient Near Eastern Donald Trump, the boastful king next ticks off the items in his investment portfolio: houses, vineyards, gardens, orchards, pools, male and female slaves, and livestock (vv. 4–7). He amasses incomparable wealth and amuses himself with singers and concubines (v. 8).

4. Quoted in Roland E. Murphy, *The Tree of Life: An Exploration of Biblical Wisdom Literature* (Grand Rapids: Eerdmans, 1990), 56.

"I too have had a strong theological education," Qoheleth says, "and I perceive that this also is but a striving after wind. I know about biblical criticism, the names of the popes, the teachings of the rabbis, the strategies of pastoral care, the rituals of the eucharist, and the debates about hermeneutics. . . . Now, as I come to the close of a blessed life, I perceive that all these things are but a striving after wind."

Phyllis Trible, "A Striving after Wind," in *Life in Abundance*, ed. John R. Donahue (Collegeville, MN: Liturgical Press, 2005), 293.

Every earthly pleasure is indulged: "Whatever my eyes desired I did not keep from them" (v. 10a).

In one of the earliest Christian critiques of slavery, Gregory of Nyssa uses bitter sarcasm to challenge the way the king lists enslaved human beings among his possessions (v. 7):

> What price did you put on rationality? How many obols did you reckon the equivalent of the likeness of God? How many staters did you get for selling that being shaped by God? . . . God would not reduce the human race to slavery, since he himself, when we had been enslaved to sin, spontaneously recalled us to freedom. But if God does not enslave what is free, who is he that sets his own power above God's?[5]

Theologians today would also condemn the king's sexual exploitation (v. 8). In seeking to gratify his desires and make himself great, the king flagrantly "sets his own power above God's," as Gregory of Nyssa puts it, heedless of the cost to his fellow human beings.

The king seems to be testing one of William Blake's "Proverbs of Hell": "The road of excess leads to the palace of wisdom."[6] On one level, the king's excess leads to its desired outcome: the acquisition of earthly success and glory. His greatness exceeds that of all his royal predecessors (v. 9). Not only does he derive pleasure from the results of what he toiled to accomplish; he finds a reward in the pleasure of the toil itself (v. 10). But though his wisdom remains with him (2:9), all is not well in his Jerusalem palace. Augustine,

5. Gregory of Nyssa, *Homilies on Ecclesiastes*, trans. Stuart Hall and Rachel Moriarty (New York: Walter de Gruyter, 1993), 74.
6. William Blake, *The Marriage of Heaven and Hell* (Mineola, NY: Dover Publications, 1994), 31.

reflecting on the Roman Empire in his time, notes that its leaders were also motivated by the desire for surpassing greatness and "labored towards honours, power and glory." While they were still alive, the imperial leaders "were honoured in almost all nations; they imposed their laws on many peoples." Even after their death "they enjoy renown in the history and literature of nearly all races."[7] By their hard work (and reckless abuse of others), they stored up treasure on earth (Matt. 6:19) and received the earthly reward they sought. But like all rewards of the earthly city, Augustine notes, it has an expiration date. Immortality achieved through the history books is a perishable commodity. Qohelet, speaking through the voice of the king, reaches an even deeper disillusionment: there is "no enduring remembrance" of those who have come before (v. 16). Historical memory is nonexistent. There can be fleeting pleasure in the toil, but the reward of human beings' labor perishes with them.

Qohelet reprises the opening question of what is gained from human toil (1:3) from the vantage point of the king's "great works" (2:4) and reaches a disheartening conclusion: there is *nothing* to be gained (2:11). The search for profit is finally human beings' attempt to establish themselves, to demonstrate the significance of their own existence, to wrest something enduring by and for themselves out of life.[8] Within the framework of Qohelet's understanding of creaturehood, it cannot be done because it denies human dependence and finitude. Human beings are not their own makers and keepers, and they cannot use creaturely things to bestow ultimate meaning on their lives. As Augustine insists, pleasure in possessions and accomplishments, and in work itself, comes when they are loved not as humanity's final end and source of value but as relative goods that receive their value as gifts from God.[9] Before the king's wisdom reaches this chastened yet joyful conclusion, it must first hit bottom.

The king's thoughts begin a downward spiral. If he whose wisdom surpassed all others (1:16) is unable to achieve anything of enduring value, then there is no hope for any who come after him (2:12).

7. Augustine, *The City of God* 5.15, trans. Henry Bettenson (London: Penguin Classics, 1972), 205.
8. This sentence is a paraphrase of Edwin Good, *Irony in the Old Testament* (Philadelphia: Westminster Press, 1965), 186.
9. See Augustine, *On Christian Teaching* 1.33, trans. R. P. H. Green (Oxford: Clarendon Press, 1995).

Why has he knocked himself out to be wise if there is finally no profit in it (v. 15)? Even if "wisdom excels folly" (v. 13), a conviction Qohelet never relinquishes, its benefits have clearly been highly overrated. How is wisdom "a tree of life" (Prov. 3:16) if eventually "the wise die just like fools" (v. 16)? The king sees that all the earthly gains of his lifetime of wise toil come to nothing in the end. As Edwin Good puts it, "The meaning of life is not to be found in a ledger, because everyone finally goes to the same place. Death writes 'Canceled' over the entire transaction."[10]

> **I am at the end of my rope. I am nauseated by life; it is insipid—without salt and meaning. If I were hungrier that Pierrot, I would not choose to eat the explanation people offer. One sticks a finger into the ground to smell what country one is in; I stick my finger into the world—it has no smell.**
>
> Søren Kierkegaard, *Fear and Trembling/Repetition*, *KW* 6 (Princeton, NJ: Princeton University Press, 1983), 200.

"So I hated life" (v. 17). The king has now reached his nadir. Even the pleasure he had earlier found in his toil (v. 10) is wiped out by the realization that he must leave it all behind after he dies, with no guarantees about what will come of it. The king's denunciation of the value of work probably hits closer to home for many readers of this commentary than his earlier dismissals of pretentions to great wisdom and the restless pursuit of wealth and pleasure. Work has received moral approbation for Christians in a way that wealth and pleasure have not. But the king recognizes that who finally benefits from his work and what legacy he leaves behind are not within his control. If the value of his life's work depends on its lasting impact after he is gone, then it too is a source of despair, not consolation (v. 20).

The king's "purpose-driven" life has crumbled. To move on, he must reject a totalizing view of human existence. In other words, he must reject the notion that "what makes a human life a single and meaningful whole is that it has been totally committed to some sort of project, [even] that of becoming a wise person."[11] Starting in verse

10. Good, *Irony*, 185–86.
11. David Kelsey, *Eccentric Existence: A Theological Anthropology* (Louisville, KY: Westminster John Knox Press, 2009), 325. See pp. 155–56, "Further Reflections: Qohelet and the Missional Church."

24, and repeatedly throughout the book, Qohelet will encourage instead an enjoyment of and gratitude for the opportunities and gifts of ordinary life (see pp. 171–72, "Further Reflections: The Command to Rejoice"). This joy has a distinctively theological rationale for Qohelet. By abandoning the king's grandiose ambition to master life and his metanarrative of continuing progress in wisdom, Qohelet finds room to acknowledge the generous hand of God. God is the source of daily sustenance and enjoyment. Fittingly, Ecclesiastes is read as part of the liturgy for the annual Jewish Feast of Tabernacles, known as Sukkot. This holiday is both a celebration of the fruits of the harvest and a reminder of God's provision for Israel during their forty-year sojourn in the desert. Joy is also found in work itself, a joy that is not dependent on the external goods of money or fame that sometimes accompany work (v. 24).

The futility of earthly striving is reinforced in verse 26. This verse should not be read as a neat doctrine of moral retribution, such that God rewards the righteous and punishes sinners, each according to their desserts. This is indeed Qohelet's hope (cf. 3:17; 8:12–13), but to read it as a statement of present reality would fly in the face of the pervasive ambiguities of creaturely existence (cf. 3:16; 9:11). Rather, verse 26 describes the way joy can elude those who set their heart on earthly things (cf. Matt. 6:21). Those who are given the wisdom to know that creaturely life has its source and sustenance in God are able to take joy in earthly things. By contrast, those who have lost their way (NRSV "sinner") are still striving to write their own ticket in life. They plod on ceaselessly with "the work of gathering and heaping" but never obtain satisfaction (cf. 5:10). As the novelist David Foster Wallace put it in a college commencement address,

> If you worship money and things—if they are where you tap real meaning in life—then you will never have enough. . . . Worship power—you will feel weak and afraid, and you will need ever more power over others to keep the fear at bay. Worship your intellect, being seen as smart—you will end up feeling stupid, a fraud, always on the verge of being found out.[12]

12. David Foster Wallace, "Plain Old Untrendy Troubles and Emotions," *The Guardian*, Sept. 20, 2008, available at http://www.guardian.co.uk/books/2008/sep/20/fiction.

Similarly, Martin Luther notes that joy is not a matter of material quantity. Those who trust in God "truly possess the whole world, because they enjoy it with happiness and tranquility," even when they in fact have very little. But those who do not trust God "do not possess it even when they have it."[13] In the midst of abundance they feel anxious and deprived. The joy in what they have is denied to them and given to those who have already found enjoyment "from the hand of God" (v. 24). This tragic paradox is for Qohelet yet another example of "vanity and a chasing after wind" (v. 26; see pp. 39–41, commentary on 5:1–25).

FURTHER REFLECTIONS
Qohelet and the Missional Church

Dietrich Bonhoeffer had a special affinity for the book of Ecclesiastes. In a portion of his *Ethics*, Bonhoeffer mocks those who act "as if human beings incessantly had to do something decisive, fulfill a higher purpose, meet an ultimate duty." This represents, he says, "a misjudgment of historical human existence in which everything has its time (Ecclesiastes 3)—eating, drinking, sleeping, as well as conscious decision making and acting, working and resting, serving a purpose and just being without purpose."[14] Qohelet repeatedly portrays the futility of a radically purpose-driven life (Eccl. 2:9–11, 18–23; 4:7–8; 5:15–17).

Ironically, this notion of continually "incessantly doing something decisive, fulfilling a higher purpose, and meeting an ultimate duty" is exactly the way Christians have often thought about the church in recent years. This is especially true of the recent emphasis on the missional church. According to missional ecclesiology, the church exists as a means to God's end of establishing the kingdom. The church's core identity is missional, reaching out in testimony and witness to the world. In fact, the Christian community succeeds in truly being the church only when it is being sent, when its whole

13. Martin Luther, *Ecclesiastes, Song of Solomon, and Last Words of David*, *LW* 15, trans. J. Pelikan (Saint Louis: Concordia, 1969), 48.
14. Dietrich Bonhoeffer, *Ethics*, *DBW* 6 (Minneapolis: Fortress Press, 2008), 365.

life is directed outward toward its ultimate duty of witness to the world. Missiologist Darrell Guder insists that "ultimately, the evangelistic mandate of the church must define every dimension of the church's life and activity."[15] Being sent is the one grand project to which the church is called.

Ecclesiastes, however, casts doubt on totalizing views of human existence. These views fail to take into account our creaturely lives and our creaturely faithfulness to the God who made and sustains us. Bonhoeffer quotes again from Ecclesiastes in another section of his *Ethics* when he insists that Christians should see bodily life "not only as a means to an end but also an end in itself."[16] Qohelet's repeated affirmations of the joys of bodily life need to be taken seriously in thinking about the Christian life. The creaturely life God gives Christians is not only a means to an end, the end of witness. The creaturely life of the church is also a good in itself, something to take joy in and to praise God for. Sharing meals, celebrating the birth of a new child, singing and making music together, rejoicing in news of a successful surgery, taking the youth group on a camping trip—these are all goods in themselves and ways in which we flourish as God's creatures. These activities are all faithful responses to God's work of giving and sustaining creaturely life. They are not distractions from a supposedly all-encompassing missional mandate.

We are not to take ourselves and our Christian duty so seriously that we leave no room for joy, for times of play, and, as Bonhoeffer puts it, "just being without purpose."[17] Joy comes not in the dazzling success of our ventures—missional and otherwise—but in our ability to receive God's ordinary, daily gifts and to recognize God as the giver of them. As Qohelet insists, "It is God's gift that all should eat and drink and take pleasure in all their toil" (Eccl. 3:13).

15. Darrell L. Guder, "Growing Evangelizing Churches," in *Teaching Mission in a Global Context*, ed. Patricia Lloyd-Sidle and Bonnie Sue Lewis (Louisville, KY: Geneva Press, 2001), 144.
16. Bonhoeffer, *Ethics*, 180.
17. Ibid., 365.

3:1–22

Life under the Sun

Ecclesiastes 3:1–8 is probably the best-known section of Ecclesiastes, thanks in part to Pete Seeger's 1959 song "Turn, Turn, Turn." Its stately poetry, whether borrowed or composed by Qohelet, stands in literary contrast to the rest of the book. Just as 1:4–7 looked at the ceaseless rhythms of the cosmos, so this poem explores the rhythms of human life. As Ellen Davis notes, there is a time and place for every *essential aspect* of human life, not literally for "every matter under heaven" (v. 1): "there is no right time for oppression or wretched suffering, for foolishness or deceit."[1] Scholars debate the meaning of verse 5a. Some see a sexual reference in scattering and gathering stones together, anticipating "a time to embrace" in verse 5b; others see a reference to a game or to a trading practice of using stones as counters. Knowing "what time it is" in one's life is a central part of wisdom's discernment. Proverbs too recognizes "a time to keep silence, and a time to speak" (v. 7b; cf. Prov. 11:12; 15:23). Most of the items in verses 2–8 are not really a matter of human choice or planning. Birth and death and the seasons for planting and harvest (v. 2) are hardly within human control at all. The lack of discernable order in the rest of the list reinforces a sense of the contingency of our lives: most occasions simply present themselves and demand our response. We do not "decide" to mourn or to dance (v. 4b); instead, something happens to us that makes one or the other appropriate. The reprise of the question of the profit of human toil (v. 9; cf. 1:3, 2:22; 6:11) shows that the alternation in human activities

1. Ellen F. Davis, *Proverbs, Ecclesiastes, and the Song of Songs*, WBC (Louisville, KY: Westminster John Knox Press, 2000), 184.

in verses 2–8 does not imply a narrative of progress. Despite the workers' constant toil, nothing lasting is gained. There is a time for "building up" (v. 3b) something new, but eventually that too must be broken down. Laughing will be followed by more weeping.

As in 2:24–26, Qohelet turns from the futility of human doing to the efficacy of divine doing. Ecclesiastes 3:11–15 repeatedly points to what God has made and done. God is the source of all that exists and all that happens. The only thing that human beings are to "do" is to find pleasure in their toil (v. 13), and even this is God's gift. The NRSV softens the Hebrew in verse 11, which says that God has made everything *beautiful* for its time. Are death, killing, hatred, and war (vv. 2a, 3a, 8) ever "beautiful"? Verse 14 heightens the discomfort by insisting that there is a perfect completeness to what God has done, so we must receive it all in reverence. We cannot simply select the parts we want of life and discard the rest. In *Shadowlands*, a film about the death of C. S. Lewis's beloved wife, Joy Gresham, the Lewis character asks at the end,

> Why love if losing hurts so much? I have no answers any more. Only the life I have lived. Twice in that life I've been given the choice: as a boy and as a man. The boy chose safety; the man chooses suffering. The pain now is part of the happiness then. That's the deal.[2]

Like Lewis, Qohelet has no answers. Life "under the sun" is a package deal, and all we can do is to endure the pain and to treasure the moments of happiness and joy that God gives (v. 12).

God has put a sense of eternity (*hāʿōlām*) in human hearts (v. 11), "a consciousness of and yearning for that which transcends the present."[3] But the present is where humanity lives. They know that there is more, but they cannot transcend their creaturely limitations and attain a God's-eye command of it all (v. 11). They can only rejoice in the fleeting moments of joy and purpose that point beyond themselves to something more. The glory is found in the ordinary. The enigmatic conclusion in verse 15 is that God lastingly

2. David M. Thompson, prod., *Shadowlands* (BBC Wales, 1985).
3. C. L. Seow, *Ecclesiastes: A New Translation with Introduction and Commentary* (New York: Doubleday, 1997), 173.

presides over all that seems futile or ephemeral to human beings. God seeks out "what has gone by" is better understood as God seeks out "that which people seek in vain."[4] What is unobtainable through human intellect or effort is apprehended and secured by God. As Kierkegaard notes, "God's wisdom is beyond all comparison with yours, and God's governance has no obligation of responsibility in relation to your sagacity."[5]

The limits of human intellect and agency address another challenge in verse 16: the reality of wickedness in the place of justice and righteousness. The governmental structures that are supposed to be bulwarks of justice and righteousness have become utterly corrupt, so the poor and weak have no recourse. Wickedness reigns in the world. Qohelet refuses to offer an explanation for this distressing state of affairs: in this respect also the world of our experience is absurd. To try to make rational sense of it is to deny its horrors. The resolution lies beyond the reach of our present experience, in God's earthly judgment of the righteous and the wicked (v. 17; cf. 8:12–13). The timing of this judgment lies in God's hands, not ours (v. 17). However, the problem for Qohelet is not simply the delay of God's earthly justice. Even if we witness divine judgment tomorrow, "just deserts for both heroes and scoundrels pale in comparison with the common fate of all the living."[6] The wicked and righteous die alike, and humanity as a whole dies just like the animals (vv. 18–19; cf. Ps. 49:12, 20). Once again, creaturely finitude seems to erase

In Daniel Quinn's novel, Ishmael, a gorilla, takes it upon himself to rid humanity ("the Takers") of the delusion that it "stands alone, unique and infinitely apart from all the rest" of creation: "Though the Takers don't know it yet, the gods did not exempt man from the law that governs the lives of grubs and ticks and shrimps and rabbits and mollusks and deer and lions and jellyfish. They did not exempt him from this law any more than they exempted him from the law of gravity, and this is going to be the bitterest blow of all to the Takers."

Daniel Quinn, *Ishmael* (New York: Bantam/Turner, 1992), 102–3.

4. Ibid., 166.
5. Søren Kierkegaard, *Works of Love*, *KW*16 (Princeton, NJ: Princeton University Press, 1998), 20.
6. William P. Brown, *Ecclesiastes*, Interpretation: A Bible Commentary for Teaching and Preaching (Louisville, KY: Westminster John Knox Press, 2000), 47.

human distinctions and achievements. At this point anyway (but see 12:7), Qohelet is resolutely agnostic about whether humanity has any advantage over (other) animals after their death (v. 21). In an echo of Genesis 3:19, Qohelet affirms the common finitude of all creatures: from dust and back to dust (v. 20; cf. 12:7). All the more reason, then, to enjoy life and work now (v. 22).

4:1–16

Power and Its Discontents

The panoramic overview of the world's vanity fades away at the beginning of chapter 4, and Qohelet's sage observations become more particular and concrete. Qohelet addresses four issues in this chapter: oppression (vv. 1–3), envy (vv. 4–6), personal isolation (vv. 7–12), and wise government (vv. 13–15). Not surprisingly, this shift toward the particular is accompanied by an increased use of proverbial forms.

Qohelet's social analysis in verse 1 could have been lifted straight from classic liberation theology: humanity is divided between the oppressed and their oppressors, and the two are distinguished by a disparity of cultural, political, and economic power. Exercising "a preferential option for the poor," Qohelet sides with the oppressed, noting their tears (v. 1). Yet whereas classic liberation theology calls for a revolutionary transformation of oppressive structures in order to forge a radically different society, Qohelet holds out no hope for this. In this way Qohelet is closer to more recent liberation theology, which "looks for ways to be faithful and persevere, even though hope for positive and substantial structural changes has waned."[1] Qohelet's call to modest forms of creaturely solidarity will be detailed in verses 9–12.

The repeated, plaintive cry in verse 1 that there is "no one to comfort" the oppressed echoes the dire distress of Judah in Lamentations, who also found no one to help or comfort (Lam. 1:2, 7, 9,

1. Nancy Bedford, "Little Moves against Destructiveness: Theology and the Practice of Discernment," in *Practicing Theology: Beliefs and Practices in Christian Life*, ed. Miroslav Volf and Dorothy Bass (Grand Rapids, Eerdmans, 2002), 163.

16, 17, 21). The word translated "comfort" should be understood as more than a consoling pat on the shoulder. To comfort is to provide succor and to advocate on someone's behalf in order to bring that person relief from suffering. The two figures to whom Israel traditionally turned for justice and deliverance were God and the king, but Qohelet sees no one stepping in to fill this liberating role. Qohelet has by now dropped the royal guise of chapters 1–2, and no king appears to "speak out for those who cannot speak" (Prov. 31:8). Even though "those who oppress the poor insult their Maker" (Prov. 14:31), God too is silent. Shaken by this hopeless situation, Qohelet reaches a despairing conclusion: it is less painful to be dead than to be alive and witness "the evil deeds that are done under the sun." Even better yet is to have not yet been born (vv. 2–3). This first "better than" proverb in Ecclesiastes contains a deep irony: what is "better" is not within the grasp of anyone who is alive.

Qohelet returns to the subject of human toil and work in verses 4–6. Taking pleasure *in* one's toil is a gift from God (3:13). By contrast, toil that is motivated by the desire to gain a competitive edge over one's neighbor (NRSV: "another") is vanity in both senses of the word: it reflects inflated pride in oneself and is ultimately without value (v. 4). Envy-driven work has no natural stopping point: there is always someone else to catch up to and surpass. This attempt to establish one's superiority over others is futile and self-consuming—"a chasing after wind." Qohelet follows this observation with two proverbs that could both have come from the book of Proverbs. The first notes the self-destructive character of the opposite extreme of compulsive work: folding one's hands and refusing to work altogether (v. 5; cf. Prov. 24:33–34). "Better than" either complete idleness or ceaseless work driven by envy is work that is kept in perspective and balanced with rest (v. 6; cf. Prov. 23:4).

Work that is driven by envy breaks down community. So does work driven by the desire to enrich only oneself. Qohelet considers those who live alone without dependents or siblings yet work ceaselessly to accumulate wealth for themselves (v. 7). Putting their trust in their riches leaves them perpetually wanting more. Rather than share what they have in ways that bring joy to themselves and others, they anxiously seek to enhance their "net worth." Their preoccupation with work deprives them of pleasure, and their riches benefit no one.

Qohelet's response to oppression, envy, and selfishness is to commend concrete forms of human solidarity: working together, lifting one another up, keeping one another warm, defending one another (vv. 9–12). The call to solidarity is in keeping with Qohelet's understanding of creation: it is impossible to transcend the vulnerability and finitude of creaturely life by grasping for power (vv. 1–2) or glory (vv. 4–6), or by hoarding treasure for oneself (vv. 7–8). Human beings are dust, and to dust they will return (3:20). To pretend otherwise is vanity. But in the meantime God the Creator calls humanity to protect and nurture one another in ordinary, daily ways. These are not grand, heroic gestures, but neither do they represent a disengagement from the suffering and needs of others. Rather, they are what Nancy Bedford calls "little moves against destructiveness."[2]

As noted above, Qohelet's despair over social oppression does not issue in a call to radical social transformation. As Elsa Tamez puts it, Qohelet sees "no feasible macrostructural solution" to society's ills, "not even an unfeasible one."[3] The endless, repetitive cycles of the cosmos undercut utopian hopes for genuinely new social and political arrangements. In the face of these structural intransigences, the only recourse is basic, small-scale forms of creaturely solidarity such as Qohelet advocates in verses 9–12. Tamez finds hope and guidance in Ecclesiastes for those in her own late-capitalist Latin American context living with little hope for a new and better day. In an "inverted society" dominated by the logic of "Save your own skin," Ecclesiastes points us to "spaces of good life and grace in the midst of a dehumanizing present, and in the face of inscrutable horizons."[4]

Compared to the robustly communal ethos of Proverbs, verses 9–12 provide a modest call, to be sure. Like many seekers today, Qohelet seems to have lost confidence in the major institutions of society. In striking contrast to Proverbs, the family is no longer appealed to as a source of wise guidance for attaining a secure and

2. Ibid.
3. Elsa Tamez, *When the Horizons Close: Rereading Ecclesiastes* (Eugene, OR: Wipf & Stock, 2000), 14.
4. Ibid., v.

ordered life. Likewise, wise and just political leadership is the exception rather than the rule. The wisdom of parents and political leaders cannot be relied on to guide a new generation. Qohelet's institutional skepticism is vividly portrayed in a parable at the end of chapter 4, in which wisdom has lost its traditional associations with wealth, age, and social standing. The poor youth is declared to be a wiser leader than the old but foolish king (v. 13). Indeed someone utterly bereft of social capital—such as an impoverished ex-convict—can earn the respect of the people and become a political leader (v. 14). Yet despite the youth's great popular following, he leaves no legacy. When he dies, so does all memory of him (vv. 15–16). Qohelet discounts the possibility of accumulated, inherited communal wisdom. Political leadership, like ordinary human life, is concerned with present duties and opportunities. In Karl Barth's words, it is about "doing the relatively better relatively well" in the here and now.[5]

5. Karl Barth, *Church Dogmatics* IV/4, *The Doctrine of Reconciliation*, trans. G. W. Bromiley, ed. T. F. Torrance (Edinburgh: T. & T. Clark, 1969), 271.

5:1–20
Fearing God

5:1–7

Biblical wisdom literature rarely addresses issues of worship. The faith in God it commends is lived out principally in the daily world of work and human relationships. But 5:1–7 recognizes that the vanity of human life extends also to religious observance. Here too human beings are tempted to try to secure themselves by their own actions and achievements. Qohelet's terse instructions on how to worship begin and end with a caution to approach God with proper respect and awe (vv. 1, 7). This rationale rests on Qohelet's understanding of the fundamental asymmetry between Creator and creature (v. 2). God has set the terms for human life, not the other way around. The human inclination to treat God as a guarantor of human values and ambitions is an idolatrous confusion.

Ecclesiastes shares Proverbs' concerns with inappropriate vows and sacrifices. Casual and hasty vows reflect a lack of reverence before God (Prov. 20:25). To vow something before the priest (NRSV: "messenger") that one has not considered carefully or, even worse, has no intention of fulfilling is to mock God (vv. 5–6). Jesus likewise will urge his followers "not [to] swear at all, either by heaven, for it is the throne of God, or by the earth, for it is his footstool" (Matt. 5:34–35). Sacrifice offered in the foolish belief that God can be bought off is also an abomination (cf. Prov. 15:8; 21:27). Qohelet says it is better to listen than to sacrifice (v. 1), because listening indicates a reverent receptivity to God rather than an attempt to manipulate God for one's own ends. As Kierkegaard notes, "Silence is the beginning of the fear of God," and in fact it is more than that: it *is* the fear of God.[1] Biblical wisdom's general concern for custody of the tongue is heightened in the case of speech to God, because foolish verbosity leads humanity into sin and incurs God's wrath (v. 6).

The excess of religious words flows from human "dreams" (vv. 3, 7): fleeting, baseless fantasies about God. In response to the temptation to set up a religious universe in which everything revolves around human perceptions and concerns, Qohelet reminds us that God is in heaven, and we are on earth (v. 2b). God does not exist to satisfy human aims and desires. God is not a mascot for our favorite causes. Since self-serving human fantasies about God are a perennial religious problem, it is not surprising that theologians in other ages have appealed to Qohelet's counsel. Karl Barth wrote his Romans commentary in response to early twentieth-century German theologians who saw a natural bridge between their highest aspirations and God and who confidently enlisted God's support for their nationalist and cultural causes. In the preface to the second edition, Barth explains his contrasting theological approach by quoting Ecclesiastes 5:2b: "God is in heaven, and you upon earth."[2] (Qohelet's advice in that same verse to "let your words be few" was evidently left behind when Barth later embarked on his enormous *Church Dogmatics*!) In the same passage, Barth appeals to Kierkegaard, who in his nineteenth-century Danish context also confronted a church complacently allied with the cultural values around it—where

The advantage of the human being over the animal is the ability to speak, but, in relation to God, wanting to speak can easily become the corruption of the human being, who is able to speak. God is in heaven and the human being is on earth and therefore they can hardly converse. God is infinite wisdom; what the human being knows is idle chatter; therefore they can hardly converse. God is love and the human being, as we say to a child, is a little ninny even in regard to his own welfare, and therefore they can hardly converse. Only in much fear and trembling is a human being able to speak with God, in much fear and trembling.

Søren Kierkegaard, *Works of Love*, 11.

1. Søren Kierkegaard, *Works of Love*, *KW* 16 (Princeton, NJ: Princeton University Press, 1998), 11.
2. Karl Barth, *The Epistle to the Romans*, trans. Edwyn C. Hoskyns (London: Oxford University Press, 1933), 10.

"the meaning of life was to make a living," and "piety consisted in going to communion once a year."[3] Rather than seeing a comfortable continuity between God's aspirations and our own, Kierkegaard posits "an eternal essential qualitative difference" between God and humanity.[4] Qohelet's understanding of God is austere and unsettling, but in the face of cavalier and domesticated assumptions about God, Ecclesiastes is a welcome tonic.

5:8–20

Interpreters wrestle with verses 8–9 on a variety of linguistic levels; this commentary will follow the lead of C. L. Seow and William P. Brown. The theme of the social oppression of the vulnerable carries over from 4:1, but this time the oppressed are explicitly identified as "the poor" (v. 8). The special responsibility of political leaders toward the poor is a central biblical theme (e.g., Ps. 72:1–4, 12–14), and verses 8–9 again reflect Qohelet's disillusionment with political leadership. Just as "the king" in 2:7–8 gave no heed to the lives of his slaves and concubines, so here too leaders are portrayed as haughty, ambitious people "who think that they can achieve anything they want at anybody's expense."[5] But their ambitions are frustrated because in their political hierarchy "there are always people who are higher than they, looking down at them".[6] The officials are preoccupied with their status in the bureaucratic system, indifferent to the needs of the people. The point of political leadership is to create the peace and security needed for the flourishing of the land and its people: "By justice a king gives stability to the land" (Prov. 29:4). This is the key to understanding the enigmatic saying in verse 9 that the king exists for the sake of "a plowed field," not for the sake of gratifying his lust for power.[7] While this is the political ideal, Qohelet laments that the reality on the ground is quite different: the poor

3. Søren Kierkegaard, *Either/Or*, *KW* 3, pt. 1 (Princeton, NJ: Princeton University Press, 1987), 34.
4. Kierkegaard, *Works of Love*, 100.
5. C. L. Seow, *Ecclesiastes: A New Translation with Introduction and Commentary* (New York: Doubleday, 1997), 218.
6. Ibid.
7. William P. Brown, *Ecclesiastes*, Interpretation: A Bible Commentary for Teaching and Preaching (Louisville, KY: Westminster John Knox Press, 2000), 59.

suffer injustice, and political officials are stuck in an endless loop of greedy ambition.

These verses then open into a larger reflection in verses 10–17 on the futility of what Augustine called cupidity: the inordinate love of creaturely things. According to Augustine, only in loving God does the heart find a secure resting place. Earthly power (v. 8) and money (vv. 10–12) cannot be possessed without the fear of losing them. When they are the ultimate aim of one's life, there can be no security or contentment. Gorging on them (v. 11) brings no lasting satisfaction, because desire for them is a bottomless pit: "The lover of money will not be satisfied with money" (v. 10; cf. 1 Tim. 6:10; Heb. 13:5). Augustine does not mean that material things, including money, are to be despised: "God does not forbid you to love these things, but not to devote your love [to them] for the attainment of happiness."[8] Ironically, those who do devote their love of power or money to attaining happiness find themselves supremely *unhappy*, consumed by "vexation and sickness and resentment" (v. 17). Happiness comes in holding earthly goods with a light hand, not in clinging more tightly. The benefit of wealth is limited to what the eyes see (v. 11), that is, to what can be enjoyed in the present.

In verse 12, Qohelet ironically contrasts the sweet sleep of hungry laborers with the restless nights that the rich spend worrying about their wealth. In a Qohelet-like way, Elsa Tamez subverts this: "It is said that in a country of sharp contrasts, no one can sleep. The poor—the majority—do not sleep because they are hungry, and the rich do not sleep because they know it."[9] There is nothing "sweet" about being poor. As Proverbs 30:8–9 counsels, "Neither poverty nor riches" is an ideal state; both extremes make it difficult to trust God. Qohelet follows this observation about the anxiety of wealth with a parable about a rich fool (vv. 13–17; cf. Luke 12:13–20; also see pp. 113–15, "Further Reflections: Jesus as Sage"). The NRSV transposes the whole vignette into the plural, but the Hebrew is singular. In this travesty of financial expectations ("grievous ill"), a rich man

8. Augustine, *Tractates on the First Epistle of John*, trans. John W. Rettig, The Fathers of the Church, vol. 92 (Washington, DC: Catholic University of America Press, 1988), 154.
9. Elsa Tamez, *When the Horizons Close: Rereading Ecclesiastes* (Eugene, OR: Wipf & Stock, 2000), 82.

hoarded his wealth (v. 13), only to lose it all in a disastrous investment (v. 14). He has nothing to show for a lifetime of relentless toil (vv. 15–16). His hands are empty, with nothing to pass on to his son—meaning that his son "has nothing in [his] hands" either (5:14). Qohelet's assertion that we come naked from the womb and go naked to our death finds echoes elsewhere in the Bible (Eccl. 5:15; cf. Job 1:21; Ps. 49:17; 1 Tim. 6:7) and is a common theme in ancient Near Eastern wisdom literature. The Egyptian *Song of Anef* declares, "No one can bring his property with him. No one who goes will come back again."[10] Once again Qohelet declares this a travesty (v. 16)—what is the point of a lifetime of sweat and toil if death consumes it all?

> **The most ludicrous of all ludicrous things, it seems to me, is to be busy in the world, to be a man who is brisk at his meals and brisk at this work. . . . What, after all, do these busy bustlers achieve? Are they not just like that woman who, in a flurry because the house was on fire, rescued the fire tongs? What more, after all, do they salvage from life's huge conflagration?**
>
> Søren Kierkegaard, *Either/Or*, 25.

Even worse, anxiety about the uncertain future robs a person of enjoyment in the present. Luther declares it "the height of vanity and misery, to cheat oneself of the use of present goods and vainly to be troubled about future ones."[11] Verse 17 paints a picture of a living death. The one who eats "in darkness" is like the stillborn child of 6:4–5 who "has not seen the sun" and "goes into darkness." Being consumed with acquiring earthly treasure is in the end to destroy oneself, both psychologically and physically.

Qohelet amply demonstrates the folly of placing one's trust in creaturely goods. What conclusion is the wise person to draw from this? One understandable response would be to despise and condemn the things of this world (see pp. 56–59, commentary on 9:1–18). Martin Luther observes that contempt for the world is "the error and dangerous opinion held by many," noting the inclination

10. Quoted in Seow, *Ecclesiastes*, 221.
11. Martin Luther, *Ecclesiastes, Song of Solomon, and the Last Words of David*, *LW* 15, trans. J. Pelikan (Saint Louis: Concordia, 1969), 8.

among Christian preachers to "inveigh against glory, power, social position, wealth, gold, fame, beauty, or women." Luther rejects this response, because it denigrates God's good creation: "For God has made all things to be good and to be useful for some human purpose." According to Luther, contempt for the world is also a misunderstanding of Ecclesiastes: "What is being condemned in this book, therefore, is not the creatures, but the depraved affection and desire of us men."[12] Another inappropriate response to the folly of trusting earthly goods is suggested by Kierkegaard. One might cynically conclude from Qohelet's observations that "life is not a process of development but a process of the downfall of the great and distinguished" and decide that the best recourse is a complete skepticism and "mistrust of life": trust nothing and no one! Kierkegaard rejects this as a "final decision on life's questions" and insists that it is also a misunderstanding of Ecclesiastes: "When Solomon says that all is vanity," the point of destabilizing our trust in earthly goods is to lead us "to finding a trust" elsewhere, namely in God.[13]

Luther's and Kierkegaard's conclusions echo the theological framework of Qohelet's own response in verses 18–20. The simple pleasures of eating and drinking and daily work are to be cherished as gifts from God. As William Brown notes, for Qohelet "the most tangible setting for joy is found around a table."[14] If God grants not only wealth but also the ability to enjoy it (v. 19), this too is a gift. When earthly goods are present, they are to be gratefully received as an acknowledgment of God's beneficence and our creaturely dependence. Luther considered 5:18–20 to be the key to the whole book of Ecclesiastes: these verses "forbid vain anxieties, so that we may happily enjoy the things that are present and not care at all about the things that are in the future, lest we permit the present moment, our moment, to slip away."[15] Qohelet's point in verse 20 is not that human beings will altogether cease worrying about their problems or the uncertainties of the future. God responds to our creaturely vulnerabilities not by erasing them but by giving us joy in the

12. Ibid.

13. Søren Kierkegaard, "From the Papers of One Still Living," in *Early Polemical Writings*, *KW* 1 (Princeton, NJ: Princeton University Press, 2009), 79–80.

14. Brown, *Ecclesiastes*, 128.

15. Luther, *Ecclesiastes*, 93.

present. Accepting our creaturely lot (v. 19) and enjoying simple gifts from God's hand keep us from cynicism and contempt for our creaturely lives.

FURTHER REFLECTIONS:
The Command to Rejoice

The enjoyment of life is a basic theme of Ecclesiastes (2:24–25; 3:12–22, 22; 5:18–19; 9:7–10; 11:8–9). James Limburg uses a musical analogy to portray its centrality: while the pedal point of the book is *hebel*, the counterpoint, "the 'joy' theme in Ecclesiastes, is really what it is all about."[16] Qohelet calls us again and again to "enjoy life" (9:9). But is joy something that can be commanded?

If joy is a sense of subjective satisfaction with life in general, then the command to rejoice makes no sense. This subjective feeling of joy cannot be commanded: it will arise on its own when things go our way in life. But Qohelet makes clear that this is not what we should expect. Throughout Ecclesiastes, Qohelet acknowledges and laments the miseries and contingencies of finite creaturehood. Life is a vanity of vanities (1:2; 12:8). The movement from hating life to finding joy in it is not propelled by the absence or the denial of life's vanity. As the seventeenth-century Christian philosopher Blaise Pascal notes, "Anyone who does not see the vanity of the world is very vain himself."[17] Rather, the command to rejoice for Qohelet is rooted in our relationship to God the Creator.

Michael Fox notes that "God's most congenial quality" in Ecclesiastes is God's desire that humanity enjoy the simple pleasures of life: "If you are doing this, it is not because you have wrested a moment of respite from a hostile deity. It is what God wishes you to do."[18] God wishes for finite, dependent creatures to have joy, and we enjoy life's pleasures as gifts from God's hand (Eccl. 2:24). Our

16. James Limburg, *Encountering Ecclesiastes: A Book for Our Time* (Grand Rapids: Eerdmans, 2006), 137.
17. Blaise Pascal, *Pensées: Thoughts on Religion and Other Subjects*, #164, trans. W. F. Trotter (New York: Washington Square Press, 1965), 53.
18. Michael V. Fox, *A Time to Tear Down and a Time to Build Up: A Rereading of Ecclesiastes* (Grand Rapids: Eerdmans, 1999), 138.

rejoicing is a rejoicing *in God* (cf. Phil. 4:4). Joy is a divine gift before it is a human task. As Kierkegaard notes, "Every man who truly wants to relate himself to God and be intimate with him really only has one task—to rejoice always."[19] This call to rejoice in God's gifts is not predicated on the confidence that God will enable us to transcend the conditions of creaturehood or that God will intervene to settle scores and make everything turn out right. It is predicated instead on a grateful acknowledgment of our creaturehood. The *hebel* that Qohelet has discovered everywhere in human life remains. Joy in God's gifts as Creator is called forth in the midst of this *hebel*. Poet Wendell Berry catches some of the absurdity of this joy when he writes, "Be joyful, even in the face of all the facts."[20]

19. Søren Kierkegaard, *Søren Kierkegaard's Journals and Papers*, vol. 2 (Bloomington: Indiana University Press, 1967), 495.
20. Wendell Berry, "Manifesto: The Mad Farmer Liberation Front," in *The Selected Poems of Wendell Berry* (Berkeley, CA: Counterpoint, 1998), 87.

6:1–9
When Life Doesn't Add Up

Qohelet continues the themes of the insatiability of desire and the uncertainties of human existence with another parable about the miscarriage of a family inheritance. This time the protagonist is a biblical patriarch on steroids: a man of honor and wealth who begets one hundred children and lives two thousand years—more than twice as long as Methuselah (Gen. 5:27)! He has received all the blessings associated with wisdom: riches, honor, abundant progeny, and extraordinarily long life. Once again, Qohelet upends the conventional expectations of wisdom: like the man in the parable in 5:13–17, this one ends up unhappy and empty-handed (6:3). The rich man in chapter 5 was done in by a bad investment. The rich man in chapter 6 loses his fortune to a stranger.

The postexilic context of both Proverbs and Ecclesiastes encouraged a heightened fear of strangers and the threat they represented to family structures and the familial inheritance of wealth. Proverbs warns repeatedly against financial transactions with strangers (11:15; 20:16; 27:13), and dalliance with "the strange woman" is presented as a deadly alternative to life with Woman Wisdom (2:16–19; 5:1–23; 6:20–35; 7:1–27). In Proverbs all turns out well: the threat posed by strangers is successfully fended off, and the young man ends up secure in Wisdom's household, enjoying wealth, honor, and progeny (31:10–31). In Ecclesiastes, it is the stranger who emerges triumphant, enjoying the "wealth, possessions, and honor" (6:2) that do not belong to him and usurping the familial claims to inheritance. The rich man with one hundred children enjoys none of the good things in his life and dies without a decent burial (6:3).

Proverbs compensates for the absence of the monarchy and the priesthood as sources of social stability by emphasizing the role of the family in passing down wisdom and conserving wealth. Ecclesiastes' lack of confidence in the institution of the family is radically unsettling (see pp. 36–38, commentary on 4:1–27), because there is nothing else on the horizon that can secure the society's flourishing. As Jonathan Lear notes,

> This inability to conceive of its own devastation will tend to be the blind spot of any culture. By and large a culture will not teach its young: "These are ways in which you can succeed, and these are ways in which you will fail; these are dangers you might face, and here are opportunities; these acts are shameful, and these are worthy of honor—and, oh yes, one more thing, this entire structure of evaluating the world might cease to make sense."[1]

Proverbs devotes itself to building such a "structure of evaluating the world" and thus has limited critical leverage on its own assumptions. Unlike Proverbs, Ecclesiastes dares to contemplate the possibility that the whole structure of evaluating the world from the vantage point of Israel's wisdom traditions might cease to make sense. "For

[In Muriel Barbery's novel, a young girl, Paloma Josse, expresses her disillusionment with life:]

> **The problem is that children believe what adults say and, once they're adults themselves, they exact their revenge by deceiving their own children. 'Life has meaning and we grown-ups know what it is' is the universal lie that everyone is supposed to believe. . . . People aim for the stars, and they end up like goldfish in a bowl. I wonder if it wouldn't be simpler just to teach children right from the start that life is absurd.**

Muriel Barbery, *The Elegance of the Hedgehog*, trans. Alison Anderson (New York: Europa Editions, 2008), 22–23.

1. Jonathan Lear, *Radical Hope: Ethics in the Face of Cultural Devastation* (Cambridge, MA: Harvard University Press, 2008), 83.

what advantage have the wise over fools?" asks Qohelet (6:8). The scandalous conclusion in verses 3–5 is that a stillborn infant has a better chance at peace and happiness than the rich patriarch who "enjoys no good" during his long life.

Like the despondent patriarch, those who toil in order to possess and profit will never be satisfied (v. 7). Being wise does not help the poor improve their circumstances either (v. 8). Just as there is no gain from ceaseless toil, so there seems to be no gain from wisdom. Fools seem to do just as well as the wise. In an echo of 5:11, Qohelet commends "the sight of the eyes," the enjoyment of what is present now, over the insatiable desire to secure ourselves through our own efforts and resources (v. 9).

6:10–7:29

Death and Life, Wisdom and Folly

God enters into Qohelet's reflections in 6:10, right at the hinge of the book of Ecclesiastes. Qohelet refers to God as "the one who is stronger," though this reference is unfortunately obscured by the NRSV plural translation ("those who are stronger"). There is nothing reassuring about God's presence. The austere theological timbre of 6:10–12 is captured by Dietrich Bonhoeffer:

> Life is beyond the realm of figures and ideas, life laughs at every attempt to calculate it, for life comes from God Himself, who cannot be calculated in his plans, who is free to do whatever he pleases.—Life is dark and beyond the grasp of human understanding, so are man's ways and fates. Who understands them? Who interprets them?[1]

God has set the terms for creaturely existence, and human beings are in no position to "dispute" with their Creator (v. 10).

William Brown suggests that what has "already been named" is humanity: "Primal man is formed 'from the dust of the ground,' *'ādām* from the *'ădāmâ* ('ground')."[2] "What human beings are" (v. 10) is dust—fragile, transient creatures who live on borrowed breath. Their words are even less substantial than they are (v. 11)! Arguments, complaints, petitions addressed to God—they are all useless. Along with Bonhoeffer, Qohelet declares that life is dark, and human ways and fates are beyond the reach of creaturely control

1. Sermon on Prov. 16:9, in Dietrich Bonhoeffer, *London 1933–1935, DBW* 13 (Minneapolis: Fortress Press, 2007), 399.

2. William P. Brown, *Ecclesiastes*, Interpretation: A Bible Commentary for Teaching and Preaching (Louisville, KY: Westminster John Knox Press, 2000), 67.

and understanding. Human creatures do not know either how best to order their short lives or what will happen after they die (v. 12). Life cannot be "figured out," much less reconfigured to suit human preferences. At this point in Qohelet's reflections, creaturely joy has disappeared. The only thing left for earthlings to do with their words is to acknowledge God's inexorable presence: "It's a cold and it's a broken Hallelujah."[3]

Though the implied answer to the question in verse 12, "Who knows what is good for mortals?" is "No one," Qohelet proceeds in 7:1–14 to share some proverbial wisdom at least about what is relatively "better" for mortals (vv. 1–3, 5, 8). Earthly life lasts only a "few days" (6:12) and death "is the end of everyone" (7:2). Wisdom cannot overcome death. But Qohelet insists that death can teach us how to live more wisely. Verses 1–6 are divided into three couplets. The first couplet contrasts the day of birth and the day of death. The day of birth is associated with celebration and feasting (v. 2). "Precious ointment" (v. 1) may refer to the practice of anointing newborn infants. Though everyone has both a day of birth and a day of death, Qohelet concludes that the impending day of death is "better." Life at birth is full of hope, but it is naïve and untested. The day of death is associated with mourning but also with a taking stock of one's life and of one's "good name" acquired over a lifetime (vv. 1–2). Death, unlike birth, is instructive for the living if they "will lay it to heart." The prospect of death can reorder life, clarifying what is important and sharpening simple pleasures. In his essay "At the Graveside," Kierkegaard likewise commends an earnestness about death. Its utter finality, its absolute and equalizing power over all people, and the radical uncertainty about its timing make it a powerful teacher for the living. "Death in earnest gives life force as nothing else does; it makes one alert as nothing else does."[4]

The second couplet (vv. 3–4) links wisdom with sorrow and mourning, and folly with laughter and mirth. This is confusing, because "mirth" is the same Hebrew word as the "joy" repeatedly commended by Qohelet (2:26; 5:20; 8:15; 9:7), and 2:26 associates

3. Leonard Cohen, "Hallelujah," *Various Positions* (Columbia Records, 1984).

4. Søren Kierkegaard, "At the Graveside," in *Three Discourses on Imagined Occasions*, *KW* 10 (Princeton, NJ: Princeton University Press, 2009), 83.

> **You think that I am smiling,**
> **but I'm practicing my death-**
> **grin.**
> **I must wear it for a rather long**
> **time.**
>
> Vassar Miller, "Memento Mori," in *If I Had Wheels or Love: Collected Poems of Vassar Miller* (Dallas: Southern Methodist University, 1991), 219.

joy with wisdom and knowledge and pleasing God. By contrast, 7:4 declares that joy ("mirth") is where the heart of fools resides. This contradiction reflects the recognition, in both Ecclesiastes and Proverbs, that joy and wisdom do not always line up. Fools find joy in folly (Prov. 15:21) while the wise recognize that "even in laughter the heart is sad, and the end of joy is grief" (Prov. 14:13). The song of fools spills into Ecclesiastes 7: 5, where it is contrasted with the rebuke of the wise, also a commonplace of Proverbs (cf. 10:17; 13:1; 15:10; 25:12). Qohelet likens the laughter of fools to the loud crackling of burning thorns that quickly fades, producing no heat (7:6).

The foolish mirth that Qohelet criticizes in verses 1–6 seems to be an escapist joy that refuses to face the facts of creaturely life. This joy is characteristic of the beginning of the "esthetic" path that Kierkegaard describes in *Either/Or,* an attempt to "abandon [one] self in joy's infinitude."[5] Rather than plumb life's deeper meaning, the esthete ceaselessly pursues a surface pleasure and gratification. However, this glib cheerfulness is soon overtaken by a numbing boredom and despair. By contrast, the joy Qohelet commends is summoned "in the face of all the facts."[6] People who come through a major trauma or face a terminal illness sometimes exhibit this kind of joy: a gratitude for simple pleasures accompanied by unflinching honesty about life's threats and risks. For the wise, a glad heart can coexist with a sad countenance (v. 3).

Verses 7–10 address threats to pursuing what is "better" in creaturely existence. Suffering and oppression can crush human spirits and even drive people to madness (v. 7a). When "what is" and "what ought to be" are fundamentally and persistently at odds with each other, human beings can experience such dissonance that the world stops making sense. As Susan Neiman notes, pervasive evil "shatters

5. Søren Kierkegaard, *Either/Or, KW* 3, pt. 1 (Princeton, NJ: Princeton University Press, 1987), 41.
6. Wendell Berry, "Manifesto: The Mad Farmer Liberation Front," in *The Selected Poems of Wendell Berry* (Berkeley, CA: Counterpoint, 1998), 87.

our trust in the world," paralyzing both our moral understanding and our moral agency.[7] Evil can also suck us in, tempting us to acts that over time warp our moral dispositions (v. 7b). Pride and anger are threats as well. The proud (v. 8b) approach the world with a sense of entitlement, assured from the start that everything will go their way. When it does not, they fly into a rage at the world's recalcitrance (v. 9). By contrast, the patient are willing to see a thing through to the end (v. 8), knowing that life contains adversity as well as prosperity (v. 14). They do not indulge in foolish nostalgia for the "good old days" (v. 10), because it accomplishes nothing. Within Qohelet's larger cosmology, there is no reason to think that times are getting permanently worse: there is nothing new under the sun (1:9–11; 3:15; 6:10). Prosperity follows adversity like day follows night.

Trouble is endemic to earthly existence. Qohelet holds out no revolutionary hopes for a fundamental reordering of society that will overcome adversity. Instead, the wise find ways to cope with it. Nicholas Wolterstorff, reflecting on his sense of helplessness in the wake of his son's death, observes,

> I have learned coping. We live in a time and place where, over and over, when confronted with something unpleasant we pursue not coping but overcoming. Often we succeed. Most of humanity has not enjoyed and does not enjoy such luxury. Death shatters our illusion that we can make do without coping.[8]

According to Qohelet, human wisdom cannot make do without coping. Wisdom is not a panacea: it does not always "make straight our paths" (Prov. 3:6). Like money, wisdom brings protection and advantage (vv. 11–12), but it provides no guarantees.

Qohelet's reflections seem a long way away from Woman Wisdom's confident declarations in Proverbs about the benefits of obtaining wisdom (cf. Prov. 8:1–36). In Ecclesiastes, as Roland Murphy notes, wisdom has "become less assured of herself." However, Murphy observes that it is perhaps better to say that "wisdom

7. Susan Neiman, *Evil in Modern Thought: An Alternative History of Philosophy* (Princeton, NJ: Princeton University Press, 2004), 9.
8. Nicholas Wolterstorff, *Lament for a Son* (Grand Rapids: Eerdmans, 1987), 72.

herself, by her own strength and with her own weapons, . . . is correcting her own principles." From this perspective, Ecclesiastes is "continuing the emphasis on the *limitations* of wisdom, which are certainly experienced and also articulated" in Proverbs (cf. Prov. 16:1, 2, 9; 19:21; 20:24; 21:30–31).[9]

The reason for Qohelet's somber judgment on human wisdom is as much theological as experiential. While the word *crooked* always has a negative valence in Proverbs (cf. 8:8; 21:8; 28:6, 18), in Ecclesiastes crookedness is part of the world that God has made (7:13). Riskiness and uncertainty are steady state features of our existence, and no human life eludes a measure of terror, disaster, and heartbreak (7:14). We cannot straighten life out or create our own utopia. Following the *New American Bible* translation of 7:14c, "so that no one may find the least fault with [God]," Qohelet's theological point is that the Creator's ways are beyond human judgment and manipulation; we are in no position to "dispute" with God (6:10). As Luther advises, "Be calm and let things happen as they happen, for they will happen as they happen."[10] The best we can do is to take life as it comes from God's hands, rejoicing in its gifts and coping with its adversity.

Having undercut the difference between wisdom and folly (6:8) in guaranteeing human flourishing, Qohelet now questions wisdom's foundational alliance with righteousness. Qohelet's confidence about the moral order of the universe has been severely tested by the empirical disconnect between righteous human actions and their outcomes. As Roland Murphy puts it, "It is a beautiful idea that evil corrupts, that good is somehow diffusive of itself." [11] But is this the way the world in fact works? "How many holes did one have to dig for others before falling in oneself? (Prov. 26:27; 28:10)."[12] What Qohelet observes turns the expectations of conventional wisdom upside down: righteous people die young, and wicked people

9. Roland E. Murphy, "Qohelet's 'Quarrel' with the Fathers," in *From Faith to Faith*, ed. Dikran Y. Hadidian (Pittsburgh: Pickwick Press, 1979), 236.
10. Martin Luther, *Ecclesiastes, Song of Solomon, and the Last Words of David*, *LW* 15, trans. J. Pelikan (Saint Louis: Concordia, 1969), 119.
11. Roland E. Murphy, *Proverbs*, Word Biblical Commentary (Nashville: Thomas Nelson, 1998), 265.
12. Ibid., 265.

Even if it is true, say, that career criminals have a higher mortality than most law-abiding citizens, when people see even a few crooks growing old and rich, they may conclude that there is no justice. And what does it matter if offenders eventually do meet the death due them? It is no deterrent to crime when an eighty-year-old mob boss is gunned down (or, worse, expires of illness) after a life of prosperity.

Michael V. Fox, *A Time To Tear Down and a Time to Build Up: A Rereading of Ecclesiastes* (Grand Rapids: Eerdmans, 1999), 58.

live long happy lives (7:15). To paraphrase 6:8, "What advantage do the righteous have over the wicked?"

Qohelet's radical advice is not to overdo wisdom and righteousness (7:16). At the same time, following traditional wisdom teaching (cf. Prov. 10:2), Qohelet insists that avoiding folly and wickedness is also advisable (7:17). The whole point of Israel's wisdom traditions is to figure out what is good for human creatures to do (Eccl. 2:3), but Qohelet finds no algorithm for guaranteeing a prosperous and happy life. Neither righteousness nor wickedness can guarantee human security. In fact, an excess of either is dangerous. Being too righteous is a recipe for self-deception and despair. Being too wicked leads to self-destruction. The only recourse is to fear God (7:18). Fearing God "cannot be called security nor can it ensure security. It is simply a basic attitude that one must have, no matter one's fate."[13]

Martin Luther's interpretation of the difficult sayings in verses 16–18 connects them with verses 19–22 that immediately follow. According to Luther, Ecclesiastes is not addressing personal righteousness but rather *political* righteousness. The counsel not to be too righteous or too wicked is addressed to persons in political authority, who must decide how to govern. Luther encourages rulers to acknowledge the "lengthy catalog of vices" on their own résumés and then say, "Look, I myself am still unrighteous, and yet I am tolerated by God and am not banished by people. Then why am I so carried away with fury that I harshly require of others what I do not achieve myself?"[14] No one on earth can claim perfect

13. Roland E. Murphy, *Ecclesiastes*, Word Biblical Commentary (Dallas: Word Books, 1992), 70.
14. Luther, *Eccesiastes*, 122.

righteousness (v. 20; cf. 1 John 1:8), and demanding perfection from others leads to a harsh forcefulness that is both unwise and hypocritical (v. 19). Good rulers have a thick skin and a keen awareness of their own shortcomings (vv. 21–22). On the other hand, permitting rampant wickedness is also bad governance: "It is good to overlook some things, but not to neglect all things."[15] Life in the earthly city, in Luther's view, requires modest expectations about the success of wisdom's endeavors: "You are foolish if you either presume that you alone can accomplish everything or despair of everything when it does not go your way."[16]

The attempt to "be too righteous" (v. 15) is characteristic of the "ethical" path that Kierkegaard describes in the second part of *Either/Or,* in which social duties and obligations are confidently taken up as the guarantee of a worthwhile life. However, like Qohelet, Kierkegaard finds it impossible for human beings "to do good without ever sinning" (v. 20). Human beings can never meet their moral obligations perfectly, no matter how hard they try. The pretense of being perfectly righteous and thus deserving of social and divine approval leads only to despair. The paradoxical consolation that Kierkegaard comes to at the end of this ethical path is that "in relation to God we are always in the wrong."[17]

In 7:23–29, Qohelet admits abject failure in the quest for wisdom. The whole passage plays on the relationship between seeking and finding, a traditional trope of wisdom (cf. Prov. 2:4; 8:17). But what Qohelet seeks—"wisdom and the sum of things" (v. 25)—is never found. And what Qohelet finds—"the woman who is a trap" (v. 26)—is not what was sought. Some interpreters, and even some Bible translators, have gone on a misogynist field day with verse 26. The *New Jerusalem Bible* ignores the definite article *hā* ("*the* woman") and translates the verse as a general statement about all women: "And I find woman more bitter than Death, she is a snare, her heart is a net, and her arms are chains. The man who is pleasing to God eludes her, but the sinner is captured by her." In his interpretation of the verse, Luther launches into a tirade against the woman

15. Ibid., 123.
16. Ibid., 124.
17. Kierkegaard, *Either/Or, KW* 3, pt. 2, (Princeton, NJ: Princeton University Press, 1987), 339.

who "arrogates wisdom and ruling power to herself." A woman, in Luther's view, is created by God "to care for children and to bring them up in an honest and godly way, and to be subject to the man." "Domineering women" who forsake their created purpose are a snare and more bitter than death.[18]

However, as C. L. Seow notes, "given the context, with its focus on wisdom and folly, it seems unlikely that Qohelet is suddenly introducing the topic of women in general, or even of a particular type of women."[19] It is better to read this section in line with Proverbs' female personifications of both Folly and Wisdom. The woman whom Ecclesiastes describes as "more bitter than death," her heart like "snares and nets" and her hands like "fetters" (v. 26), is reminiscent of Woman Folly in Proverbs (2:16–19; 5:20–23; 7:21–27). The woman who is utterly elusive (Prov. 7:28), by contrast, is Woman Wisdom. It should be remembered that wisdom is not easy to find even in Proverbs. The search for Woman Wisdom can be frustrated (Prov. 1:28), and the "woman of strength" in Proverbs 31 who incarnates wisdom is extremely valuable precisely because she is difficult to find (31:10). In Ecclesiastes, the quest for Woman Wisdom is a failure of almost comical proportions. Like a madcap scene from a Shakespearean comedy, Woman Folly chases after Qohelet, who is desperately seeking Woman Wisdom. Only Woman Wisdom can deliver Qohelet from Woman Folly's snares, but she is nowhere to be found.[20] The search for wisdom ends up empty-handed. As Johanna van Wijk-Bos notes, "There is in the end no counterpart to the woman who is a snare and brings destruction, woman folly, . . . at least not that Qohelet can find."[21]

There are puzzling grammatical issues of gender in this passage. In verse 27, the verb *says* is in the feminine form, as if the speaker, Qohelet, were a woman (in 1:2 and 12:8 the masculine verb form is used). What, if anything, should be made of that? The word

18. Luther, *Ecclesiastes*, 130–31.
19. C. L. Seow, *Ecclesiastes: A New Translation with Introduction and Commentary* (New York: Doubleday, 1997), 262.
20. I am indebted to the analysis in Seow, *Ecclesiastes*, 68–69.
21. Johanna van Wijk-Bos, "Reading Qohelet: Finding a Woman among a Thousand" (paper presented at the International Meeting of the Society of Biblical Literature, London, July 5, 2011).

translated "man" in verse 28 is the Hebrew *'ādām*, which everywhere else in Ecclesiastes denotes humanity as a whole. If verse 28 is to be read as a derogatory contrast between men and women, why is this generic term used? Seow ascribes verse 28b to a misogynist copyist. Van Wijk-Bos suggests the following translation: "One human being in a thousand I have found, and woman in all these I have not found."[22] She invites contemporary readers to find in this verse an invitation to free themselves from the kind of gender essentialism exhibited by Luther and others. Perhaps this essentialism is one of the "schemes" devised by human foolishness (v. 29). Whereas Qohelet acknowledges some crookedness in God's work in verse 13, here it is affirmed that God is not to blame for human failures in wisdom, because God has created humanity "straightforward." Human schemes "are rooted in false and self-destructive 'accountings' of life and conduct."[23] Yet the explanation for humanity's persistent attempts to live at cross purposes to God's intentions is "far off, and deep, very deep" (v. 24), well beyond the reach of human wisdom. Like Augustine, Ecclesiastes laments the absurdity of the human condition: we are "in love with [our] own ruin, in love with decay."[24]

22. Ibid.
23. Brown, *Ecclesiastes*, 84.
24. Augustine, *Confessions* 2.9, trans. Maria Boulding (Hyde Park, NY: New City Press, 1997), 68.

8:1–17
God and the King

The Hebrew text of Ecclesiastes 8 is difficult, and English translations vary significantly. The chapter begins with the rhetorical questions "Who is wise?" and "Who knows?" that are answered in verse 7 by "no one knows" and clinched at the end of the chapter by the insistence that even the wise (who claim to know) do not really know (v. 17). Joseph Khalil interprets the opening verses of chapter 8 to be Qoheleth's response to overly confident preachers, noting preachers' special share in "the persistent human desire to overstep one's bounds with God."[1] Khalil points out that the NRSV translation of verse 1b, "Wisdom makes one's face shine," leaves out the word *human*. According to the Hebrew, it is human wisdom that makes the face shine. Khalil suggests that Qohelet is being ironic in contrasting bogus human wisdom with the wisdom that comes from God. Wisdom that is not from God is vanity and will perish. Human wisdom can shine with a false pride, but only God's shining face (cf. Num. 6:25–26) is the source of genuine assurance and blessedness.[2]

The dangers of overly confident preaching are felt particularly in the homiletic temptation to discern God's retributive justice in situations of human suffering. In this respect, some preachers seem to have the whole divine road map spread out in front of them and so are in a position to give the rest of us confident progress reports. Qohelet, by contrast, reminds us that wisdom about God's mysterious ways in the world regularly eludes us. "Even though those who

1. Joseph S. Khalil, "Qoheleth's Response to the Overconfident Preacher: A New Approach to Ecclesiastes 8:1–3" in *Word and World* 32, no. 3 (Summer 2012): 277–85, quoting 278.
2. Ibid.

are wise claim to know, they cannot find it out" (v. 17). In particular, Qohelet holds preachers back from theologies that reflexively look for sin as the explanation for every occasion of human suffering. In the Bible, that malignant theology surfaces among Job's friends and even among Jesus' own disciples, who asked him, "'Who sinned, this man or his parents, that he was born blind?'" (John 9:2). In our own time, we hear it over and over again in the face of everything from hurricanes to terrorist attacks to the HIV/AIDS pandemic. In chapter 8, Qohelet pulls the rug out from under this overly confident theology, insisting that the "how" and the "when" of God's retributive justice elude human understanding.

Some interpreters read "the king" in verses 2–4 as a reference to God, but it is probably better to see Qohelet as drawing uncomfortable parallels between the arbitrary power of a human despot and the unfathomable ways of a sovereign God (cf. Prov. 16:14; 19:12; 20:21; 24:21–22). Dealings with both require prudence. Contrary to the NRSV translation, a more plausible meaning of verse 2 is that one must obey the king "*in the same manner* that one would keep an oath sworn to God."[3] Verse 3 presents more textual difficulties. The "the matter [that] is unpleasant" may refer to seditious activity against the king that could result in one's death. Qohelet's advice is to be prudent and avoid rash actions (Seow translates verse 3a as "Do not persist in a harmful thing"). The reason for caution is that the king "does whatever he pleases" (v. 3b), a phrase that occurs elsewhere in the Bible with reference to God's omnipotence (Ps. 115:3; 135:6). No one with any sense dares interrogate the king and question his actions, saying, "What are you doing?" (v. 4; cf. Job 9:12). Verse 4a literally says, "The word of the king is power." Keeping the king's command is therefore wise even when the command is unjust, so as to "meet no harm" (v. 5) from the king's wrathful punishment.

There is no single "biblical view" of the appropriate relation of people of faith to political authority. John Mansford Prior notes that "Ecclesiastes aims for a practical ethic adequate for repressive and uncertain times. The sage aims to be supremely adequate rather than

3. C. L. Seow, *Ecclesiastes: A New Translation with Introduction and Commentary* (New York: Doubleday, 1997), 279.

prophetically ideal, for striving after ideals is futile."[4] The quiet realism of Qohelet stands in contrast to the apostle Paul's insistence that political authority has been "instituted by God" and that to disobey it is tantamount to disobeying God (Rom. 13:1–5). On the other hand, Qohelet's perspective also contrasts with the call for courageous resistance against the blasphemous political authority of the "beast" in Revelation 13:1–18. Ecclesiastes urges a watchful resilience that avoids extremist words and actions and hopes for the ultimate triumph of God's justice.

The king's arbitrary and oppressive control over his subjects cannot be challenged in the present, but Qohelet holds out hope for a future reckoning. The point of verse 5b is not that the wise themselves "will know the time and way" of this reckoning, but rather that the wise trust God to render judgment in *God's* own time and way (cf. 3:16–22). When troubles lie heavy on human life and political resistance is dangerous and futile, the only consolation is that God will act at a time and in a manner of God's choosing (v. 6). Like the king, God cannot be questioned or second-guessed. Even the wise cannot predict how God will bring justice or what it will look like (v. 7). Yet God's power trumps that of the king. The power of the king over his subjects may seem absolute, but even the king does not have power over life and death (v. 8). (The word translated "wind" in the NRSV can also be translated "spirit" or "breath of life.") The most powerful king will one day lose his battle with death (v. 8b). He will not emerge victorious over this "last enemy" (1 Cor. 15:26). The king's wicked attempts to secure himself by abusing his authority over others will ultimately not deliver him (v. 9).

Qohelet, like the sages of Proverbs, trusts that eventually God's justice will triumph. One day, "it will be well with those who fear God" (v. 12), and "it will not be well with the wicked" (v. 13). But in the meantime, all Qohelet can see is injustice and oppression. Though they do not deserve a dignified burial, the wicked are honored in their death as well as in their life. Job likewise complains about the respect paid to the wicked at their death (Job 21:32–33). Seow speculates that "in the time of Qohelet, some people who were

4. John Mansford Prior, "Ecclesiastes," in *Global Bible Commentary*, ed. Daniel Patte (Nashville: Abingdon Press, 2004), 177.

considered important . . . were publicly eulogized at the synagogues before they were buried."[5] Meanwhile, the righteous are honored neither in death nor in life. The wheels of justice turn so slowly that evil runs rampant (v. 11). The wicked do evil "a hundred times" and continue to prosper (v. 12). Righteous people are punished, and the wicked are rewarded (v. 14). With gritted teeth, Qohelet stands by Israel's traditional wisdom that those who fear God will flourish and the wicked will perish, even when reality stands in stark contradiction to this hope (vv. 12b–13; cf. pp. 71–73, "Further Reflections: Preaching on Proverbs 10–15 without Sounding Like Job's Friends"). Life isn't fair, and there is not much that humanity can do about that. The injustice of the world cannot be resolved or removed in a permanent way by human efforts. In the midst of this frustration and heartache, Qohelet once again commends the simple pleasures that accompany human work (v. 15). This enjoyment is not a hedonism born of despair but a humble receptivity to God's gifts. God does not deliver justice on humanity's schedule, but God remains the giver of life and bestows creaturely pleasures for our enjoyment. Enjoying life's simple gifts is certainly preferable to wearing ourselves out trying to comprehend the means and timing of God's work (vv. 16–17).

> **You do not know what God intends to do to you or to someone else, whether tomorrow you will die or live or get sick or what other evil may befall you. If we had knowledge of God's prolonging or shortening our lives, we would be very badly off in every way.**
>
> Martin Luther, *Ecclesiastes, Song of Songs, and the Last Words of David*, 173.

Acknowledging our creaturely ignorance and limitations and simply resting in God is difficult in a culture like ours that prizes measurable progress toward goals. Even religious communities are not immune to these pressures. In 1965, in a rather ironic meditation on his life as a monk, Thomas Merton observed,

> The monastic life as a whole is a hot medium. Hot with words like *must*, *ought*, and *should*. Communities are devoted to high-definition projects: "making it all clear!" The clearer it gets the

5. Seow, *Ecclesiastes*, 285.

> clearer it has to be made. It branches out. You have to keep clearing the branches. The more branches you cut back, the more branches grow. For one you cut, you get three more. On the end of each branch is a big question mark.[6]

Like monastics and overly confident preachers, religious people in general often have a hard time accepting the limits of their wisdom and insight into the things of God. But according to Qohelet, "the inability to know is the God-ordained plight of the human race."[7]

This plight of not knowing is key to the "religious" path that Kierkegaard explores in the last part of *Either/Or*. Faith in God exceeds the limits of our intellect—it is absurd. Yet faith also makes a new way of life possible. The person of faith fully acknowledges the sadness and pain of the world and grasps the hope for transcending it. But faith then makes possible a return to the finitude of earthly existence with new zest for life's ordinary pleasures. Trust in God runs deeper than the pain of the world and the frustrations of our inability to know. This trust makes it possible to receive God's gift of joy in the midst of everything. As Kierkegaard notes in a journal entry, "It takes moral courage to grieve; it takes religious courage to rejoice."[8]

6. Patrick Hart and Jonathan Montaldo, eds., *The Intimate Merton: His Life from His Journals* (San Francisco: HarperSanFrancisco, 1999), 243–44.
7. Khalil, "Qoheleth's Response," 278.
8. Søren Kierkegaard, *Søren Kierkegaard's Journals and Papers*, vol. 2 (Bloomington: Indiana University Press, 1967), 493.

9:1–18
Earthly Joy

The syntax of verse 1 is difficult, and it is not clear whether the source of "love or hate" is God or humanity. If "love or hate" is read as a reference to the hidden motives behind human deeds, it anticipates the reference to human love, hate, and envy in verse 6. This reading reflects Qohelet's skepticism about estimates of human wisdom and righteousness: we can judge only appearances, and we do not have access to what drives human behavior. However, most commentators think that "love or hate" refers to the indeterminacy of God's attitude toward humanity, and this commentary will follow this theologically problematic reading. "The righteous and the wise and their deeds" are all in God's hands, but it is not clear from a human perspective whether God regards them with love or hatred. Qohelet portrays God as terrifyingly inscrutable. In the Bible God is occasionally said to hate evildoers (Ps. 5:5), but the suggestion that God hates the righteous flouts one of the most basic biblical assumptions (Ps. 5:12; 32:10–11; 34:15–17; 146:8; 1 Pet. 3:12).

Qohelet refuses to dismiss this deeply unsettling possibility. Rampant injustice and universal human mortality conspire to undermine human assurance of God's love for the righteous: the wicked and righteous do not get what they each deserve in life, and then "the same fate comes to all" (v. 2). Based on what Qohelet has seen, how is confidence in God's love for the righteous reasonable? The people of Israel reach the same conclusion in the wilderness, when they grumble, "'It is because the Lord hates us that he has brought us out of the land of Egypt, to hand us over to the Amorites to destroy us'" (Deut. 1:27). But they are immediately given counterevidence and admonished for their lack of trust (Deut. 1:29–33), whereas Qohelet's doubts about God's character remain unchallenged.

The righteous and the wicked, the religiously scrupulous and the slackers, all suffer the same fate. The earnest religious and moral distinctions of Proverbs, briefly rehearsed in Ecclesiastes 8:12–13, are once again deconstructed here. What happens to people in the end is not a function of their degree of virtue or religious observance. Goodness is not rewarded, and evil is not punished. Qohelet pronounces this an outrageous "evil" but seems resigned to it. Unlike the writers of the Psalms, Qohelet issues no passionate calls for God to intervene on the side of justice. Human life under the sun is a moral chaos, and Qohelet foresees no life beyond in which everything gets sorted out and tidied up (see pp. 204–7, "Further Discussion: Death and Life Everlasting").

The word in verse 4 translated "hope" in the NRSV is better rendered "trust" or "assurance" (cf. 2 Kgs. 18:19), but it is a bitter consolation: what the living can trust is that they too will die. Given this reality, living the life of a dog, a despised animal in the ancient Near East, is better than being a dead lion. The sensibilities of the pious are further offended in verse 5, with the assertion that there is no more reward for the dead and that "even the memory of them is lost." This last claim denies one of the profoundest features of the Jewish and Christian ways of being in the world: the call to remember. In a radical statement of the absurd ephemerality of human existence, Qohelet strips away even the traditional consolations of human society. We can hope to leave no memory or legacy behind us, either through our children or through our work. In death we stand alone and forgotten, bereft of "any share in all that happens under the sun" (v. 6; cf. 1:11).

Surprisingly, what follows Qohelet's most despairing assessment yet of the human condition is an equally strong positive exhortation for how to live in the present (vv. 7–10). In one of the rare imperative passages in the book, Qohelet once again urges the enjoyment of whatever fleeting moments of pleasure come along (cf. 3:12, 22; 5:19; 8:15). People are to eat, drink, and be merry, assured that "God has long ago approved what you do" (v. 7). As Martin Luther sums it up, "As long as we are obliged to live in the midst of such perversity, it is best for us to be happy and relaxed." Luther also finds the assurance of "a gracious God, who approves our works and actions," to be a soothing balm for people of faith who have despaired of attaining righteousness and wisdom.[1]

There is no definite article before *'iššâ*, the Hebrew word translated "wife" in the NRSV, so it is possible to render Qohelet's phrase in verse 9 as "enjoy life with a woman you love." Some interpreters see an allusion to the exploits of Ecclesiastes' purported author Solomon, who "loved many foreign women" (1 Kgs. 11:1; cf. Eccl.2:8), but it seems unlikely that even a renegade sage like Qohelet would advocate casual promiscuity. Whether the love Qohelet is advocating is marital or not, this phrase supports the exegetical decision not to read 7:26–28 as a derogatory comment on actual women (see pp. 46–47, commentary on 7:1–27). Life in relationship is part of the enjoyment God intends for human creatures.

Qohelet's commendation of celebration, feasting, the extravagance of white garments, and joy in relationships finds parallels in other ancient Near Eastern literature, notably the famous epic poem *Gilgamesh*. In that ancient Babylonian tale, Gilgamesh grieves the death of his friend Enkidu and confronts the prospect of his own mortality. He receives this advice from the wise woman Siduri:

> Thou, Gilgamesh, let full be thy belly,
> Make thou merry by day and by night.
> Of each day make thou a feast of rejoicing,
> Day and night dance thou and play!
> Let thy garments be sparkling fresh,
> Thy head be washed, bathe thou in water.
> Pay heed to the little one that holds on to thy hand,
> Let thy spouse delight in thy bosom!
> For this is the task of [humanity].[2]

Within the ancient Near Eastern context, Qohelet sounds a distinctive note by urging also the enjoyment of work (v. 10)—not joy

1. Martin Luther, *Ecclesiastes, Song of Solomon, and the Last Words of David, LW* 15, trans. J. Pelikan (Saint Louis: Concordia, 1969), 148.
2. J. B. Pritchard, ed., *Ancient Near Eastern Texts Relating to the Old Testament* (Princeton, NJ: Princeton University Press, 1969), 90.

in the successes and rewards of work, which have already shown to be unreliable and short-lived, but joy in work itself. Freed of the pretensions and anxieties that often accompany human striving, hearers are urged to apply themselves to the work at hand with all their might, because the earthly time in which to do work is itself a fleeting, precious gift.

Kierkegaard likewise distinguishes "incidental work" from "essential work." The first is of value only if it is successfully completed. But essential work is part of "the living of each day as if it were the last and also the first in a long life." This work is worth doing "whether one is granted a lifetime to complete it well or only a brief time to have begun it well."[3] Both Qohelet and Kierkegaard remove work from the realm of vain ambition and grudging duty and recast it as an integral part of a joyful openness to what earthly life offers. It is one of the tasks and joys of creaturely existence that are absent in Sheol (v. 10).

Qohelet's unabashed commendation of creaturely pleasure in verses 7–10 may seem out of tune with other voices in the biblical canon and the Christian tradition. Isaiah mocks those who blithely proclaim, "Let us eat and drink, for tomorrow we die," heedless of God's impending judgment (Isa. 22:13), and the apostle Paul quotes this verse from Isaiah to criticize those who deny the resurrection of the dead (1 Cor. 15:32). Some Christian commentators reflect their deep reservations about Qohelet's celebration of the ordinary pleasures of human life by giving a libertine reading of verses 7–10. The fourth-century biblical commentator Jerome, for example, who wrote his commentary on Ecclesiastes to provoke "the saintly Blesilla" to a contempt of earthly existence, gives this sardonic paraphrase:

> Walk about adorned in white garments, anoint your head, embrace with joy whatever delights your femininity, pursue this vain, brief life with a vain, brief relish, quickly seize whatever it is that pleases you lest it perish, for you will have nothing more beyond this that you currently enjoy.[4]

3. Søren Kierkegaard, "At the Graveside," in *Three Discourses on Imagined Occasions*, *KW* 10 (Princeton, NJ: Princeton University Press, 2009), 96.
4. Jerome, *Commentary on Ecclesiastes*, in J. Robert Wright, ed., *Ancient Christian Commentary*

Jerome here reflects the larger Christian and classical antiquity tradition of *contemptus mundi*, "contempt for the world." In Christian versions of it, hope in the resurrection is expressed by pursuing an ascetic, contemplative life that disdains the world of the flesh.

By contrast, Dietrich Bonhoeffer, writing from a Nazi prison and facing the realization that he would not be released, drew on Ecclesiastes to *resist* the temptations of the *contemptus mundi* tradition. Rather than "rushing a few steps ahead" to the joys of resurrected life, Bonhoeffer insists that Christians are to "remain in step with God" and "love God in our *life* and in the good things God gives us." Bonhoeffer continues,

> To say it clearly—that a person in the arms of his wife should long for the hereafter is, to put it mildly, tasteless and in any case is not God's will. One should find and love God in what God directly gives us; if it pleases God to allow us to enjoy an overwhelming earthly happiness, then one shouldn't be more pious than God and allow this happiness to be gnawed away through arrogant thoughts and challenges and wild religious fantasy that is never satisfied with what God's gives.[5]

Bonhoeffer appeals to Qohelet's insistence that God "has made everything suitable for its time" (3:11) to counsel a genuine gratitude for "earthly happiness in God" that does not deny Christian hope and even longing for eternal life with God.

If there is one verse that sums up the whole book of Ecclesiastes, it is verse 11. This verse gathers up all the desirable attributes that are supposed to benefit human life—physical prowess, wisdom, and skill—and declares that none of these guarantees human flourishing. They are not to be counted on because "time and chance happen to [us] all." We are helpless in the face of cosmic contingencies. Like fish in a cruel net and birds in a snare (v. 12), we never see calamity coming until it is too late. Qohelet does not repudiate human

---

on Scripture: Proverbs, Ecclesiastes, Song of Solomon (Downers Grove, IL: InterVarsity Press, 2005), 263. Martin Luther inveighs against this tradition of reading Ecclesiastes in *Ecclesiastes, Song of Solomon, and the Last Words of David*, 4.

5. Dec. 18, 1943, letter to Eberhard Bethge, in Dietrich Bonhoeffer, *Letters and Papers from Prison, DBW* 8 (Minneapolis: Fortress Press, 2010), 228–29.

wisdom in verses 11–18 but clearly warns us not to expect too much from it.[6]

Qohelet's insistence that time and chance happen to everyone is not what either the sages of ancient Israel or the strategic planners of today want to hear. Human beings like to think that their creaturely life is within their control. As Reinhold Niebuhr writes,

> Modern man lacks the humility to accept the fact that the whole drama of history is enacted in a frame of meaning too large for human comprehension or management. It is a drama in which fragmentary meanings can be discerned within a penumbra of mystery; and in which specific duties and responsibilities can be undertaken within a vast web of relations which are beyond our powers.[7]

Qohelet affirms the importance of human wisdom and skill but insists that they are not up to the challenge of fully understanding and managing life. If we think they are, we are like fish about to be "taken in a cruel net" (v. 12). Wisdom is needed to acknowledge the limits of wisdom.

Qohelet's reflections in these verses have important implications for ethics and social policy. In a "regular verbs" world, it is easy to assume that people get what they deserve. The battle *is* to the strong, and riches *are* to the intelligent (v. 11). From this perspective, the best political course is to give people the freedom and opportunity to strive for their own well-being. However, the "deeper wisdom" of Qohelet (see pp. 87–104, commentary on Prov. 16:1–22:16) insists that it is dangerous to overestimate our ability to control and manage our lives. "No one can anticipate the time of disaster" (v. 12). This suggests a rather different approach to public policy. As Robert Shiller comments,

> Overcoming the false sense that each individual's fate is fully deserved is vital, not only because it inures us to our own risks but also because it prevents us from appreciating the kinds of policies that society needs to adopt to deal with these risks

6. Michael V. Fox, *A Time to Tear Down and a Time to Build Up: A Rereading of Ecclesiastes* (Grand Rapids: Eerdmans, 1999), 92.
7. Reinhold Niebuhr, *Irony of American History* (New York: Charles Scribner's Sons, 1952), 88.

> and blinds us to the arbitrariness and absurdity of the misfortunes that others face. Only then can we really confront those risks and take timely actions against them.[8]

Following the deeper wisdom of Qohelet, public policy must leave room for both the regularities of wise actions and their consequences *and* for the caprice and absurdity endemic to human life.

In verses 13–16 Qohelet tells yet another wry parable about the (limited) benefits of wisdom (cf. 4:13–16; 5:13–17; 6:13–16). In telling parables, Qohelet engages in what Kierkegaard called indirect communication, a mode of communication whose purpose is to "deceive the hearer into the truth"[9] by inviting her to enter into a story that slyly unsettles her assumptions. Qohelet uses parables to gain critical leverage on the commonplaces of Israel's wisdom traditions. As in the parable in 4:13–16, wisdom is pitted against political might. In chapter 9, a poor wise man is up against a great king who lays siege to his little city. The NRSV translates verse 15b in the indicative: "He by his wisdom delivered the city." However, Seow suggests a more conditional rendering that fits better with verses 15c–16: "He by his wisdom *might have* delivered the city."[10] Had anyone listened to the poor wise man, had the townsfolk not despised his wisdom, the city could have been delivered. Qohelet maintains that it is better to heed quiet words of the wise than to listen to the foolish bellowing of the powerful (v. 17). Wisdom is better than brute force (v. 18a). But the sad fact of the matter is that wisdom is often impotent against the world's folly and violence: it takes only "one bungler" to "destroy much good" (v. 18b). Tearing down is easier than building up. Hurting others is easier than healing them. The hearer of the parable, expecting to have her assumptions about the benefits of wisdom reinforced, is left disconcerted and saddened. In a sane world, "wisdom is better than might" (v. 16), but unfortunately that is not the world in which Qohelet lives. "Tragic failure seems to be wisdom's lot."[11]

8. Robert J. Shiller, *The New Financial Order* (Princeton, NJ: Princeton University Press, 2003), 45.
9. Søren Kierkegaard, *Søren Kierkegaard's Journals and Papers*, vol. 1 (Bloomington: Indiana University Press, 1967), 274, 288.
10. C. L. Seow, *Ecclesiastes: A New Translation with Introduction and Commentary* (New York: Doubleday, 1997), 310.
11. William P. Brown, *Ecclesiastes*, Interpretation: A Bible Commentary for Teaching and Preaching (Louisville, KY: Westminster John Knox Press, 2000), 97.

10:1–20

Collected Sayings

Chapter 10 is a hodgepodge of "collected sayings" (12:11) reminiscent of Proverbs. This is the only chapter in the book of Ecclesiastes in which the ubiquitous word *hebel*, translated *vanity* in the NRSV, does not appear. Verse 1 is the source of the English phrase "the fly in the ointment." Qohelet's point is similar to that of 9:18: a little folly can corrupt and ruin much "wisdom and honor." Right and left are not neutral distinctions in the Bible. As soon as we find out that the Benjaminite leader Ehud is left-handed (Judg. 3:15), we anticipate the treachery that follows (Judg. 3:21–23). It is no accident that the unfortunate goats end up on the left hand of God in Matthew's parable (Matt. 25:31–36). Likewise, here in verse 2, the wise go to the right, and the heart of the fool inclines to the left. Qohelet's point is that there is a visible, intractable difference between the wise and the foolish that is evident to everyone, even when fools are simply walking down the street (v. 3).

Verses 4–7 reprise the topic of wise behavior in the presence of rulers (cf. 8:2–5). It is better to respond to the ruler's anger with composure than to flee in terror (v. 4). Appeasement is the wise strategy for underlings (cf. Prov. 16:14). Qohelet next launches into a lament about an upside-down world from a distinctly aristocratic point of view. While the rich and wise are supposed to occupy the "high places" in society, and the poor and foolish, the "low places," what Qohelet observes instead is the reign of folly and the social humiliation of the rich (v. 6). Slaves enjoy the majesty of traveling by horseback while princes walk on foot (v. 7; cf. Prov. 19:10; 30:22). Qohelet has already unsettled the traditional alliances between wealth and power, on the one hand, and wisdom on the other (4:13–16; 9:13–18) but still finds the overturning of social hierarchies galling. Other biblical passages will celebrate these kinds of social reversal as good news for the poor and oppressed (cf. 1 Sam. 2:1–10; Luke 1:46–55).

A series of proverbs in verses 8–9 lift up everyday disasters: falling into a pit, getting a snakebite, being hurt by a heavy stone or log. The first, verse 8a, about falling into a pit one has dug plays on a common wisdom metaphor for getting one's just deserts (cf. Prov. 26:27). The reader may expect that the proverbs that follow will also reinforce this sense of moral order: as you sow, so shall you reap. Instead, Qohelet uses these proverbs to reinforce the unsettling message of human susceptibility to "time and chance" (v. 11). The ordinary routines of life can bring sudden calamity, even for the wise and righteous. "Wisdom helps one to succeed" (v. 10c) by following sensible precautions like sharpening one's tools (vv. 10a–b), but it provides no guarantees. Snake charmers are helpful too, but they are of little use to the one who has been bitten by a snake "before it is charmed" (v. 11). Once again, the conclusion is that life cannot be secured by our own efforts.

The contrast between wise and foolish speech, another wisdom commonplace, dominates verses 12–15. Verses 12–14a are reminiscent of similar injunctions in Proverbs (12:6, 13; 10:8, 14). Fools expend great amounts of energy babbling about what will happen when they know nothing, not even the way to town (v. 15). By contrast, the wise are circumspect. They refrain from empty words, not pretending to know what the future will bring. Only fools are "wise in their own eyes" (cf. Prov. 26:12).

A contrasting jeremiad and beatitude about political leadership follows in verses 16–17. The word translated "servant" in verse 16a can also mean "child," but given the contrast with "nobleman" in verse 17a, the NRSV rendering is preferable. Woe to a country whose king is unfitted for leadership and whose princes devote the morning to feasting rather than attending to the needs of the people (cf. Prov. 31:4–5)! Blessed is the country whose king is of noble bearing and whose princes feast after a day's work, and in moderation! Two related proverbs on laziness and feasting reinforce issues of leadership. The household calamities brought on by indolence (v. 18) are at the same time metaphors for political rule: the structures of government are also prone to collapse when neglected. Verse 19 makes clear that feasting, wine, and money are good things when they are not abused. The chapter ends with the cautionary reminder that cursing the rich and powerful, even in private, is dangerous business. "Even the walls have ears."

11:1–6
Living Life Forward

Qohelet picks up the theme of the uncertainty of life once more at the beginning of chapter 11, reminding us that we "do not know what disaster may happen on earth" (v. 2; cf. 9:12). The question then is how to make the most of life, given that we cannot foresee or control what will happen. Qohelet's response in verses 1–6 is that we must do whatever work is before us with all our might (cf. 9:10), not waiting until we have assurance about how it will all turn out. As Kierkegaard notes,

> Philosophy is perfectly right in saying that life must be understood backward. But then one forgets the other clause—that it must be lived forward. The more one thinks through this clause, the more one concludes that life in temporality never becomes properly understandable, simply because never at any time does one get perfect repose to take a stance—backward.[1]

It is impossible to wait until life becomes "properly understandable" to act. Though there is disagreement among scholars about what verses 1–2 are about, many interpreters find here a reference to sharing one's "bread" with the needy. Qohelet's point is that this sharing is not to be done in a calculating way, but freely and generously. What is done in love

> **Do good, throw your bread on the waters, and one day you will find it.**
>
> Arabic proverb, quoted in William P. Brown, *Ecclesiastes*, Interpretation: A Bible Commentary for Teaching and Preaching (Louisville, KY: Westminster John Knox Press, 2000), 101.

1. Søren Kierkegaard, *Søren Kierkegaard's Journals and Papers*, vol. 1 (Bloomington: Indiana University Press, 1967), 1030.

is never wasted, even if it is impossible to predict what one will get back. William Brown notes that verse 2 may be translated, "Give a portion to seven, or even eight."[2] This translation ties verses 1–2 together with the theme of generous benevolence. Given the way in which "mortals are snared at a time of calamity" (9:12), it is wise to spread one's resources widely, not knowing in advance where they will be most needed.

Rain comes, and trees fall (v. 3), but it is impossible to predict when and how. Rather than being paralyzed by this uncertainty, human beings must move ahead with sowing and reaping. God is the source of all that happens on earth, but human beings are given no blueprint for God's work (v. 5). Even what happens in the present is beyond human comprehension. The movement of the "wind" (v. 4a) is as mysterious as the coming of "breath" (v. 5a) into a fetus (both words are translations of the Hebrew word *rûaḥ*). Present and future, life and death, are all in God's hands. We are to be about our daily business, not knowing what blessing or calamity may befall us. Qohelet urges honest work, both day and night (v. 6). As the apostle Paul will write, "Whenever we have an opportunity, let us work for the good of all" (Gal. 6:10). The sages of Proverbs are more confident about the "payoff" of honest work (cf. Prov. 14:23), but Qohelet is equally adamant about its importance.

2. Brown, *Ecclesiastes*, 103.

11:7–12:8

The Sweetness of Youth

The remaining teachings of Qohelet, before the epilogue in 12:9–14, can be summed up by the title of Guy Lombardo's song "Enjoy Yourself (It's Later Than You Think)."[1] Life "under the sun" is often difficult and frustrating, to the point that Qohelet can despair of life itself (2:17) and long for the darkness of death (6:4–5). But in general, Qohelet insists that "light excels darkness" (2:13) and that its sweetness (11:7) should not be wasted by compulsive toil that leaves no time for joy (5:17). Knowing that the long darkness of Sheol awaits (11:8), Qohelet urges us neither to deny ourselves the pleasures of earthly life nor to take them for granted.

The words addressed to a "young man" starting in 11:9 stand in some contrast to the prudence and caution one usually associates with adult counsel to youth. As James Limburg notes, there are "no words about working hard, saving money, disciplining oneself in sexual and other affairs."[2] Instead, Qohelet exhorts the young man to rejoice, follow the inclinations of his heart, and banish anxiety from his mind (vv. 9–10). This exhortation echoes the vain attempt of the king in chapter 2 to "make a test of pleasure" (2:1) and the warning in Numbers 15:39 not to forget God's commandments. But here the point is not to rebel against God or wrest some lasting "profit" for oneself, but simply to enjoy the fleeting pleasures of youth. As Luther insists, "Joy is as necessary for youth as food and

1. http://www.elyrics.net/song/g/guy-lombardo-lyrics.html.

2. James Limburg, *Encountering Ecclesiastes: A Book for Our Time* (Grand Rapids: Eerdmans, 2006), 136.

drink, for the body is invigorated by a happy spirit."[3] Live life to the utmost while you still can!

In the NRSV translation, God's coming judgment is a damper on the call to pursue one's desire (v. 9b): Go ahead and enjoy yourself, *but* remember God's judgment. However, the Hebrew does not require this. The verse could as well be translated, "Follow your heart and the desire of your eyes *and* know that God will call you to account." God is not a killjoy in Ecclesiastes: the pleasures of earthly existence are gifts from God's hand (2:24). In fact, enjoying them is part of our accountability to God. This reading is in accord with Augustine's insistence that a heart oriented to God leaves room for great freedom and delight in creaturely things. As Augustine puts it in a sermon on 1 John 4,

> Love, and do what you will: whether you hold your peace, through love hold your peace; whether you cry out, through love cry out; whether you correct, through love correct; whether you spare, through love do you spare: let the root of love be within, of this root can nothing spring but what is good.[4]

No earthly joy or happiness will harm those who remember God the Creator (12:1). They will be like Woman Wisdom, "rejoicing in [God's] inhabited world and delighting in the human race" (Prov. 8:31).

The call to remember (12:1) is not directed toward the Torah or the "mighty acts" of God in Israel's history but toward God's presence as Creator. In the joy of God's presence, sorrow (NRSV: "anxiety") and pain dissipate. As Luther insists, "Joyfully enjoy the joyful things when they are present, but do not be crushed by the difficult things when they come."[5] Youth should be enjoyed, but it cannot be extended indefinitely. The days of youth do not last: they are ephemeral (*hebel*, 11:10). What follows them is decline and death.

3. Martin Luther, *Ecclesiastes, Song of Solomon, and the Last Words of David, LW* 15, trans. J. Pelikan (Saint Louis: Concordia, 1969), 177.
4. Augustine, *Homily 7.8 on the First Epistle of John*, in *Nicene and Post-Nicene Fathers*, 1st series, vol. 7, ed. Philip Schaff (Buffalo, NY: Christian Literature Publishing Co., 1888), 504. I am using the revised translation supplied at New Advent: http://www.newadvent.org/fathers/170207.htm.
5. Luther, *Ecclesiastes*, 177.

This decline is expressed in the beautiful poetry of 12:2–8. These verses are susceptible to several interpretations; they have been seen to depict everything from an "aging body, a crumbling house, an approaching thunderstorm, a passing funeral," to "the eschatological destruction of the cosmos."[6] An interpretation of verse 3 as an allegory of an aging human body seems plausible: "the *strong men* are the legs, the *guards* are the arms; the *women who grind* are the teeth, the *windows* are the eyes."[7] The images in the following verse are harder to interpret, but they point to decline and dissolution. The precious water of life, evoked in the images of bowl, pitcher, fountain, and cistern in verses 6–7, eventually dries up or becomes unobtainable. In the end, the dust of creaturely life returns to dust, and creaturely breath, "to God who gave it" (v. 7). Sibley Towner suggests that someone reading verses 1–7 in worship do so "in the mode of a clock running down," gradually lowering the pitch and speed of the voice till it fades away completely.[8] The repeat of the opening refrain of Ecclesiastes, "Vanity of vanities" (1:2) in verse 8 links the ceaseless repetition of the cosmos with its demise. As William Brown comments, "Ecclesiastes is essentially an obituary of life itself."[9]

FURTHER REFLECTIONS
Death and Life Everlasting

The horizon for both Proverbs and Ecclesiastes is earthly life. Neither book posits a realm beyond physical death in which the suffering and injustice of earthly life are resolved. Proverbs acknowledges the existence of earthly suffering and injustice but holds out hope that God's will is (eventually) done on earth. Both Job and Ecclesiastes contest the adequacy of Proverbs' scheme for making sense of lived

6. William P. Brown, *Ecclesiastes*, Interpretation: A Bible Commentary for Teaching and Preaching (Louisville, KY: Westminster John Knox Press, 2000), 108.
7. *The New Oxford Annotated Bible with the Apocryphal/Deuterocanonical Books*, New Revised Standard Version, ed. Bruce M. Metzger and Roland E. Murphy (New York: Oxford University Press, 1991), 851, note on Eccl. 12:1–7, emphasis added.
8. Sibley Towner, "The Book of Ecclesiastes," NIB 5 (Nashville: Abingdon Press, 1997), 356.
9. Brown, *Ecclesiastes*, 104.

experience, but neither questions Proverbs' earthly horizon. Nor do they reject Proverbs' general expectation of earthly righteousness. Rather, Job and Ecclesiastes refuse to let the assurances of Proverbs' broader sapiential framework "diminish the significance of individual suffering in the here and now."[10] Qohelet responds to this suffering and injustice with a sense of helplessness and resignation while an anguished Job protests and argues with God. In neither book is hope transferred to a realm beyond physical death.

Later Jewish and Christian readers whose trust in such a realm is an integral part of their faith have struggled with how to approach these biblical books. Interpreters often succumb to two opposite temptations. One temptation is simply to reject biblical wisdom's theological worldview as being opposed to what other parts of the Bible and later tradition say about God and human hope, and being therefore of little value; for Christian commentators, this often means labeling wisdom's approach as "sub-Christian." Robert Roberts, for example, urges those who profess Christ to be "so loosely attached to the present soil" that they are "ready to leave at a moment's notice." He contends that to be "deeply rooted in this world," as were the sages of Israel, is to be rooted in despair.[11] The opposite temptation is to try to force wisdom's teachings into alignment with later theological views. For example, when Proverbs declares that "righteousness delivers from death" (11:4), this is sometimes interpreted as anticipating New Testament hopes for life beyond finite creaturehood. Similarly, the *Targum*, an interpretive Aramaic translation of the Hebrew Bible, takes Qohelet's claim that the dead "have no more reward" (9:5) as applying only to the wicked, thus preserving the hope of appropriate reward for the righteous dead.[12]

Neither dismissing biblical wisdom's perspectives nor forcing them into alignment with later views seems to do justice to the authority of Scripture. As David Kelsey notes, "the canon is a chorus

10. Michael V. Fox, *A Time to Tear Down and A Time to Build Up: A Rereading of Ecclesiastes* (Grand Rapids: Eerdmans, 1999), 69.
11. Robert C. Roberts, *Spiritual Emotions: A Psychology of Christian Virtues* (Grand Rapids: Eerdmans, 2007), 61.
12. Leonard S. Karavitz and Kerry M. Olitsky, *Kohelet: A Modern Commentary on Ecclesiastes* (New York: UAHC Press, 2003), 93.

that is sometimes dissonant."[13] It is better to allow canonical wisdom to enter into our theological comfort zone and raise some awkward questions about the ways the doctrine of everlasting life has functioned. Clearly, in addition to providing hope and comfort, the Christian teachings about everlasting life have been subject to dangerous misuse. Here are three ways in which biblical wisdom can help correct distortions in understandings of Christian hope:

First, wisdom's agnosticism about what lies beyond death challenges quid pro quo religion—the idea that faith is a kind of bargain we enter into with God, in which our earthly attempts at piety and morality are rewarded with everlasting life. To put it bluntly, faith pays. This makes everlasting life just another goal for human achievement, encouraging invidious comparisons along the way between the self-designated faithful and everyone else. In situations of oppression and injustice, a quid pro quo view can also function to justify earthly suffering and frustration by the promise of heavenly compensation. Worst of all, this view denies the graciousness of God, whose unfathomable love is finally the only basis of our hope for life beyond death.

Second, wisdom's uncompromising account of the precarious contingencies of human life reminds us that the doctrine of everlasting life should not be used to offer false comfort to those who resent human limitations and deny the reality of death. The whole created cosmos of which we are a part is intrinsically marked by finitude and death. Our hope for everlasting life permits no evasion of life's vulnerabilities and death's hard reality. Finitude is part of God's good creation. Even on the other side of death, we remain creatures existing in radical dependence on God.

Third, biblical wisdom's exuberant call to make the most of earthly life resists any pious tendency to denigrate its value, as the *contemptus mundi* tradition does. Earthly life is not a waiting room for the life that really matters. Reflecting on the death of his son Eric, Nicholas Wolterstorff feels acutely that "his sudden early death is not just our loss but his: the loss of seeing trees, of hearing music, of reading books, of writing books, of walking through cathedrals,

13. David Kelsey, *Eccentric Existence: A Theological Anthropology* (Louisville, KY: Westminster John Knox Press, 2009), 345.

of visiting friends, of being with family, of marrying, of going to church. . . ."[14] Our confidence that we will enjoy transformed life with God after death does not devalue our life here. As Bonhoeffer wrote, "Only when one loves life and the earth so much that with it everything seems to be lost and at its end may one believe in the resurrection of the dead and a new world."[15]

14. Nicholas Wolterstorff, *Lament for a Son* (Grand Rapids: Eerdmans, 1987), 49.
15. Dec. 5, 1943, letter to Eberhard Bethge, in Dietrich Bonhoeffer, *Letters and Papers from Prison*, *DBW* 8 (Minneapolis: Fortress Press, 2010), 213.

12:9–14

A Word from Qohelet's Sponsors

The voice shifts abruptly in verse 9, and most scholars agree that these last verses are the work of another editorial hand (or hands). Until now, the phrase "Qohelet says" (1:2; 7:27; 12:8) has been used to introduce the first-person reflections of Qohelet. In these final verses, Qohelet is spoken about in the third person as a wise man who collected wisdom teachings and taught others. Only chapters 7 and 10 seem to fit the description of Qohelet's work as one of "weighing and studying and arranging many proverbs" (v. 9). The long personal ruminations in the rest of Ecclesiastes are not proverbs, nor do they seem to aim at writing "words of truth plainly" (v. 10). Verse 11 is particularly difficult, and the NRSV phrase "collected sayings" has been translated variously. Assuming that the "one shepherd" (v. 11) refers to God, the point of the verse is to authenticate Qohelet's teachings and give them sacred status: these writings, idiosyncratic as they may seem, are given to us by God. They belong to Israel's larger wisdom tradition and are "pleasing" (v. 10) in the sense of being an appropriate and legitimate part of that tradition. The warning against excess in "making many books" (v. 12) is a reminder of the folly of human pretensions to wisdom: the scholar and the fool are often equated in Renaissance Christian imagery. This warning can also be read as a back-handed compliment to Qohelet: what is here is sufficient for study and reflection.

If verses 9–12 commend Qohelet's teachings, at least indirectly, the concluding two verses (vv. 13–14) seem to function more as "damage control." For those scandalized by Qohelet's skepticism about the value of human righteousness and the certainty of divine judgment

(7:15–16; 8:14; 9:1–2), there is a reassuring exhortation to keep God's commandments and anticipate God's righteous judgment on every good and evil deed. The bewildered, sometimes despairing reflections of Qohelet on the vexations of earthly life are declared finished: "All has been heard" (v. 13). Without these more conventional pronouncements, perhaps Ecclesiastes would not have made it into the biblical canon (see the discussion on p. 140 in the introduction to Ecclesiastes). So we can be grateful that these words were added, even if they attempt to blunt the sharp edges of Qohelet's teaching. More important, the epilogue reframes Qohelet's words as an authentic part of Israel's wisdom tradition without revising and censoring them. As Roland Murphy notes, "If Qohelet has a 'quarrel' with his teachers, we may not evaluate it as anti-wisdom. The writer of the epilogue, closer to the scene than ourselves, had no problem in counting this work as wisdom, as a wisdom that still spoke to his generation."[1]

1. Roland E. Murphy, "Qohelet's 'Quarrel' with the Fathers," in *From Faith to Faith*, ed. Dikran Y. Hadidian (Pittsburgh: Pickwick Press, 1979), 243.

Afterword

Writing this commentary has changed me. The discipline of paying close attention to a whole text of Scripture rather than flitting about from verse to verse, as theologians are wont to do, has been formative. John Calvin famously declares the psalms to be "An Anatomy of all the Parts of the Soul."[1] I have come to feel the same way about the canon of Scripture as a whole. Writing a theological commentary on two books that have been largely neglected in contemporary Christian reflection has made me realize that we neglect a part of our soul when we systematically ignore parts of the canon.

It is easy for theologians to criticize what they see as the genealogical temptation among some biblical scholars, the assumption that digging down to the earliest strands of the text, or to the authorial intention or historical situation behind the text, is the key to the true meaning of the text. This tends to keep the text simply in the past, depriving Scripture of its living voice in the community. However, the corresponding temptation among theologians is evolutionism, the assumption that what comes later is definitive for our faith and practice.[2] Evolutionism tempts Christian theologians to bind or silence the multiple texts of Scripture, especially the texts of the Old Testament that are difficult to accommodate within a particular theological orbit. Christian theologies that revolve exclusively around the categories of sin and redemption, for example, tend to find little use for Proverbs and Ecclesiastes.

1. John Calvin, *Commentary on the Psalms* (Grand Rapids: Baker, 1979), 1:xxxvii.
2. Rowan Williams has highlighted the twin dangers of genealogy and evolutionism in his essay "Historical Criticism and Sacred Text," in *Reading Texts, Seeking Wisdom: Scripture and Theology*, ed. David F. Ford and Graham Stanton (Grand Rapids: Eerdmans, 2004).

In this commentary, I tried to avoid both temptations. It is the *interpreted* text that forms the touchstone of our identities as Christians, and I have self-consciously read Proverbs and Ecclesiastes in conversation with a larger Augustinian theological tradition. But I have tried to avoid what Karl Barth describes as "the constant danger that the Bible will be taken prisoner by the church, that its own life will be absorbed into the life of the church, that its free power will be transformed into the authority of the church, in short, that it will lose its character as a norm magisterially confronting the church."[3] In other words, I have tried to let the larger theological tradition guide my reading of Proverbs and Ecclesiastes while at the same time letting these biblical books enlarge and unsettle my reading of the theological tradition. Readers will have to judge to what extent I have succeeded.

My ecclesiology has been enlarged and unsettled enough by my work on Proverbs and Ecclesiastes that I am now attempting to write what I am calling a wisdom ecclesiology. Paying close attention to two biblical books whose horizon is creation has convinced me that Christian reflection on the church has tended to operate with a truncated doctrine of God: it has given center stage to God's work as Redeemer and Consummator while ignoring God's primordial and ongoing graciousness to us as Creator. What Phyllis Trible says of Ecclesiastes is true of Proverbs as well: the sages of Israel "speak to us, both Jews and Christians, in and through the Scriptures that have nourished, shaped, challenged, and disturbed our lives for millennia." Their words are "spoken from faith to faith."[4] I expect that they still have more to say to me.

3. Karl Barth, *Church Dogmatics* I/1, trans. G. W. Bromiley, ed. T. F. Torrance, 2nd ed. (Edinburgh: T. & T. Clark, 1975), 106.
4. Phyllis Trible, "A Striving after Wind," in *Life in Abundance*, ed. John R. Donahue (Collegeville, MN: Liturgical Press, 2005), 293.

For Further Reading

Brown, William P. *Character in Crisis: A Fresh Approach to the Wisdom Literature of the Old Testament.* Grand Rapids: Eerdmans, 1996.

———. *Ecclesiastes.* Interpretation: A Bible Commentary for Teaching and Preaching. Louisville, KY: Westminster John Knox Press, 2000.

———. *The Seven Pillars of Creation: The Bible, Science, and the Ecology of Wonder.* Oxford: Oxford University Press, 2010.

Chrysostom, John. *St. John Chrysostom Commentaries on the Sages.* Vol. 2, *Commentary on Proverbs and Commentary on Ecclesiastes.* Brookline, MA: Holy Cross Orthodox Press, 2006.

Davis, Ellen. *Proverbs, Ecclesiastes, and the Song of Songs.* WBC. Louisville, KY: Westminster John Knox Press, 2000.

Fox, Matthew V. *A Time to Tear Down and a Time to Build Up: A Rereading of Ecclesiastes.* Grand Rapids: Eerdmans, 1999.

Good, Edwin M. *Irony in the Old Testament.* Philadelphia: Westminster Press, 1965.

Gregory of Nyssa. *Homilies on Ecclesiastes.* Trans. Stuart Hall and Rachel Moriarty. New York: Walter de Gruyter, 1993.

Kelsey, David. *Eccentric Existence: A Theological Anthropology.* Louisville, KY: Westminster John Knox Press, 2009.

Limburg, James. *Encountering Ecclesiastes: A Book for Our Time.* Grand Rapids: Eerdmans, 2006.

Luther, Martin. "Notes on Ecclesiastes." In *Luther's Works,* vol. 15, translated by J. Pelikan, 3–193. Saint Louis: Concordia, 1969.

Murphy, Roland E. *Proverbs*. Word Biblical Commentary. Nashville: Thomas Nelson, 1998.

———. "Qohelet's 'Quarrel' with the Fathers." In *From Faith to Faith,* edited by Dikran Y. Hadidian, 235–45. Pittsburgh: Pickwick Press, 1979.

Newsom, Carol A. "Women and the Discourse of Patriarchal Wisdom: A Study of Proverbs 1–9." In *Gender and Difference in Ancient Israel,* edited by P. L. Day, 142–60. Philadelphia: Fortress, 1989.

Seow, C. L. *Ecclesiastes*. Garden City: Doubleday, 1997.

Tamez, Elsa. *When Horizons Close.* Maryknoll, New York: Orbis Books, 2000.

Van Leeuwen, Raymond C. "The Book of Proverbs." NIB 5:19–264. Nashville: Abingdon Press, 1994.

———. "Wealth and Poverty: System and Contradiction in Proverbs." *Hebrew Studies* 33 (1992):25–36.

Washington, Harold. "The 'Strange Woman' of Proverbs 1–9 and Post-Exilic Judean Society." In *Second Temple Studies 2: Temple and Community in the Persian Period,* JSOT Supplement Series 175, edited by Tamara C. Eskenazi and Kent H. Richards, 217–42. Sheffield: JSOT Press, 1994.

Yoder, Christine Roy. *Proverbs*. Nashville: Abingdon Press, 2009.

———. *Wisdom as a Woman of Substance: A Socioeconomic Reading of Proverbs 1–9 and 31:10–31*. New York: Walter de Gruyter, 2001.

Index of Ancient Sources

Old Testament

Deuterocanonical Books

Index of Subjects